The Transition to College Writing

Keith Hjortshoj
Cornell University

Bedford/St. Martin's   Boston ◆ New York

For Bedford/St. Martin's

Developmental Editor: Karen S. Henry
Production Editor: Elizabeth M. Schaaf
Production Supervisor: Joe Ford
Marketing Manager: Brian Wheel
Editorial Assistant: Caroline Thompson
Production Assistant: Kendra LeFleur
Copyeditor: Barbara G. Flanagan
Text Design: Claire Seng-Niemoeller
Cover Design: Donna Lee Dennison
Composition: Karla Goethe, Orchard Wind Graphics
Printing and Binding: Haddon Craftsmen, Inc.

President: Charles H. Christensen
Editorial Director: Joan E. Feinberg
Editor in Chief: Karen S. Henry
Director of Marketing: Karen Melton
Director of Editing, Design, and Production: Marcia Cohen
Managing Editor: Elizabeth M. Schaaf

Library of Congress Control Number: 00–106445

Manufactured in the United States of America.

5   4   3   2   1
f   e   d   c   b

For information, write: Bedford/St. Martin's, 75 Arlington Street, Boston, MA 02116 (617-399-4000)

ISBN: 0–312–14916–6

Acknowledgments
From *Women's Work: The First 20,000 Years: Women, Cloth, and Society in Early Times* by Elizabeth Wayland Barber. Copyright © 1994 by Elizabeth Wayland Barber. Used by permission of W. W. Norton & Company, Inc.
Jessie Bernard, "The Good-Provider Role: Its Rise and Fall." Copyright © 1981 by the American Psychological Association. Reprinted and adapted with permission

Preface for Instructors

Several readers of this book have observed that I could almost shorten the title to *The Transition to College*. Such a change would require a much larger volume than this, but I have chosen to view writing through a wide-angle lens that includes the surroundings in which college students write, read, and learn. And this is not a still image but a moving picture. For teachers and administrators, college might be a familiar, settled environment that changes slowly. But college freshmen, especially, are rapidly moving and reinventing themselves in unfamiliar surroundings, where most of the survival skills they developed in the past are open to question. For them, college is and should be a wonderfully disruptive experience in which writing is a central medium of transformation: a way of making connections among many dimensions of learning in all fields of study.

Although this moving picture creates a new kind of book about writing in college, writing teachers have always been involved in helping students negotiate the transition to college. The establishment of freshman composition requirements earlier in this century acknowledged the central importance of language skills for new populations of college students, unfamiliar with the traditions and standards of higher education. Over the past twenty years or so, "writing across the curriculum" programs have begun to distribute this responsibility beyond freshman English into other courses in other disciplines. When teachers in any field pay real attention to student writing, they always confront problems of adjustment that concern reading, thinking, and learning as well. They also suspect, at least, that some of the most common weaknesses they observe in student writing result not only from lack of experience but also from prior experience: from the use of rules, skills, and strategies the writer previously learned, often in preparation for college. In recent years, many "bridge" or dual-credit programs, positioned between high school and college, have focused directly on the problems of transition in the development of learning skills.

In this book I've simply tried to make these complex dimensions of writing explicit and clear to students at all stages of the transition to college: from the senior year of high school through the first year of college, in writing and writing-intensive courses of all kinds. While I offer these perspectives directly to students, I hope they will also facilitate the teaching of writing and other learning skills, in and beyond the writing course.

In another sense, this book simply redistributes insights I acquired from three kinds of teachers.

~ I'm most grateful to the hundreds of undergraduates I've known at Cornell University. It's difficult to convince these students that they are also my teachers, but they continually remind me that both teaching and learning are two-way streets. Without them this book would not have had anything to say.

Faculty members and graduate teaching assistants in a wide range of disciplines at Cornell, from English to astrophysics, have broadened and enriched my view of the diverse academic environments college students enter. Collaboration with them has also given me a second chance to get a liberal education. Several of these teachers wrote assignments presented at the beginning of Chapter 4. Assignments by Lynda Bogel (film studies), William Barnett (philosophy), Catalin Kaser (linguistics), and Paul Doremus (political science) were included in a volume of assignment sequences Katherine Gottschalk compiled for a graduate course called Teaching Writing. Others were contributed by William Kennedy (comparative literature), Dan Usner (history), and Yervant Terzian (astronomy). In the same chapter, the Senator Wisdom assignment was written by astronomer Martha Haynes, who raises assignment writing to the level of an art form.

Close attention to students and interdisciplinary collaboration are essential features of the Knight Institute for Writing in the Disciplines and the Writing Workshop at Cornell. In Cornell's writing programs I've learned to teach not only from my students but also from constant discussions with my colleagues Joe Martin, Kathryn Gottschalk, Mary Gilliland, Barbara LeGendre, Judy Pierpont, Elliot Shapiro, and former members of the staff, along with Steven Youra in the college of Engineering. Through the Knight Institute's Consortium for Writing in the Disciplines, led by Jonathan Monroe, these ongoing discussions include teachers from colleges and universities throughout the United States and abroad. Ken Pickens at

Ithaca High School has helped to illuminate his end of the bridge college students have crossed, and he has deepened my respect for the skills and responsibilities of high school teachers at large.

Finally, I'm deeply grateful to the publishers and editors at Bedford/St. Martin's for their patient help in getting the potential value of this work in focus. Karen Henry, Joan Feinberg, and Chuck Christensen deserve much of the credit for steering this project through substantial revision. Nancy Sommers, George Otte, Gilda Teixido Kelsey, and other reviewers gave me essential advice and encouragement in the process. Barbara Flanagan, Elizabeth Schaaf, and Karen Henry made copyediting and the final stages of production as painless as they can ever be. Thanks to Joan Schwartz and Erika Merschrod at Cornell for their generous help with illustrations and examples of scientific writing.

Contents

6 Investigative Writing   152

7 Rules and Errors   187

Introduction:
The Turning Point

That burning day when I got ready to leave New York
and start out on my journey to college! I felt like Colum-
bus starting out for the other end of the earth. I felt like
the pilgrim fathers who had left their homeland and all
their kin behind them and trailed out in search of the
New World.   — Anzia Yezierska, *Bread Givers*

To exist is to change, to change is to mature, to mature is
to go on creating oneself endlessly.
                                — Henri Bergson, *Creative Evolution*

Are You Prepared for College?

When Anzia Yezierska entered Columbia University in 1904, going
to college was a rare opportunity, especially for a young woman
born in a Russian Jewish ghetto in Poland and raised in a tenement
on the Lower East Side of Manhattan. At the beginning of this
century, high school was still very high on the educational ladder.
In 1910, only 2.7 percent of Americans over the age of twenty-five
had completed college, most of them from wealthy families in the
eastern states, and the average American had completed only eight
years of school. Because only about 4 percent of high school graduates continued their education, there were fewer than a thousand
colleges and universities in the United States, with an average enrollment of only 250 undergraduates. To be one of those students
was a great privilege, set apart from the ordinary lives of working
Americans. "All the young people I had ever seen were shut up in
factories," Yezierska recalled in her autobiographical novel Bread
Givers. "But here were young girls and young men enjoying life,
free from the worry for a living."

1

By contrast, if you are entering college this year you represent the majority, about 63 percent, of high school graduates nationwide. Each fall nearly 3 million high school graduates begin their studies at more than 3,600 American colleges and universities, with an average enrollment of 3,900 students. More than 14 million students are currently enrolled in undergraduate or graduate programs in the United States. What was once a rare privilege has become a statistical norm and for many careers a necessity.

School systems have changed accordingly. Some of you have been heading in the direction of college since primary school, where you were already enrolled in accelerated programs. In high school, many of you have taken honors or advanced placement courses designed to prepare you for undergraduate studies in particular fields. You have taken batteries of standardized tests, perhaps two or three times, possibly with the help of coaching services. Parents, friends, teachers, and guidance counselors have probably helped you to identify the schools that best match your interests, credentials, and financial resources. During the application process, many of you studied published guides to colleges, along with catalogues and brochures, and visited campuses to get a clearer view of undergraduate life at the schools that interested you.

In other words, the majority of public and private high schools today have also become college "prep schools," joined in a complex matchmaking system with offices of admissions in higher education. In contrast with my own thin application to a state university in 1962, filled out in ballpoint pen, the applications I now read with university admissions officers each spring are plump credential files, filled with detailed aptitude and achievement scores, Advanced Placement scores, high school transcripts and class ranks, lists of honors and activities, letters from teachers and guidance counselors, and essays. Admissions officers use this record of high school achievements, interests, and aptitudes to choose the members of the next freshman class.

On the whole, this matchmaking system works remarkably well. In its survey of freshmen who entered college in the fall of 1998, *The Chronicle of Higher Education* found that more than 90 percent were attending their first- or second-choice schools. In general, these students were both satisfied with their choices and optimistic about their futures. Only 12 percent expected to transfer to other colleges. Only 1 percent expected to fail a course or drop out of college even temporarily. From this perspective, we might imagine that going to college has become an ordinary, predictable experience, effectively regulated by educators at both ends of a transition that has become straight and smooth.

But research and experience tell a somewhat different story. According to a 1995 survey by the American College Testing Service, even at the most selective schools 14 percent of freshmen discontinue their studies, at least temporarily, by the beginning of sophomore year. For all colleges and universities nationwide the figure rises to 35 percent. College freshmen, including those who stay in school, obviously run into a variety of problems they did not anticipate. And while the abundance of detailed information about high school performance makes college admissions look like an exact science, on the basis of this record we cannot reliably predict how individuals will perform in college. Students with weak high school backgrounds often do extremely well. Students with superb credentials sometimes have the most difficulty adjusting to undergraduate studies. In spite of all the advanced placement and honors programs now designed for the college-bound, professors at every type of undergraduate institution still complain, much as they did a hundred years ago, that their students are unprepared for the kinds of writing, reading, and thinking required in college.

The basic reason is quite simple, and it is a cause for celebration as well as concern. *Even the best high schools cannot fully prepare you to be a college student, because in some very fundamental ways a college or a university is a different kind of learning environment in which you must become a different kind of student.*

In other words, preparations for college have led you to one of the major turning points in your life, but until you get there you can't see around this corner. When you actually make the turn, you begin a new segment of your education afresh, in an unfamiliar environment where you will encounter new challenges and responsibilities, discover new opportunities, and form new relationships. As you turn in this new direction, much of the knowledge and skill you previously acquired will remain useful, but the credentials that brought you to this point will suddenly become irrelevant. When college admissions officers close your application folder and put it in the ACCEPTANCE pile, it is unlikely that anyone will ever look at your high school record again. Previous triumphs, struggles, and failures are in this sense erased, and what you do from now on is all that matters.

As you enter freshman year, the one thing you can be sure of is that you will change in the coming years, but no one can predict for certain how quickly or effectively you will adapt to this new environment. In unfamiliar circumstances, some people become very alert, flexible, and adventurous, while others become very cautious, clinging to familiar patterns of thought and behavior. They try as much as possible not to change, even though, as the philosopher Henri Bergson observed, change is unavoidable.

The challenge of adapting to undergraduate work is therefore a *normal* difficulty, to which no one is entirely immune. And when almost every aspect of your life has altered, it is sometimes hard to distinguish academic challenges from other new responsibilities, other demands on your time and attention. You might imagine that Natalie Portman, the actress most familiar as Queen Amidala in *Star Wars: The Phantom Menace*, would have no difficulty performing a new role as a college freshman at Harvard. In a Gannett News Service interview in November 1999, however, Portman described the same adjustment problems that other students experience:

> It's learning to balance my time between various aspects of living on my own and my studying. There's so much schoolwork, but I also have social activities, extracurricular activities, and taking care of the housework. When the weekends come, I find I have to do the laundry, clean the bathroom, vacuum, and shop so I have food to eat. All those are difficult to adjust to when you're used to just saying, "Mom, I'm hungry."
>
> I find I have a lot more responsibility, including dealing with time management. (3B)

This challenge is a cause for celebration because the opportunity to change is still the greatest benefit college offers you, just as it was for Anzia Yezierska nearly a century ago. High schools cannot be like colleges. Colleges should not be like high schools. Very few of you would want college to be a direct continuation of high school, even if you enjoyed those years and feel the loss of friends and relations in the familiarity of your home. Like foreign travel, this disruption of familiar routines offers you the opportunity to become a somewhat different person, with new skills, interests, relationships, and responsibilities.

Like other travelers, furthermore, you face the necessity of figuring out what you should bring with you on this journey and what you should leave behind. I'm referring not just to belongings but primarily to ways of thinking and learning and to strategies for reading and writing. Some of the skills and strategies that were successful in the past will remain valuable. Some will no longer work. Your success in college will therefore depend not just on the strength of your background but also on your ability to reorganize your time, change your approaches to learning, abandon ineffective methods, and develop new ones. From this perspective, college teachers find their students continually "unprepared" for undergraduate work simply because their expectations of students differ from those of high school teachers and even from those of other college teachers. You can't predict and adapt to these diverse expectations immediately, and for this reason "preparation" for college will be an ongoing process throughout and beyond your freshman year.

A Brief Overview

The central purpose of this book is to help you make the transition in the most important dimension of college work: the use of written language, especially in writing but also in reading.

You probably associate writing and reading most closely with the field of English and might view writing as one requirement for graduation. A basic premise of this book, however, is that writing and reading are essential to learning in *all* of your courses — in chemistry or economics as well as in English or history. Among these courses, the kinds of writing and reading you do will vary a great deal. As you travel from high school to college and from one undergraduate course to another, the meanings of *writing, reading, studying,* and *learning* will change, and these variations will determine what it means for you to be a good student.

While writing this book I've kept my own students, through twenty-five years of teaching, foremost in my mind. I've recalled the skills and motivations they brought with them to college, the problems they encountered in their studies, and the most successful strategies they used for solving these problems. I thought especially of the many bright, capable freshmen I've known who, during their first semester, felt overwhelmed by the volume and variety of work, confused by the differing expectations of their teachers, or discouraged by their first grades on papers and exams. I've considered the changes that allowed these students to write, read, and study more efficiently, with greater composure and better results. I tried to understand how the approaches to learning they developed as sophomores, juniors, and seniors differed from the approaches they used as entering freshmen, and I have tried to describe these differences in the following chapters.

While writing I have also kept in mind the many teachers I know, at my university and at other schools, in almost every field of study offered to undergraduates. What kinds of writing, reading, and learning do these teachers expect of their students? What would it mean for you to be a good student in their courses, and how do their expectations differ? What general patterns can I observe among their teaching goals, assignments, and dissatisfactions with student work? What kinds of student writing and thinking do they most admire? What can I tell you about these teachers and learning environments that most of you need to know to make the process of adapting to college work more efficient and less frustrating?

My attempts to answer these questions became the basis for the following chapters.

Chapter 1 provides a general orientation to the variations among the instructors and courses you will encounter, including the most basic differences between high school and college work, the most common types of college classes, the roles of language in these classes, and the kinds of writing instruction most often available to undergraduates.

Chapter 2, "Footstools and Furniture," describes the basic formula for writing essays taught in many high schools and explains how you can put the best features of this model to work in more diverse, complex, and sophisticated forms of writing assigned in college classes.

Chapter 3, "How Writing Gets Done," recognizes that the products you turn in to teachers result from the methods you use for writing. This chapter describes the process of writing, the methods college students typically use, and alternative methods that will improve your work.

Chapter 4, "What Do College Teachers Expect?," explains some general standards for academic writing and distinguishes the most common forms and purposes of writing assignments in the sciences, social sciences, and humanities. Using examples of assignments from these fields, the chapter will also help you to determine the specific kinds of writing teachers expect from you.

Chapter 5, "Reading: How to Stay on Top of It," describes the diverse reading strategies that successful students use for different purposes, as alternatives to the linear, passive reading methods that college freshmen often try to use.

Chapter 6, "Investigative Writing," explains what teachers are looking for when they assign research papers and how you can develop methods for meeting their expectations, using college libraries and other resources. This chapter includes essential guidance for quotation, citation, and the use of Internet sources, along with a discussion of the causes and effects of plagiarism in college work.

Chapter 7, "Rules and Errors," helps you reduce error by developing your intuitive knowledge of the structure and flow of written English. The chapter also discusses some of the false rules that lead to error and explains how to use handbooks of grammar.

Chapter 8, "Looking Ahead," anticipates the further changes you will need to make as a writer as you move through advanced levels of undergraduate study, toward graduate programs and professions.

How to Use This Book

In some respects the transition to college begins in high school, when you turn your attention in the direction of college with investigations, preparations, and applications. Adjustment to college does not occur all at once: the transition continues well beyond your arrival on campus and the beginning of your first semester. Students often tell me that they feel really at home on campus, for the first time, when they return for their sophomore year. Having been away for the summer, they realize that the place has gradually become familiar. When they come back they resume familiar routines and relationships. They see that over the previous year acquaintances have gradually become friends. The expectations of teachers have become more predictable, and balancing their social lives with their studies and other responsibilities has become easier. Because they know where they are, they feel more fully there when they come back, and over following semesters this familiarity continues to grow.

The Transition to College Writing is therefore designed both for those of you who are on your way to college and for those of you who have already arrived. It is also designed both to be read through, from beginning to end, and to use as a reference, in or outside a particular course. If you are heading for college, you might use this book in a senior English course or read it on your own as a general description of what lies around the corner. When you arrive, you can then refer to specific chapters to remind yourself of expectations and strategies most relevant to your studies. Some of you might receive *The Transition to College Writing* when you begin your undergraduate studies, for use as an orientation to writing and reading in following semesters.

For some of you this will be an assigned text in freshman composition or in other courses that require extensive writing. Your teacher will use this book for specific purposes, but I encourage you to use it as a reference for other courses as well, during and beyond your freshman year. The chapters on writing methods, reading, research papers, and errors, for example, will apply to requirements in a wide range of courses. All writing teachers hope that the skills and strategies you develop in a composition class will help you to write successfully in all of your courses. One of the main purposes of this book is to establish these vital connections between writing instruction and the uses of written language throughout the curriculum.

Mapping Exercises

In unfamiliar territory, good maps are essential, and the exercises at the end of each chapter (and referred to at appropriate points within the chapter) illustrate what I mean by "mapping" the domains of writing in college. Like other features of *The Transition to College Writing*, these exercises can be used either in or outside a particular course.

Your writing teacher will make other assignments, designed to give you practice with various types of writing. A few of the mapping exercises in this book will serve the same purpose, but most ask you to investigate some aspect of writing, reading, and learning or of the contexts in which you pursue these activities. Their main purpose is to heighten your awareness of what you are doing and how you are doing it and to link the value of your writing class with the rest of your academic work. Whether you do these exercises on your own or as course assignments, they should strengthen your working knowledge of the concepts presented in the text.

Freshmen?

In a book that encourages alertness to language, I should briefly explain why I continue to use the term *freshmen*, even though the *men* portion of the word is more than a century out of date. Over half of college freshmen in the United States are now women, and the proportion of women increases in subsequent years of college because men are more likely to discontinue their studies. An article called "What's Wrong with the Guys?" in the February 1996 issue of *Postsecondary Education Opportunity* pointed out that if the proportion of women attending college continues to increase as it has been increasing since 1870, the percentage of men in college will reach zero in the year 2144. Then the term *freshwomen* will be entirely accurate.

Meanwhile, I use the conventional *freshmen,* with some apology and reluctance, because I like the *fresh* part of the word and dislike the alternatives. The neuter *freshpeople* and *freshpersons* sound ridiculous. The most widely used option, *first-year student,* is cumbersome and bland. Its acronym *FYS,* which educators use in professional literature, seems impersonal and bureaucratic. We obviously need a new term altogether, but I can't think of one, and inventing a new term usually creates more confusion than it resolves.

In the nineteenth century, however, a new student was often called simply a *fresh* and in the beginning of the twentieth century a *freshie.* These terms, like *freshman,* had some demeaning connotations. *Fresh* can mean clueless, immature, still green and unseasoned, unfamiliar with the campus scene. Until the 1960s, freshmen at many colleges had to identify themselves by wearing sillylooking "beanie" caps and were subjected to hazing from older students. These forms of initiation emphasized their disorientation and vulnerability and suggested that although they had gone off to college from their high schools and families, they didn't fully belong there.

I'm glad that most of this ritual degradation has ended, but the *freshness* of this transition is a wonderful quality, much more appealing than its opposite, *staleness:* what happens to people and things when they've been around too long. While I want to reduce the confusion and frustration of undergraduate work, I also want you to keep the freshness of college — its richness and unexplored potential — alive for as long as possible. In this sense I hope you will remain freshmen and freshwomen throughout your college years.

1 Orientation

> The foundation for a successful undergraduate experience is proficiency in the written and the spoken word. Students need language to grasp and express effectively feelings and ideas. To succeed in college, undergraduates should be able to write and speak with clarity, and to read and listen with comprehension. Language and thought are inextricably connected, and as undergraduates develop their linguistic skills, they hone the quality of their thinking and become intellectually and socially empowered.
>
> — Ernest Boyer, *The Undergraduate Experience in America*

If It's Tuesday, This Must Be Biology

When you first arrive on campus, *orientation* literally means finding your way around an unfamiliar spatial, social, and administrative terrain: locating the dining hall, the laundry room, offices, and classrooms, sorting out your academic requirements, and figuring out how to register for courses. All colleges and universities provide orientation programs to help you negotiate this bewildering maze of facilities, schedules, rules, and procedures. These programs also introduce you to the social environment, through organized activities and introductions to student organizations. When the official orientation period ends, other students, teachers, and advisers will continue to help you recover from that initial feeling, especially at large universities, that you are utterly lost.

Orientation to the academic, intellectual life of the campus takes longer, because no one can give you a guided tour of this complex dimension of your college or adequately describe it in a brochure.

Maps of the campus locate academic departments. The course catalogue lists the faculty, courses, and requirements. Schedules for the semester tell you when and where classes meet. To that extent the curriculum is clearly defined in time and space. When you have created a schedule and located all of your classes, you have completed one kind of orientation and can begin the process of accumulating the credits you need for graduation. In following semesters, as you register for new classes in different departments or at higher levels, the process of moving through the curriculum will become easier, almost routine.

In a deeper sense, however, academic life transcends the boundaries defined by maps, catalogues, and schedules. Even in a small liberal arts college the curriculum represents an effort, at least, to encompass all space and time, all cultures and languages, the whole physical universe, the origins and forms of all life on this planet, and all dimensions of human thought. Your astronomy course might meet three times each week at 10:00 A.M. in a particular place, but this course also will take you to the beginning of time and to the outer limits of space. History of Architecture meets in a particular building, but the course will expose you to traditions of building in many cultures throughout history. Your psychology course, like others, will require thought, memory, and the use of language, but this course is also *about* human thought, memory, and language. Readings in your literature class will open whole realms of experience and imagination beyond the confines of your own life and time. Other courses will carry you beneath or beyond the ordinary dimensions of sense perception: to the invisible, subatomic structure of the entire universe, to the minute functions of neural networks, to the scale of whole ecosystems, or to global climate changes over centuries.

College brochures have these great riches in mind when they describe the freshman year, especially, as a time of exploration and discovery, freedom, intellectual expansion, and personal growth. Education, like travel, is supposed to broaden the mind.

Neither education nor travel automatically has this effect, however, if it is confined to the sort of packaged, whirlwind tours (meals and lodging included) in which all the routes and stops are plotted out in advance, with no time to wander off the beaten path, no time to revisit places that intrigue you. Education does not broaden the mind very much if history or geology is simply a class you attend in a certain building at a certain time on Mondays, Wednesdays, and Fridays or if "making connections" between subjects means simply getting from one class to the next on time, like a busy commuter, before it takes off without you.

Having traveled through many countries foreign to me, I know how easy it is to become trapped in your itinerary, focusing most of your attention on getting from one place to another, worrying about currency and luggage or about finding time to eat and sleep, often struggling to speak and understand an unfamiliar language. Having passed through my freshman year in a daze, I know how easy it is to become trapped in a surreal experience of college governed by the course catalogue — to become preoccupied with schedules, requirements, and grades (the currency of higher education) while struggling to understand alien, academic dialects. I suppose this is why students refer to everything outside their experience of college as "the real world": a place where economics, for example, is not something you got a B in last semester or plan to take next fall to complete a distribution requirement, but an important aspect of life, interwoven with others.

Because the pace of instruction is usually hectic and the opportunities available can be overwhelming, during your first year of college you will probably fall into narrow routines by necessity, in the effort to manage your time and priorities. To make these routines visible, I ask fall-term freshmen to draw personal maps of the campus, based on their own experience of the place. Then I tell them to ask other students to draw such maps as well, so we can compare differing perspectives of the same environment. Although the details vary, new students typically produce sketchy drawings of a few paths connecting a few buildings, among great blank, uncharted spaces. Straight lines lead from a dormitory to a dining hall, to particular academic buildings, to one of the libraries, sometimes to a gym or to athletic fields. **[Exercise 1]** (Exercise numbers in **boldface** refer to related exercises at the end of the chapter.)

I teach at a university with a big campus — 745 acres, with more than 260 buildings — and there are parts of it I have never explored. I'm not at all surprised, therefore, that fall-term freshmen have explored so little.

When I give the same mapping assignment to sophomores or juniors, however, although the paths and locations are more clearly defined, the great blank spaces usually remain. These advanced students have figured out where they are and where they are going throughout the day, but they rarely depart from their established routes and routines.

For this reason I sometimes ask my students to veer off the trails they have drawn, to explore one patch of *terra incognita* and describe what they find there:

> Visit one of those places off your map, where your schedule would never take you. Wander into the art studios, the greenhouses, the science library, or the law school, and tell us what you discover. Fill in one of the blank spaces.

I encourage you to do this as well, because the familiarity of the well-marked path can offer an illusory kind of security. If you remain on that path too cautiously, you won't feel lost, but in a broader sense you won't know where you are, why you are there, or what other opportunities are readily available. "If you really want to know where you are and what you are doing," I sometimes tell my students, "you need to find out where you aren't, what you are not doing, and why you have chosen the path you are on." In other words, you need to explore, and in some respects this book is entirely about exploration, for the purpose of gaining as much as you can from the wealth of opportunities that surround you.

Some Basic Differences between High School and College

In the Introduction I said that high school cannot fully prepare you for college because high schools and colleges differ in some fundamental ways. Here I'll describe the most basic differences I had in mind.

As I make these generalizations, I'm aware that colleges and universities vary a great deal, and so do high schools. "College" is not a single kind of environment, and the transition to college is not a single kind of experience. This variation is perhaps the most basic reason high schools cannot entirely prepare their students for college.

High schools themselves vary greatly in size — from fewer than a hundred students in some rural and private schools to urban and suburban districts with enrollments of several thousand. But variations in higher education are even more extreme. Among the 3,600 colleges and universities in the United States, about 350, almost 10 percent, enroll fewer than 200 students. At the opposite end of the scale, 125 universities are at least 100 times larger, enrolling 20,000–50,000 students at a single campus. As a consequence, some of you might enter colleges smaller than your high schools, while others enroll in universities larger than the towns in which you were raised. About 80 percent of you will attend colleges in your home states, and some of you will travel only a few miles from your homes, where you might continue to live while you are in school. Others will cross the entire continent or arrive from other countries, moving from large cities to small towns or from rural areas to large cities. College tuition varies radically as well, from less than $2,000 a year to more than $20,000, and so do standards for admission, curricula, housing, physical and social environments, and patterns of diversity in the student body.

These variables were no doubt important factors in your choice of a college. They also determine the kinds of adjustments you will have to make as an individual, in ways that high schools cannot wholly predict. When I describe general patterns of change, therefore, I am also describing types and degrees of variation.

College courses are not direct continuations of high school instruction.   Standardized tests create illusions of uniformity and continuity, partly because many of the high school courses designed as preparation for college work actually prepare students to pass the standardized exams essential for college admissions. In some basic subjects these courses do provide excellent foundations for introductory college work. A good high school calculus or precalculus course will be a great asset to you in your first year of college mathematics and science. The same will be true for good high school courses in chemistry, biology, physics, and computer science. The periodic table, the principles of genetics, and the laws of motion will not change between your senior year of high school and the first year of college. Nor will the dates of important historical events or the structures and vocabularies of English, French, or Spanish.

Even in these basic subjects, however, methods of instruction and evaluation will vary considerably. Freshman courses in English literature, psychology, American history, or philosophy will not necessarily cover the material you studied in high school versions of these courses; nor will they proceed with the same assumptions about what is important and true.

In addition, many of the subjects you study in college do not exist in the high school curriculum. The average university encompasses about fifty academic departments and interdisciplinary programs, each with its own faculty, roster of courses, prerequisites, and requirements for undergraduate majors. At the freshman level in social science departments, for example, introductory courses often represent more specialized fields of study: microeconomics, international politics, cultural anthropology, social psychology, or the sociology of religion. **[Exercise 2]**

While high school teachers are generalists, college teachers are specialists. Your college professors will not directly coordinate their courses with high school instruction because most of them know very little about the high school curriculum. Professors who teach introductory courses in their departments are specialists in certain types of research. They are not just biologists, but particular types of molecular biologists, neurobiologists, or geneticists; they are not just historians, but specialists on particular periods and features of English, American, Brazilian, or West African history. These teachers view introductory courses not as extensions of high school but as points of departure into advanced studies.

Principles of "academic freedom" encourage variation in college teaching. "Academic freedom" means that within broad guidelines for fairness and responsibility, individual college professors are free to decide what and how they teach. College courses, especially in private schools, are not governed by the kinds of state and local mandates that standardize secondary education, and college professors are not required to pass through formal teacher training and certification. As a consequence, two professors in the same political science department, for example, might teach an introduction to political theory with very different course designs, texts, assignments, and examinations. One might emphasize factual knowledge, through formal lectures and short-answer exams. The other might emphasize critical thinking and discussion, assigning position papers and a research project in place of exams.

This variation is most dramatic in the freshman year. In your first year or two, most of your courses will satisfy distribution requirements, designed to ensure broad exposure to the sciences, social sciences, and humanities. In a single day, therefore, you might travel from a large lecture course in chemistry to a writing class taught as a seminar or workshop and then to a small lecture course in cognitive psychology that includes student participation and to a biology lab where you work on experiments with a partner. Your friends, meanwhile, are probably taking other courses of diverse sizes and designs — in anthropology, education, philosophy, astronomy, nutrition, or calculus. The following semester you will take different courses, some of them in different departments, with different teachers who have their own unpredictable ideas about what and how you should learn. At large schools, especially, individual professors will have little or no idea what you are doing (or how much you have to do) in other courses.

College work requires new kinds of motivation and self-discipline. In their first year, most of my students face the necessity of finding new reasons for getting their work done and new ways of making productive use of their time among many potential distractions. When they were in high school, their parents, teachers, and school officials made sure they were attending classes, completing assignments, and meeting requirements from one day or week to the next. They also worked hard for the purpose of getting into college.

When they arrived, most of those structured expectations vanished. On any particular day they were free to skip class, postpone work on assignments, and spend their time in many other tempting ways. Because colleges give students much greater freedom and responsibility, they could fall behind in their work, sometimes even to the point of failing classes, without any intervention from their teachers. Problems with time management and motivation account for a large proportion of the attrition from college in the first year, often among students who were very successful in high school.

If you have difficulty finding the motivation and discipline you need to concentrate on your studies, you will have to sort through these issues very deliberately.

> On a particular evening, given many options and the freedom to use your time in other ways, why should you work on a writing assignment for your English class or study for an exam in biology?
> **[Exercise 3]**

In their answers to this question, my students tell me that they redefine some old motivations and discover some new ones. Even without direct parental supervision, most students work partly to live up to their parents' expectations, to avoid disappointing them, and to justify the expense of college. Career goals and admission to graduate programs replace college admissions as motivations to study. New academic interests, the high expectations of teachers, the challenges of difficult courses, and competition with peers provide other incentives.

Above all, successful students find internal motivations and discipline to replace the external factors that kept them focused in high school. These students tell me that they do not want to disappoint themselves or waste opportunities and that they feel pride in learning to be both independent and responsible.

One of my students found a basis for self-discipline the hard way. Throughout his freshman year, Lloyd was continually distracted from his studies by opportunities to spend time with his new friends in college, without any of the restrictions his parents and teachers imposed when he was in high school. As a consequence, he missed classes, failed to complete assignments, and received such poor grades that the university suspended him for a year.

When Lloyd returned to college and came to see me, I immediately noticed that he had matured over his year of suspension. He was more serious and direct, and he told me that he was doing well in all of his classes. When I asked Lloyd how he spent that year out of school, he told me he had taken a job as assistant to a gruff, silent mason and had spent the year loading and unloading concrete blocks, forty or fifty hours each week, without any conversation. Bored throughout the day and too exhausted at night to go out, he had plenty of time to think about the past and future. He decided that when he returned to school he should think of his academic work as a much better job than hauling concrete blocks. And if he didn't take this job seriously and put in his forty to fifty hours each week, this time he would be fired for good. This resolve successfully created work habits he had lacked, and in following semesters Lloyd found other, more substantial reasons for paying attention to his studies.

Course Designs and Teaching Styles

Variation in the sizes and designs of college courses deserves special attention, because some types of classes might be unfamiliar to you, and each requires specific learning strategies.

Compared with those in college, high school courses are remarkably uniform. In the great majority of high school classes, regardless of the subject, fifteen to thirty students sit in chairs arranged in rows, facing the teacher and the chalkboard; in small private schools the number of students might be lower. Within this typical classroom, teachers use a variety of methods, but the basic format for instruction is fairly consistent throughout American high schools of all sizes.

By contrast, I know a college freshman this semester whose classes vary from nine students in his writing seminar to eighteen hundred in an introductory psychology course. In his writing seminar this student, his eight classmates, and his teacher sit around a seminar table and casually discuss the course material, exchange papers, break into pairs or trios for some activities, or stand up to give presentations. In his psychology course, held on the same days, he sits in silence with hundreds of other students in a huge auditorium, silently listening to the lectures, taking notes, or watching films and demonstrations — all in preparation for examinations. In his architectural design class, he works on models and drawings for his projects in a large studio filled with drafting tables, workbenches, and power tools. Students complete these projects alone or in groups, often late at night; during the class hours the professor and teaching assistants move around the room, offering advice. In each of these classes he must be a particular kind of student.

Courses with eighteen hundred students are rare, but at large universities introductory courses for freshmen commonly enroll two hundred students or more. At small colleges, class sizes might range from five to fifty students, much closer to the range in high school, but the designs of these courses still vary a great deal. Looking across the whole spectrum of colleges and universities, we can observe some types of classes that you are likely to encounter at almost any school.

Lecture Courses

Because the lecture is both a type of course and a style of teaching, lecture courses can be fairly small or extremely large. In some respects size does not matter, because in such courses the professor speaks and the students listen, look at information on the chalkboard or projections, and take notes. Whether you are one of forty students or four hundred makes little difference. While some professors take questions during or after the lecture, your main job is to pay attention and record the information you will need to remember. Lecture courses are offered in all fields of study, usually in large classrooms or auditoriums with fixed seating in rows facing a lectern or stage.

Discussion or Review Sections

Lecture courses that enroll more than forty students often include smaller weekly discussion sections led by the professor or by a teaching assistant. In the sciences these are sometimes called "review sessions," devoted mainly to clarifying lectures and readings. In the sciences and in other fields, however, good discussion leaders will encourage you to explore the course material in greater depth through exchanges with your classmates. This is your chance to participate in the course, and in some cases a portion of your grade in the course will be based on your participation. Some discussion leaders also use these sections to return exams and papers, discuss writing assignments, or give quizzes.

Lecture/Discussion Courses

In classes smaller than about forty students, professors often encourage student participation during lectures. They pause occasionally to invite questions, use part of the class period for open discussion or informal writing, break the class into smaller discussion groups, or organize formal debates.

Laboratory Sections

Introductory lecture courses in the sciences usually include laboratory components, sometimes listed as separate courses. Although the experiments and equipment in these courses will be somewhat more complex, the functions and basic designs of lab courses in college are similar to those in high school. Facilities limit lab sections to no more than twenty or thirty students, who complete a series of experiments either alone or with lab partners. These experiments are often correlated with principles taught in the lecture portion of the course, and the lab sessions, like discussion sections, sometimes include quizzes and question periods. All laboratory courses require you to record experimental procedures in notebooks or other records, and most require that you write lab reports on your experiments. I'll discuss lab reports in Chapter 4.

Studios

Studio courses in the fine arts, architecture, and other design programs are in some ways similar to laboratory classes in the sciences. In both cases you are actively engaged in learning through activity, and the work you produce through that activity (paintings, drawings, or models) is the basis for evaluation. Studio classes, like labs, are usually informal, with a lot of casual conversation among students and teachers. In most cases they are also longer than regular classes — from two to four hours.

Seminars

Seminars typically enroll fewer than twenty students and are held in small rooms with movable chairs, usually arranged around central tables as in conference rooms. If there is no table, teachers often arrange the chairs in a circle. Students therefore face one another, to encourage discussion, and the teacher usually sits with the students as a discussion leader and participant. Students often do not take notes in these classes, and because learning occurs through discussion, teachers expect that all students will participate actively. For this reason participation will often be a substantial part of your grade.

Tutorials and Conferences

A tutorial is an individual meeting with your teacher; while this kind of instruction is more common in British universities, teachers in American colleges sometimes arrange tutorials for individuals or small groups of students. In American schools these meetings are usually called "conferences," and teachers in small classes might schedule two or three each term. In addition, professors and teaching assistants hold office hours when they are free to talk with students about specific questions or issues. These meetings will often concern papers you have written or readings for the course.

Because individual conferences with teachers are less common in high schools, you might not be aware of your role in these meetings. When students enter a teacher's office, they are often reluctant to say what they want or what they think, and they let the teacher fill the silence. Teachers expect students to be prepared and do at least half of the talking in these meetings. In tutorials and scheduled conferences you should know clearly in advance what you want to say about a paper you have written, about readings you want to discuss, or about issues you want to clarify. You should also take advantage of office hours as opportunities to learn directly from your teachers, especially if you are confused about course material.

The various types of courses usually correlate with enrollment size and classroom design. If you register for a course held in a seminar room with an enrollment cap of eighteen students, for example, you can reasonably expect that the course will be taught as a seminar. Your teacher, in turn, will probably expect you to participate actively in discussions. As I mentioned with reference to academic freedom, however, individual instructors are free to teach courses according to their own preferences, teaching habits, and skills, in ways that are sometimes unpredictable.

I know a few professors who can lead lively discussions with as many as one hundred students in a lecture hall, and others lecture habitually to very small classes billed as seminars. On the way to my office, I pass a small classroom furnished with about twenty-five movable school chairs (the kind with a little writing table attached and a shelf under the seat), a library table with a portable oak lectern, and a chalkboard. One summer a history professor was teaching a class of only three students in this room. Every time I passed he was standing behind the table, bent over his notes and gripping the sides of the lectern as though he were steering a ship through a gale, lecturing in full voice. His three students sat just beneath him with expressions of mild alarm, silently taking notes.

The following summer, a graduate teaching assistant used this classroom for discussion sections of a large political science course. She usually sat on the front of the table, the lectern banished to a corner on the floor, with her twenty students seated around the room in a large circle. Often an animated discussion was in progress, punctuated by laughter, but occasionally the students were writing intently in their notebooks while the teacher watched in silence. One morning the students were clustered in little groups working on what appeared to be drafts of their papers, the teacher moving from one group to another. The room was filled with loud conversation.

In the same classroom the next fall, an English literature course was usually in progress when I walked past. The professor sat with his twelve students in a smaller circle. Now and then he was standing at the chalkboard, explaining something, but more often he and his students were engaged in quiet conversation. One day he was reading to them from what appeared to be a novel. The students listened thoughtfully with their notebooks open, but without taking notes. Another morning a student was reading from typed pages — probably from a paper she had written.

In small classrooms, lecture halls, and labs throughout the campus, teaching and learning take many other forms, not reliably correlated with departments or enrollments. I know a psychology professor who teaches a class with more than one hundred students "like a talk show," as she says. There is a central aisle in this amphitheater, where shy and sleepy students typically settle into the back rows, and she can move up and down this aisle with a microphone, calling on individuals to speak to the class. "In my course," she tells her students, "there is nowhere to hide!"

And instruction goes on outside these classrooms as well. In good weather many teachers take their students outdoors, where they sit in circles on the grass. Groups of biology students might do field studies among the gardens, trees, and wetlands, collecting samples and taking notes, and art and architecture students might be working on drawing and design projects.

During the week, you will move among three or four of the general types of courses I have described, each with some unique features as well. In each class you will have to figure out, as quickly as possible, what it means to be a good student, and as you go from a large lecture in one period to a discussion-based seminar in the next, you will have to change the quality of your presence. **[Exercise 4]**

These adjustments are among the most important and neglected keys to success in college. If you do not make them deliberately, you will tend to slide into an all-purpose default mode that leads many college teachers to complain that the freshmen in their classes are too passive and unresponsive, too reluctant to speak out and take initiative. When my small writing seminars begin, I can often tell which students have just come from a large lecture. They still appear to be sitting invisibly in the back row of an auditorium, waiting for me to do all the talking and keep them interested for the next hour. Because I expect my students to assume half of the responsibility for the quality of our class, those who do not adjust to this expectation rarely do well, even if they are very capable.

Language and Learning

In all types of courses, in every department, language is the primary medium of teaching and learning. Some classes also rely on other media: visual representations (such as pictures, diagrams, and films), demonstrations, hands-on activities (such as lab experiments), or mathematics and statistics. But about 90 percent of instruction in college is verbal, and the ways in which you use language as a student — as a writer, reader, speaker, and listener — will largely determine your levels of performance in all of your courses.

Several years ago, a Korean student helped me to realize the overwhelming importance of language in education, and in our lives more generally. A college freshman, Linda told me that when she moved to the United States and entered the sixth grade, she spoke and understood barely a word of English. Her suburban school had no English as a Second Language program, and none of the students and teachers spoke Korean. Other students were assigned to escort her to her classes, but when she got there she had no idea what was going on. She couldn't understand what the teachers and students were saying. She couldn't read textbooks, assignments, or writing on the board. She couldn't take notes in class or do homework. She couldn't ask questions or make friends with other students. She couldn't figure out how much she knew or didn't know in particular subjects — whether she belonged in the sixth grade or, as she often felt, back in kindergarten. "I felt completely stupid and helpless," Linda told me, "until I got to math class."

In that class, the teacher put a math problem on the board and stood back, speaking to the students as though he were asking them to solve it. With enormous relief, Linda realized she had learned to do this kind of problem two years earlier in Korea. To demonstrate to everyone that she had a mind that worked, she walked straight to the board, solved the problem, and returned to her desk. The teacher nodded and smiled with approval. Other students smiled at her too and looked impressed. That moment gave Linda confidence, for the first time, that she was smart enough to survive in this country. Mathematics was a language she knew. But in this foreign place, becoming a good student meant learning to use English just as well.

In its diverse forms, language was no less essential to learning when Linda was attending school in Korea, using her native language. It was no less important for her fellow students in the United States, and it is no less important for you, whether English is your native language or not. In familiar situations, however, we take most of these uses of language for granted or call them by other names:

- Attending class
- Taking notes
- Studying
- Doing homework
- Taking exams

- Asking questions
- Participating in discussion
- Getting help
- Paying attention

In every type of class, you are engaged in some or all of these linguistic activities, along with more obvious uses of language such as writing papers. In every course you take, the ways in which teachers and students use language determine the kinds of instruction and learning that will occur. Even in her mathematics class, Linda could not learn new material easily until she could understand what her teacher was saying, read explanations in her textbook, and ask questions.

If you consider these uses of language, therefore, you can analyze what is going on in your courses, how their designs and expectations differ, and what it means to become a good student in each of them. *In each case, who is speaking, listening, writing, and reading? What forms do these uses of language take?*

In a large lecture course, for example, the professor usually speaks and writes on the board, sometimes distributing course descriptions, assignments, and other handouts that he or she has previously written. Students usually listen in silence, read the information on the board and in handouts, and write in their notebooks. Outside class, they do assigned readings, speak to one another about the course material, and complete written assignments such as papers, problem sets, and other homework. Prior to exams they read over their course notes, review assigned texts, and perhaps study together. During most exams they are also writing: completing short-answer or essay questions to demonstrate what they have learned.

In laboratories, discussion sections, or seminars the uses of language differ. Students might speak in class while teachers listen; they might read drafts of other students' papers or follow instructions in a lab manual. In every case, however, learning occurs through linguistic exchange. **[Exercise 5]**

Even in a large lecture class, furthermore, there are different ways of being engaged in these activities, some more effective than others. In following chapters I will describe some of the distinct ways of writing and reading for different purposes. Here I examine these variations in one important type of writing that all of you will need to do.

A Note on Note Taking

During a lecture, almost everyone is writing in a notebook. But are these students actually doing the same thing?

They are not, as a painful memory from my first year at the University of Colorado reminds me. At my assigned seat in the required Western Civilization class, I was listening to an unbroken stream of historical information, trying to figure out what I should write in my notebook. I couldn't record everything the professor was saying, and when I tried to do so I fell behind, losing track of his lecture. Finding no solution to the problem, I occasionally wrote something down, more or less at random, in an anxious scrawl.

In the seat next to me, a sophomore listened attentively to these lectures and at the same time calmly produced detailed outlines, in green ink and tidy print. One day she turned to me and said, in a not entirely convincing tone of admiration, "I think it's *amazing* that you can remember all this information with so few notes. I need to write down almost everything or I forget it."

I don't need to tell you who got an A in the course and who got a C–. The notes I took in class were almost useless when I tried to study for the essay exams, which asked us to explain the roles of historical figures, the causes of wars, the connections among events. My notebooks resembled the ones Mike Rose rediscovered, from his first "disengaged and half-awake" semester at Loyola University, and described in his book *Lives on the Boundary*:

> The one from English is a small book, eight by seven, and only eleven pages of it are filled. The notes I did write consist of book titles, dates of publication, names of characters, pointless summaries of books that were not on our syllabus and that I had never read . . . and quotations from the teacher ("Perception can bring sorrow"). The notes are a series of separate entries. I can't see any coherence. My biology lab notes are written on green-tint quadrille. They, too, are sparce. There is an occasional poorly executed sketch of a tiny organism or of a bone and muscle structure. Some of the formulas and molecular models sit isolated on the page, bare of any explanatory discussion. The lecture notes are fragmented; a fair number of sentences remain incomplete. (42)

Rose eventually became a professor of English at UCLA, but by the end of his second semester of college he was heading toward academic probation. So was I. What were we doing wrong? What and how did we change?

If you think of note taking *as a kind of writing* — a use of written language — you can more easily understand and resolve some of the problems that freshmen commonly encounter in lecture courses, and you can understand these problems not as matters of intelligence and capability, but as questions of strategy.

The central problem is that note taking forces you to do at least two things at once: *listen* and *write*. (Sometimes you also need to *read* information on the board or on handouts.) If you use note taking to record everything the teacher says, you will soon fall behind, and in your struggle to catch up you will miss substantial portions of the lecture, including important connections. For this reason stenography — the effort to write down everything — is a lost cause. Listening and writing will be at odds.

Fortunately you don't need to record everything. Instead, you need to take notes on the most important points and the connections between them, to help you reconstruct an understanding of the lecture material a week or a month later. For this purpose, you need to give listening priority over writing: *to put writing in the service of listening, understanding, and remembering.*

The best teachers make this process fairly easy, by delivering well-organized lectures at a reasonable pace, using the chalkboard or overhead projections to outline, emphasize, or illustrate important material. Some professors even distribute lecture notes in advance, so their students can listen and think with full attention. Others, like my Western Civilization professor, deliver masses of information at a rapid pace, without pauses or visual aids. In such a class, especially, the following suggestions from some of the most successful undergraduates will be useful.

Do assigned readings before the lecture, not after.   When professors assign readings for topics on the course syllabus, they often assume that you will come to the lectures with background knowledge of the topic gained from the readings. Research on learning indicates that relevant background knowledge greatly increases our ability to make sense of and remember new information. If you have completed reading assignments in advance, therefore, you will find it much easier to understand and take notes on the lectures. If lectures correspond closely with assigned texts, you will also need to take fewer notes when you recognize material available in the readings.

Listen for the structure of the lecture.   This is what my classmate was doing, as she calmly produced those neat outlines in her notebook. While I was struggling to record whole sentences verbatim, without knowing why, she was often looking up at the teacher, listening for central themes, subtopics, lists of examples or causes. At the end of the period she left with a frame of reference for understanding and remembering the lecture and for correlating the lecture with readings. I left with fragmented bits of stenography that made very little sense a week later.

Fill in details and perspectives shortly after the lecture. For reasons I'll explain in Chapter 5, your memory of a lecture will fade very quickly, even if you feel that you understand everything at the end of a class. Because what you wrote down will be about all you will have left a day later, at your first break after a class read over your notes and fill in missing details, observations, and connections. Conscientious students often say they "recopy" their notes shortly after a lecture, but they are really doing more: reorganizing, clarifying, adding information they didn't have time to record, and noting questions they need to resolve.

Adapt your note-taking strategies to the type and design of the course. In my freshman year, my course notebooks looked very similar — all of them filled with clumps of scrawled quotations from the lecture itself, broken occasionally by diagrams I copied from the board. In later, more successful years my methods varied a great deal from one course to another. If exams were based heavily on information in lectures, I took extensive notes and reviewed them to make sure they were complete. In courses that required essays based upon the interpretation of issues, I spent more time listening and thinking about the discussion, paraphrasing central arguments and noting questions or references for further reading. Occasionally I took no notes at all or spent the time recording my own ideas in response to an issue.

Review your notes with friends in the class. These review sessions have two main functions. Friends might have noted important information or connections that you missed, or understood the material from a different, valuable perspective. Research on note taking suggests that, on the average, individual students write down only about 35 percent of important information. In the process of explaining this material to each other you will also strengthen both your understanding and your memory. **[Exercise 6]**

Forms and Functions of a Writing Class

In primary school, learning to write and read made it possible for you to learn geography, history, science, and every other subject. As I explained in the previous section, this is still true, even if you take these skills for granted. By the time you entered high school, however, direct *attention* to writing and reading probably occurred in your English class, where you also studied literature. Preparation for writing in college and for standardized tests of writing and verbal skills occurred in your English class as well.

In college, the great majority of freshman writing courses are offered through English departments, but the goals and forms of these courses differ from those of high school English.

One major difference is that college writing teachers are *not* preparing you for standardized tests, which reduce writing and verbal skills to specific, measurable forms. Instead, freshman writing courses usually serve the purposes of general education: to help you write, read, and think more effectively in all of your other courses. In this respect, the goals of a freshman writing course are closer to those of language instruction in primary school, where "language arts" were essential to all subjects. Because writing takes many forms in the undergraduate curriculum, college teachers will assign writing of diverse types. Another difference in college is that almost all freshman writing courses are taught as seminars, where you will participate in discussions and exchange work with other students.

A 1990 survey conducted by the South Coast Writing Project at the University of California Santa Barbara revealed some of the most common differences between high school and college writing instruction. Writing teachers in the University of California system and in surrounding high schools were asked to rate the importance of many features of writing and writing courses. Here are some of the most striking differences, statistically rated "extreme":

- High school teachers were much more likely to emphasize the interpretation of literature and to use literature as reading material, while college teachers assigned papers on a much wider range of topics and readings.

- The majority of high school teachers believed that writers should "know what they want to say before they begin to write," while a larger majority of college teachers disagreed, emphasizing exploratory writing and revision "for discovering what a writer has to say."

- Half of the high school teachers stressed specific formulas for structuring essays (such as the "five-paragraph theme" that I will discuss in the next chapter), while 93 percent of the college teachers discouraged the use of these formulas.

- Seventy-two percent of the high school teachers expected that students should write all of their college papers "in a formal, academic style, using a sophisticated vocabulary," but only 13 percent of college writing teachers agreed.

- While half of the high school teachers believed that the use of the first-person *I* would be inappropriate in college writing, 95 percent of college writing teachers disagreed.

I should note that there were also *similarities* in teaching methods and values between the two groups, including the idea that student writers should draw on their own interests and beliefs and the expectation that students would write for a variety of audiences. Because this was a regional study conducted some years ago, we can't assume that it represents all high schools and colleges in the present or that college writing teachers represent the expectations of all college teachers.

The major findings of this study do correspond, however, with problems of adjustment to college writing that my students face, and in following chapters I will give you advice for making these adjustments.

The designs and goals of writing classes have actually become more diverse in American colleges over the past ten years, partly as a result of a movement called "writing across the curriculum" or "writing in the disciplines." In many cases these terms simply mean that your freshman writing class will include writing and reading for a variety of fields. At other schools you might take a general writing course as a freshman but will be required to take one or more designated "writing-intensive" courses in particular fields of study before you graduate. Here at Cornell University, more than a hundred different freshman writing courses are offered in about thirty departments, so writing teachers at Cornell, as at some other schools, might be sociologists, philosophers, or psychologists. George Mason University and other colleges use freshman writing courses to help students work on assignments in "linked" courses in fields such as computer science, interior design, and engineering. Many liberal arts colleges such as Brown and Swarthmore assign trained undergraduate "writing consultants" to advise students on writing projects in many of their courses, including the sciences.

All of these programs recognize that writing is not a single set of skills you bring with you to college. Instead, learning to write effectively is an ongoing process that requires constant adjustment to diverse expectations.

To help you understand and meet these expectations, the majority of college writing programs also have writing centers, where you can get help with specific problems and assignments. At these writing centers, staff members or peer tutors are usually available for consultation on writing projects, and many of these centers offer other services, such as courses, workshops on particular skills, libraries of writing resources, Web sites, or online exchanges. [**Exercise 7**]

Do not hesitate to use these resources or to consult with your writing teacher when you run into problems in other courses. Writing courses, requirements, and facilities exist because language problems are completely *normal*, especially in the first year of college. Entering students have always had trouble adapting to the unfamiliar standards for writing and reading in higher education. When Harvard began to use an entrance examination for writing skills in 1874, more than half of the entering freshmen failed the exam.

EXERCISES

Exercise 1.   If you are attending college, draw a "personal map" of your campus — the way you picture it in your mind — and ask two other students to do the same.

Then compare the features of these maps, what they include and leave out, and write about what you notice. How much can you tell about the other two students from their maps? How much can they tell about you?

Exercise 2.   Make a list of the classes you took or are taking in your senior year of high school. If you are a college freshman, make a list of the courses you are currently taking. If you are not yet in college, you can make a list by looking at a college course catalogue, selecting courses that satisfy freshman requirements, and reading the course descriptions. (You can find course catalogues in your school or public library or on college Web sites.)

Compare these two lists, thinking of the content of the courses. How much continuity and discontinuity do you find? If the subjects are the same, are the contents and requirements directly related?

Exercise 3.   In a couple of pages, do a "motivation inventory" by answering the following questions for high school and then for college: On a particular evening, why should you work on a writing assignment for your English class or study for an exam in biology? What is or was your motivation in your junior or senior year of high school? In college, how have these motivations changed, or how do you think they will need to change?

Exercise 4.   For college freshmen: Using my descriptions of course types as a guide, identify the specific types of courses you are currently taking. For each course, write a paragraph describing what it means to be a good student in the course. What kinds of skills, motivations, and participation does the course require?

Exercise 5.   For one of your classes, in high school or in college, create a "map" of language use. In this class, who is speaking, listening, reading, and writing? What specific forms do these uses of language take?

Exercise 6.   Compare your notes for a particular day of class with those of a friend in the same course. Describe the differences in content and form between the two sets of notes on the same material. Which features of these approaches to note taking are most effective for the course?

Exercise 7.   In the reference section of your school library, look at the course catalogues from two colleges or universities — your own and another if you are now in college. At these two schools, where do writing courses and requirements fit into the curriculum? In what department or departments are required writing courses offered? How are they described in the catalogues? Are there significant differences between the two schools?

2 Footstools and Furniture

There is a general theme that freshmen in college experience throughout their first year: you have to adapt, but not necessarily abandon, what you've learned in high school to fit into your new college environment.

— A college junior

What Is Good Writing?

Many of your college teachers assume that you learned the "basics" of good writing in high school. They also assume that your freshman writing course will review and supplement the skills you need to write well in your other courses. For this reason, teachers who assign writing in fields such as history, anthropology, or biology might not tell you how to complete those assignments effectively.

You probably have learned some basic strategies for completing the kinds of essays teachers assign. When you apply that knowledge to particular assignments, however, you might find that your teachers had different expectations. The "basics" they thought you should have learned for writing in their courses might differ from the ones you were taught, and an approach that works well in one college course might not work in another. Following methods of organization you learned in high school, you might produce an essay that, according to your teacher, "lacks organization." Yet in another course the same strategy might satisfy your teacher's expectations. The effort to meet these diverse, unpredictable expectations leads some students, like this senior, to conclude that there are no reliable standards for good writing:

It's all luck. I used to think I was a good writer, but now I don't know. Sometimes I work for days on a paper, and the teacher hates it. Sometimes I whip it off in a couple of hours and it turns out great.

Maybe it's my mood. Maybe it's the teacher. I don't know. It's always a gamble, so I avoid writing whenever I can, and when I can't avoid it I just do it, and see what happens.

For the purpose of resolving these doubts I'll first reduce the problem to more manageable proportions. Among your teachers and fellow students you will probably encounter two ideas about good writing that seem to conflict:

1. All good writers and all good writing should follow some basic principles. For example, *All good writing should have a thesis, clearly stated in the introduction. Following paragraphs should each present a point that supports this thesis, and the essay should end with a logical conclusion. Writing throughout the essay should be clear, concise, and correct.*
2. Features of good writing vary from one situation to another. These variations depend, for example, on the *subject* of the writing, its *purpose*, and the *reader's expectations*. The *form* of writing used in a field of study often structures those expectations. As a consequence, the features of good writing in a literature course will differ greatly from the features of good writing in business or astronomy, and what seems clear to one audience might not be clear to another.

These statements appear to conflict, but writing is similar to other complex skills we master gradually. If you learned to play a musical instrument, for example, you started with very simple compositions that strengthened basic skills necessary for moving on to more complex forms and styles. As you became more accomplished, the basic skills you first learned remained important, but standards for performance changed, and the range of music you could play expanded. Although it was once important for you to learn to play those simple pieces well, you wouldn't choose to perform them in an advanced recital.

A different analogy might help to resolve this apparent contradiction in the case of writing: Imagine that you have learned woodworking skills by perfecting the construction of a good footstool. Your instructor has chosen this task to teach you basic principles of woodworking: the selection of materials, the use of tools, methods of shaping and joining parts, and techniques for completing a nicely finished product. With practice and guidance, you have learned these lessons well. In the final tests of your skill, you produce footstools that are solid, functional, and unblemished. You have become adept, your teacher informs you, at the basics of woodworking.

Now suppose that on the strength of this success, you take a job at a large furniture factory. In addition to the occasional footstool, the various departments produce many styles of tables and chairs, beds, wardrobes, dressers, cabinets, and bookcases. There are also different lines of these products, some purely functional, others ornate, elaborately joined, and highly polished. Different departments employ different materials and methods and maintain different standards for quality. "Eventually," the manager says, "you'll work in one of these departments, depending on your abilities and preferences. But for the first year or two we want you to try several of them, to give you a sense of the whole range of our operations and all of your options."

For more than a year, then, you move from one department to another, working as an apprentice in all of them. Many of the tools, materials, and procedures are familiar to you. Most of the types of furniture you are supposed to build have legs and tops, like a footstool, but some do not, and there are also drawers, doors, shelves, and frames, hinges and pulls, dovetail or mortise and tenon joints, different glues and dowels for different purposes, and varied finishes for different styles of furniture. In each department you are a novice and make mistakes. And as you attempt to carry the knowledge you have gathered from one department to another, you find that expectations vary. One supervisor wants you to follow detailed instructions; another expects you to be creative. One department emphasizes the quality of materials and simple, sturdy construction; another is concerned with style and the development of original, interesting designs. These standards for the production of "good furniture" differ, yet each supervisor describes these standards as though they were absolute.

"Don't get discouraged," an experienced worker reassures you. "Eventually you'll pass through this phase and settle into one kind of job. For now, just pay attention and learn as much as you can." And indeed, as the range of your experience expands, you gradually become better at adapting the skills you have already acquired to new tasks.

In the business of higher education, the departments I have in mind, of course, are academic ones, and their main product (apart from college graduates) is writing. Every academic field has its own literature. These literatures include specialized journals in which scholars must, as the saying goes, "publish or perish." They also include books written primarily for colleagues in the profession, textbooks, and books and articles for more general audiences. In the field of psychology, for example, scholars in various subfields publish articles in dozens of highly specialized research journals such as *The Journal of Personality* and *Social Psychology*, in journals that represent the entire discipline such as *American Psychologist*, and in magazines for the general public such as *Psychology Today*. All of these periodicals have their own guidelines for the length, form, and style of articles they publish. Many other types of informal and official writing (such as research notebooks, grant proposals, reports, and professional correspondence) add to the great demands of writing in the working lives of scholars in every field. In academic communities, writing is the primary medium through which the work of scholars becomes known. **[Exercise 1]**

In an introductory biology class no one will expect you to write according to standards for publication in *Nature, Evolution,* or *The American Journal of Physiology*. In any field, the standards for student writing and for professional writing differ. But professional literatures do shape the kinds of assignments you will be asked to complete. Like our apprentice woodworker, you will spend your first year getting basic experience in a variety of departments before you decide, on the basis of performance and preference, which field you will pursue. In the process, you might be asked to produce historical arguments, philosophical discussions, scientific reports, literary analyses, social science research papers, business case studies, autobiographical essays, poetry, or fiction. Most of these forms of student writing derive from professional literature of one kind or another. And although individual teachers might imagine that their standards for "good writing" are universal, they are not. As you move from one course and department to another, writing assignments will lead you to write for very different audiences, in different forms and styles, for different purposes.

What are the components of a good piece of writing, and how are they assembled? What qualities are teachers looking for when they assign writing: creativity? logic? factual content? brevity and simplicity? elaboration? evidence that you have learned what you were taught? Evidence that you can think independently, with originality? Should good writing be simple and functional, or should it be elaborately, stylishly designed? Should its significance be clear to everyone or only to certain types of readers? Diverse standards for writing can't be reduced to a single form or procedure any more than woodworking can be reduced to the construction of footstools.

To become adept at building furniture, therefore, you have to stop making footstools, even though many of the skills you learned for making them remain useful.

The Limitations of the "Footstool Essay"

I suspect that most of you have identified the footstool in this analogy: a basic form of essay, composed of a few parts assembled in a certain order. In your junior high and high school English courses you probably learned that every essay should have three parts: an *introduction*, a *body*, and a *conclusion*. "As a writer in high school," one college freshman recalled in a slightly macabre way, "I was told to follow a certain formula, introducing the topic with an introduction, concluding with a conclusion, and filling the space in between with a body."

The "formula" this student refers to is sometimes called the "five-paragraph theme" or the "keyhole essay" (a term coined by Sheridan Baker in a writing text titled *The Practical Stylist*). According to this formula, the introduction should take the shape of a funnel, beginning with a broad statement of the topic and narrowing to a thesis statement at the end. This statement lists the subtopics, or "points," of the following paragraphs, and the body of the essay raises these points in order. The final paragraph should begin somewhat narrowly, perhaps as a reiteration of the thesis, and broaden in the form of an inverted funnel to some kind of conclusion. The typical choice of three supporting points plus the introduction and conclusion accounts for the term "five-paragraph theme," and "keyhole" roughly describes the overall shape of the essay, which my students often diagram like Figure 1.

High school teachers often use some version of this formula to prepare students for the Advanced Placement English exam and other timed assessments of writing ability because it provides a structure for writing a brief essay on almost any subject. Whether you are writing arguments, summaries, explanations, or comparisons, on the causes of a war, the advantages of managed health care, or the duties of a citizen, this model allows you to begin with a basic outline. Once you have identified a central thesis and three supporting points, you know that you should begin with some general observations about the topic, narrow the introduction to a topic sentence that lists your supporting points, discuss these points in order in the body paragraphs, return to your thesis in the con-

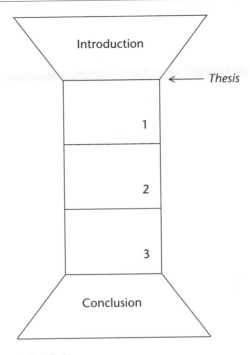

FIGURE 1

clusion, and end with further generalization. If you "say what you are going to say, say it, and say you've said it" (as some teachers instruct their students), neither the writer nor the reader can possibly get lost. If you follow these simple instructions, your essay should turn out every time, like a ready-mixed cake. **[Exercise 2]**

This basic outline is so easy to use that students often bring it with them to college and use it habitually as a template for writing essays. As an all-purpose recipe, however, this formula does not work very well or for very long. We can observe some of its limitations in the following essay written by an entering freshman in response to a timed (50-minute) writing assessment asking students to "discuss factors that facilitate or hinder learning":

> In order for people to learn there must be a
> good learning atmosphere. Many things can affect the
> atmosphere in which people try to learn. Some of
> them are class sizes, stress, and the professor's
> way of teaching. A bad learning atmosphere hinders

learning because people can't concentrate and absorb the material to be learned.

Large classes hinder learning. Large classes cause the student to get less individual student-professor contact. They also put the student farther from the teacher so it's harder to focus on him/her. The student would have a greater distance between him/her and the front of the room where the professor is speaking.

Stress from outside of class hinders learning. Stress also could distract students in class by giving them other things to think about. It might also cause headaches that would hinder or prevent proper concentration. If students have large amounts of stress it messes up sleeping patterns. This could cause students to fall asleep in class, or be too tired to learn properly. Stress hinders learning because of the effect it has on both the mind and the body.

Professors who speak in a language only they can understand hinder learning. Students then spend too much time trying to figure out what the professors are saying. This causes the students to not be able to take proper notes. Students might also lose interest in the class that is needed for them to survive. Students might continue to fall below an ever increasing pile of work as they try to understand. Students' ability to learn is hindered when professors speak in a language only the professors can comprehend.

Learning is hindered when the atmosphere isn't conducive to learning. This happens when the student has too many stresses outside of class. It also happens when students are in large classes because students don't get as much contact with the professor. Professors who speak in a language only they

can understand hinder learning because the students
try to understand them instead of the material. The
atmosphere of the classroom is hindering learning
when things such as these occur.

This is a particularly rigid, skeletal example of a "five-paragraph theme," yet it conforms to the "basic" requirements for clarity, organization, and correctness (apart from a couple of minor errors) taught in many high schools. I suspect that the student who wrote it believed that he was doing exactly what he should do to demonstrate to college teachers that he could write a decent essay.

The assessment readers, however, considered it the work of a weak writer who might not be able to meet the demands of college work. Use of the five-paragraph formula made this essay seem an empty formality rather than a thoughtful response to the question. It is too obvious that the writer was simply manufacturing an introduction and conclusion and "filling the space in between with a body," severed into three parts. Paragraphs consist of flat, disconnected statements of nearly the same length, and "say what you are going to say, say it, and say you've said it" becomes a recipe for redundancy. In fewer than two pages the essay says almost everything at least three times, as though readers suffered from attention deficit disorder.

Actually this diagnostic essay tells us very little about the student's writing ability. It tells us instead that on this occasion he used a simplistic formula that interfered with thought and communication. Once he had chosen the requisite thesis and three supporting points, writing became a task of filling in the blanks in a standard outline. While he was writing he did not think more deeply about the topic, establish connections among the supporting points, or ask himself whether "stresses outside the class," for example, can be considered features of the "atmosphere of the classroom." A conclusion that simply reiterates the introduction confirms that the essay takes the writer and the reader nowhere.

The assessment readers' main concern, therefore, was that this writer might be inflexibly wedded to a model that would undermine his responses to assignments in college courses — that he would produce a "footstool" when teachers expected a more complex, specific form. **[Exercise 3]**

Student writers who have moved beyond these formulas recognize both their functions and their limitations. One college junior realized that the prescription for good writing that he learned in his senior year of high school was really a prescription for getting through the AP English test:

> At the time, I believed that what I was learning were the "laws" of writing that every college student everywhere used to write effective papers. It is true that what I had learned worked perfectly for my specific purpose; it was exactly the style the Advanced Placement test-givers and my instructor wanted and encouraged. Although the style and rules that I learned are not totally useless (I use them sometimes to give my writing organization and direction if it is straying), they had negative consequences on style and creativity.
>
> For some reason unbeknownst to me, many of the rigid rules I observed had to do with the number three.
>
> Rule #1: Each paragraph should have at least three sentences.
>
> Rule #2: There should be at least three paragraphs to the body of a composition.
>
> Rule #3: The writer should strive to have three forms of proof or evidence for each of the three supporting ideas of the thesis.

This student's ability to look back and examine what he was taught as a way of moving forward represents the kind of flexible, reconstructive attitude that college writing teachers encourage.

What Remains True?

All of us who teach freshman writing courses are familiar with the five-paragraph formula, and most of us believe that our students need to move beyond it, into a wider range of forms and styles. We know that formulas do not automatically generate the kinds of thought, cohesion, fluency, and interest that characterize effective writing, and even a quick glance at published work reveals that good essays do not always consist of five paragraphs and three supporting points. Thesis statements do not always land at the end of the first paragraph, and a "thesis" can take many forms: a question the essay will try to answer, a statement of intention, an observation, or a strong argument, among others. Conclusions rarely mirror introductions. Successful writers pursue arguments, explanations, and other types of work in a great variety of forms that we cannot reduce to any one kind of outline or recipe. Using a single formula for all writing will bring your development to a screeching halt.

On the other hand, we know from experience that if such formulas represent in your minds the "basics" of academic writing, we cannot simply say "Abandon this formula!" without creating confusion and loss. Prohibiting the use of this model or any other standard format suggests that everything you previously learned about writing is wrong. And if these principles do not represent the basics of good writing in college, what are the *real* basics you can rely on? Writers who were left entirely to their own devices in high school, without models and standards, face equally difficult problems of adjustment, as one college junior recalled, in reference to his AP English class:

> *Sometimes I regret having been given so much leeway in writing. It seemed that sometimes I could do no wrong. My writing became more and more embellished. . . . Clichés and pretentious claims were the tricks of my trade. None of my teachers bothered to tell me that half of the time I wasn't even saying anything in my writing. I dealt in trite, pseudo-intellectual discourse when direct, honest answers would have been much more effective.*
>
> *College came as something of a shock.*

Fortunately, you can explore the complexity of writing without rejecting everything you previously learned. And there is nothing inherently wrong with a footstool as long as you don't try to use it for every purpose. It has its own design and functions, and like other objects it can be made well or badly, out of materials strong or flimsy, assembled with care or disregard. With some adaptation, skills you developed for one purpose might become useful for a very different purpose. As I'll explain in Chapter 4, for example, the basic shape of the "keyhole essay" will be most appropriate not for writing papers in an English class (where you probably learned it) but for writing science lab reports.

With some reinterpretation, furthermore, the notion of three basic sections — *introduction, body,* and *conclusion* — represents some valid observations about the structure and development of almost every kind of writing you will read and produce in college. Effective writing usually has a recognizable *beginning, middle,* and *end.* It starts somewhere, goes somewhere, and ends up somewhere. In this respect almost all writing, from short stories to scientific reports, has a quality of *narration*. It tells some kind of story, and the particular kinds of stories that academic writers tell largely define what it means to know something in that field. Historical narratives differ from philosophical or scientific ones, but all have some very general features in common:

1. *Beginnings* are points of departure, and even if they do not explicitly map the routes the writing will take, they tell us where this journey will start, point us in a certain direction, and provide some bearings for the next move. **[Exercise 4]**

2. The *middle* portions of an essay (or, for that matter, of a short story, a report, or a book), should carry the reader smoothly from the point of departure through a series of connected passages. As readers, we shouldn't feel that the route we are taking is completely arbitrary. Even if we do not know *en route* exactly where we will end up, we should feel that the writer is taking us somewhere in a particular direction. We shouldn't feel lost, either in a fog or in a thicket; if paragraphs can be rearranged without disrupting the flow of the writing, that usually means there is no flow to disrupt. We are just reading a bunch of paragraphs, a random collection of points, disconnected clusters of information. **[Exercise 5]**

3. *Endings*, then, are destinations. They might or might not present formal conclusions; they might offer new questions, explain what remains unresolved, or point out some new direction for further exploration. But they do give readers a sense of having arrived somewhere: at some new understanding or a new way of thinking about the topic. **[Exercise 6]**

Thinking about where a piece of writing will start out, where it will go, and where it will end up is a good idea, whether you are working within or without a prescribed format. While all-purpose formulas for writing ensure a measure of skeletal, structural organization, they do not automatically provide this essential quality of *movement* through and between sections — a quality that results from the relations among ideas you have thought through. This principle of movement partly explains why the five-paragraph assessment essay presented earlier was unsuccessful. The problem was not that it contained five paragraphs or three points. The main problem was that it ended up precisely where it started out. It didn't go anywhere.

For comparison, consider this response to the same writing assessment question— to "discuss factors that facilitate or hinder learning":

Many factors contribute to an environment where learning occurs. Comfortable settings, skillful teachers, and motivated students all facilitate learning. When all of these factors are positive, something like a chemical reaction happens in the minds of students.

Even one negative factor, however, can keep this reaction from happening. Students who have no desire to learn can't be taught, even by the most inspiring teachers. On the other hand, even when students are fascinated with the subject a poor teacher can make learning almost impossible.

Unfortunately this happened to me in my senior physics class. Most of us were very interested in science and wanted to go on to college with a strong background in physics. Mr. Gabler failed to satisfy our interests because he spent most of every class period telling us stories about his own experiences that often had nothing to do with science. He seemed to think we needed to be entertained rather than taught, but actually I believe he was the one who was bored with physics and with teaching. I think he was trying to entertain himself.

Because Mr. Gabler was such a poor teacher I had to learn physics mostly on my own, by studying the textbook at home. This means that learning can happen without teachers and outside the classroom. If the classroom was uncomfortable, or if the other students caused distractions, I could probably learn more by studying alone. If you are motivated to learn something you can find ways to learn unless some factor makes that "chemistry" impossible.

These examples tell us that missing factors do
not hinder learning as much as negative factors do.
Although a nice classroom, other good students, and
a skillful teacher can all contribute to a good
learning environment, learning can happen without
them. On the other hand, a horrible classroom, disruptive students, and a bad teacher can actually
prevent learning.

This assessment essay is similar to the first in some ways. In the
opening paragraph it introduces three factors that influence a learning environment, and it mentions these factors both in the following paragraphs and in the conclusion. It also has five paragraphs
and is therefore a "five-paragraph theme."

Unlike the first essay, however, this discussion of learning moves
from the opening statements through a series of connected points
to a real conclusion. In other words, it has a real *beginning*, *middle*,
and *end*, and as a consequence it takes us somewhere, beyond the
place where we started out. It has a *point of departure*, a *direction*, and
a *destination*.

We also have a sense that the writer was actually thinking about
the question both before and while she wrote. She wasn't just di-
viding the topic into three parts, according to a formula, and filling in the blanks. In fact, I suspect that when she wrote the first
paragraph she wasn't entirely sure where the discussion would end
up. The conclusion that "missing factors do not hinder learning as
much as negative factors do" probably occurred to her while she
was explaining what happened in and outside her physics class. If
she had followed the common formula, discussing three separate
points in disconnected paragraphs, this idea may not have occurred
to her at all.

In a timed assessment or essay exam, of course, you won't have
much time to think, and using a formula might seem to be the
safest alternative. In some cases students begin essays in an exploratory fashion that leads nowhere or becomes too complex for them
to finish in the allotted time.

But teachers recognize these hazards of exploratory thinking,
just as they recognize the use of formulas that minimize thinking.
*The great majority of your college teachers want you to use writing as a
way of thinking and conveying your thoughts about a subject, not as a
demonstration that you can follow a simple recipe.* **[Exercise 7]**

Breaking Out of a Rigid Structure

The main problem with the "footstool essay," therefore, is not that it consists of five paragraphs, three sections, and three supporting points. Instead, the problem is that student writers often use this formula habitually as a substitute for thought about the topic or question. Used in this rigid way, a prescription for writing will limit thought, limit the movement of your essays, and limit your development as a writer. While reliance on the formula might allow you to assemble an assessment essay or respond to an essay exam question quickly, students who depend on this model often have trouble writing longer papers that require more complex arguments and analysis. Using the same strategy whenever you get an assignment also becomes tedious. When students tell me that they no longer enjoy writing, they often mean that they no longer enjoy the routine ways in which they write.

None of these limitations apply to the idea that *a good essay is a vehicle for thought that moves from a clear point of departure, in a certain direction, toward a destination.* That conception of what you are doing can apply to writing of all kinds, of any length, at all levels of complexity.

And this is what high school teachers are trying to get across when they teach students highly structured models for writing essays. They are trying to emphasize some basic principles of organization that you can later use to develop essays of great variety. Unfortunately, students often miss the point of this instruction and assume that if they divide a topic into three subtopics the essay will more or less write itself. When they have let a prescribed formula determine the content, as I'll explain in the next chapter, they lose the flexibility and freedom they might have gained in the process of writing.

Some types of writing do occur within specific organizational frameworks that look like recipes, and I'm not encouraging you to ignore these prescribed structures. Scientific reports, for example, should carry the reader through a series of sections, with particular functions, in an order that is fairly predictable. Business reports and some kinds of correspondence, such as cover letters, have similarly predictable formats. Some writing assignments will tell you how your essay should be organized and what kinds of information it should contain. In order to write well, you must write within these guidelines, and in later chapters I'll describe some of them.

Even in these cases, however, the prescribed structure is only one feature of good writing. The quality of thought, information, and explanation is another. The way writing flows within and be-tween sections also affects the quality of the work as a whole. It is a serious mistake, therefore, to imagine that if your paper conforms to a prescribed format you have written well.

EXERCISES

Exercise 1. Go to the recent periodical section of your school library or public library, find five issues of different professional journals in a variety of fields, and photocopy the first page of the first article in each. Arrange these pages on a table and read them, paying attention to similarities and differ-ences in the ways they introduce the subject, the writing style and language, graphic features, and other details. Make a list of ten differences you notice among these examples of professional writing.

Exercise 2. In a couple of pages explain what you were taught about writ-ing essays in high school. Does the diagram of the "five-paragraph theme" or "keyhole essay" in this chapter look familiar? If it does, did your teachers show you ways to adapt or elaborate the model? If it does not, were you taught other forms or rules for organizing effective essays?

Exercise 3. To recognize how the formula structures your thinking and writing, write a conventional five-paragraph theme either for or against com-petitive grading in schools. Argue either that grading improves learning or that grading interferes with learning. Begin in the conventional way, with some generalizations about grades or learning, divide your argument into three points, discuss these points in body paragraphs, and restate your posi-tion in the conclusion.

Then in retrospect, assess what you gained and lost in using this ap-proach.

Exercise 4. To test my descriptions in this section, analyze the ways in which some published essays actually work. Choose three essays or articles from an anthology of readings used in your writing class, from other collec-tions of essays, or from magazines.

First look at *beginnings*. You should be able to identify the introductory section of each essay, from the first sentence to the point at which the author has finished telling readers what the essay will be about. How do these au-thors actually start out — with generalizations (as the five-paragraph model predicts) or with a specific anecdote, example, or question? Are these intro-ductory sections a single paragraph or several? What are their "shapes" in terms of the general and specific? How and where do the authors tell you the "thesis" or topic of the essay? Is this delivered as a statement or as a question? Does the introduction list the "points" that will follow in the body?

Exercise 5. Now look at the *middle* sections of the same essays or articles. Do the paragraphs that follow the introduction represent a simple list of supporting points, or do they follow in some other kind of logical order? How do these writers get from one place to another in the middle sections? Can you identify transitions? Could you move paragraphs within the essay without damaging its flow?

Exercise 6. Finally, you should be able to identify the *endings* or concluding sections of the same essays. Do they repeat assertions in the beginnings, or do they represent "destinations" that leave you with the sense that the essay has taken you somewhere? Are they shaped like inverted funnels, ending with generalization? What are the functions of the last sentences?

Exercise 7. Now write another brief essay about the advantages or the disadvantages of competitive grading in education. This time set the formula aside. Just think about the question until you find that you have a position from which you can start writing, begin by explaining what that position is, and then try to explain and support your position in a series of connected paragraphs. In the conclusion explain where the discussion has led you, or perhaps what issues remain.

In retrospect, what are the main differences between your essay in Exercise 3 and this essay? While you were writing the second, did you feel that you had to resist using the formula for structuring the essay?

3 | How Writing Gets Done

> When you write, you lay out a line of words. The line of words is a miner's pick, a wood-carver's gouge, a surgeon's probe. You wield it, and it digs a path you follow. Soon you find yourself deep in new territory. Is it a dead end, or have you located the real subject? You will know tomorrow, or this time next year.
>
> — Annie Dillard, *The Writing Life*

Product and Process

The word *writing* refers both to the product and to the process: to the finished work we read and to the activities through which the work gets written. In the first sense we might say, "Her *writing* is clearer than mine." In the second sense we might say, "He can't go out tonight because he's *writing* a history paper." In this chapter we will examine the second meaning of the term: the process of writing.

How do writers actually produce the papers, articles, or books we read? When the student is staying home for the evening, writing his history paper, what exactly is he doing? How do his methods differ from those of other writers, including his history teacher? And how do these methods affect the qualities of the finished products? These are some of the questions we will consider.

Is the Shortest Distance Always a Straight Line?

I'll begin with a very basic problem of logic that applies to writing and to many other aspects of our lives that we wish were completely predictable but are not.

I'm referring to the ways in which we think of all processes — everything we do that occurs over time, from a beginning to an end we can at least imagine.

Undergraduate education itself is one of these processes. When you start out as a freshman you already have an end in sight, four years down the road: graduation. You can think of every course you take, every semester you finish, as a step along that straight path toward the end you envision. Some of you have clearly defined career goals as well. If all goes according to plan, you will take courses that lead you directly to an undergraduate degree in biology or economics, for example, with grades and test scores that will deliver you directly to medical school or to an MBA program, from which you will enter a career in medicine or banking. You can think of the future, then, as a line on which you move toward a certain destination, through specific stages. We think of many shorter-term processes in this linear way as well. A building project usually proceeds in a series of stages toward a projected end: a certain kind of product. We plan trips with the assumption that we will follow specific routes to particular destinations at certain times.

I call these linear processes *Euclidean* because a theorem derived from the Greek mathematician Euclid asserts that *the shortest distance between two points is a straight line*. If you know where you are (Point A) and you know where you will end up (Point B), the shortest way to get there appears to be a straight line, without backtracking, delays, or digressions. This Euclidean logic governs the way we try to do most things that have a clear goal or product we can imagine, and it governs the way intensely goal-oriented people do almost everything, including writing.

But there are some serious, potentially hazardous limitations to this logic, which works only if we assume a couple of conditions that do not always apply to the real world. It assumes, first of all, that we know where both points are: not only where the line begins but also where it will end. Otherwise we have no way of knowing what direction the straight line should take. It also assumes that the points reside in empty space, free of obstacles — hills and valleys — or diversions. Measurement "as the crow flies" has little practical value in a mountain range, and going straight makes little sense if we don't know where we are going.

When we start any kind of process we tend to worry about the hazards of *not* having goals and plans. Choosing a destination, plotting a straight course, and strictly following that course seem to be the best way to get things done with a minimum of time, frustra-

nd confusion. We tend to forget the potential costs of choosing goals prematurely or of staying on the straight and narrow path. Here are four potential costs:

- The goals or products we envision at the beginning of the process aren't necessarily the best ones. In some cases they aren't even feasible.
- The straight path might seem to be the safest and most efficient, but it usually isn't the most interesting. Staying on it often keeps us from exploring other possibilities.
- Things rarely go exactly as we planned. If we are wedded to specific goals and plans, unavoidable diversions, obstacles, and delays can make us feel that we are lost or that we have failed.
- In some kinds of processes we can't predict the outcome, so every direction, every move we make, is exploratory. In these situations, people who believe they must have a clear goal in mind feel that every move is hazardous. **[Exercise 1]**

You've probably noticed that these limitations of linear, Euclidean logic relate to previous arguments I've made about preparations for college, orientation to college work, and the weaknesses of the "footstool essay." In all of these cases, progress rarely follows a straight path from Point A to Point B. Because the transition to college is a turning point, not a direct continuation of high school, your destination lies around a corner. Many of the goals, skills, and learning strategies you bring to this new environment will necessarily change, in ways you can't entirely predict. As a consequence, successful movement through college rarely follows a straight path, and students who cling too rigidly to goals and plans often feel derailed by unexpected obstacles and diversions, including new opportunities. In an essay called "College Pressures," William Zinsser described the hazards of linear thinking among students at Yale in the 1970s:

> *Mainly I try to remind them that the road ahead is a long one and that it will have more unexpected turns than they think. There will be plenty of time to change jobs, change careers, change whole attitudes and approaches. They don't want to hear such liberating news. They want a map — right now — that they can follow unswervingly to career security, financial security. Social security and, presumably, a prepaid grave.*

What I wish for all students is some release from the clammy grip of the future. I wish them a chance to savor each segment of their education as an experience in itself and not as a grim preparation for the next step. I wish them the right to experiment, to trip and fall, to learn that defeat is as instructive as victory and is not the end of the world. (276)

Many college writing teachers still assign Zinsser's essay because the attitudes and pressures he described have not substantially changed. I've known many college freshmen who envisioned such narrow, carefully planned routes to graduation and careers that a bad grade on one exam made them feel that their lives were ruined. As often as not, however, these goals were illusions, little more than vague ideas about the future that changed radically over the following years. When they looked back as seniors at the winding paths they had taken to unexpected destinations, their despair as freshmen over a C in calculus or economics seemed absurd to them.

In later chapters I'll explain the limitations of linear approaches to reading, research, and other skills you will use in your studies, along with alternative strategies. In reference to writing, we have already observed that an all-purpose formula for writing essays severely limits thought and expression, both in the process and in the product. The prescription for writing a five-paragraph theme told the student who wrote that first assessment essay exactly where Point A and Point B were and how he would get from one point to the other. Because he started out with the idea that he knew exactly where he was going, he had no further thoughts along the way, and as a consequence the essay went nowhere. Now we'll explore this faulty logic more deeply.

A Logical Deception

More than other processes, writing tricks us into linear approaches for two reasons:

- The product itself is linear.
- We can think of writing as captured speech.

A published article is a linear sequence of words, sentences, and paragraphs. When you read such an article, you usually begin with the first word and proceed to the last; if the writing is good, these words and sentences will flow smoothly from beginning to end, from Point A to Point B, in an unbroken stream. If you read that article aloud, furthermore, it will sound like fluent speech, as though the author wrote it continuously from beginning to end in the pace and voice of a public lecture.

When you read finished writing from beginning to end, therefore, you probably imagine that it was also *written* from beginning to end: that the author knew before she started exactly what she wanted to say, began to write with the first word you see, and continued writing to the last word on the last page. You might imagine that really good writers, like good speakers, can do this beautifully, with little need to pause or to revise what they say. Bad writers, like bad speakers, must frequently pause, stammer, and retract what they said in the awkward effort to write clearly. The linearity of the product and its association with speech lead people to believe that good writing results from natural eloquence, talent, or inspiration. These factors also lead us to *attempt* to write in the way we read and speak: from the first word to the last, in a continuous sequence.

But these ideas about the process, derived from the product, are for the most part fictions. As you read this chapter, for example, you probably imagine that the first sentence you read was the first one I wrote, and so on to the end. I also hope, at least, that the chapter sounds as though I were speaking to you clearly, continuously, without interruptions or backtracking. In fact, while I hope this will be the last draft of the chapter, it is already the fourth or fifth, and this version bears little resemblance to the first. While working on this draft I have already changed the beginning once, and I will certainly go back to make further changes to these sections before I finish. The first sentence you read might have been the last one I wrote. In other words, *the linearity of the product does not describe the process, and in this respect writing is not like speech.* A recording of speech would tell you the exact order in which words and sentences spilled forth. A written text does not.

As a record of language use, in fact, the product of writing deliberately *conceals* the process. All of those messy drafts and revisions were necessary phases in the process of completing this chapter, but I don't want to inflict them on you, the reader. Instead, I went through all of that effort, confusion, and revision to make reading effortless, clear, and continuous. Like all good performance, good writing creates an *illusion* of ease and continuity. To create this illusion, actors, dancers, and musicians have to spend many hours in rehearsal. When they perform, they do not want you, the audience, to witness all of the missed lines, awkward moves, and bad notes through which they prepared for this performance. They want you to imagine that what they are doing onstage is effortless.

Like other performing arts, therefore, writing gives you the opportunity to compose, rehearse, and revise before the real performance: the moment when the audience actually reads what you have written. As the French critic Roland Barthes pointed out in an essay called "Writers, Intellectuals, Teachers," "Speech is irreversible: a word cannot be *retracted*, except precisely by saying that one retracts it. . . . All that one can do in the case of spoken utterance is to tack on another utterance." Barthes means that if you are conversing with a friend, everything you say reaches that person immediately. If you say something confusing or offensive, something you regret, you can't take it back to revise it; you can only say something in addition to clarify the statement or repair the damage: "What I really meant was . . ." or "I'm sorry. That came out wrong. I didn't really mean it that way."

If you write a letter to this friend, however, until you drop it in the mail slot you are completely free to say anything that occurs to you, without any effect on the audience, your friend, because *in the process of writing the audience is not there.* Even if you feel that you are communicating directly with your friend, you are not. Even if you write this letter continuously in one draft, without making any changes, until you actually release the envelope into the mail slot you have complete control over its destiny. Even at that last moment you can take the letter back, read it over, make changes, tear it up, write a new version, or decide not to say anything. No one will ever know what changes you made, what you did or did not do, in that process.

The same freedom applies to a paper you write for a teacher. If a teacher assigns a four-page paper due a week later, you are free to use the available time in any way you choose. If you decide to produce a rough draft immediately and then forget about it for a couple of days, when you return to the project you might decide that it needs major or minor changes or perhaps that you want to start over from a completely different angle. If you find that you don't understand the assignment, you can talk with your teacher about it, discuss it with friends, or take a draft to the writing center for advice.

If you postpone work on the assignment until the night before it is due, you have simply limited the available choices. While you are writing, with the deadline looming, you might feel that you have to complete the paper in a single draft and that your teacher is already peering over your shoulder, reading everything you say, but this is still an illusion. As I'll explain later, many choices are yet available to you, and what you do in those remaining hours of "rehearsal" is still free from scrutiny and judgment. Until you turn the paper in to your teacher, you still have complete control over your use of language. You are not yet onstage.

In writing, the quality of the product will result directly from the choices you make in the process. The specific methods writers use vary greatly, according to their preferences, purposes, and circumstances. An individual will not use the same methods for writing a personal letter that he uses for writing a long essay or a book, and two people might use very different, equally effective methods for completing the same kind of project. In general, however, the most successful writers are those who make the best use of the freedom the writing process offers in a given situation. Weak writing, in turn, usually results from poor uses of the writing process, not from the lack of ability or "talent." The linearity of the product tricks us into thinking that beautiful writing just came out beautifully from the minds of brilliant writers. When you read work that you most admire, remember the analogy to a fine actor, dancer, or musician onstage. Remember that the fluent quality of what you are seeing or hearing results from weeks of invisible, messy rehearsals. **[Exercise 2]**

The Phases of the Writing Process

If a friend called while you were working on a writing assignment and asked what you were doing, you would probably just say, "I'm writing a paper," as though writing were a single activity. In fact, at particular moments in the process of working on that paper you might be doing very different things:

- Making notes or outlines
- Reading source material
- Pausing to think about what you are going to write
- Composing new sentences
- Reading over sentences you previously wrote
- Making changes to those sentences or to larger passages
- Checking your work for errors and other problems

Other activities would depend on your individual methods for getting writing done. For example, some people prefer to compose and revise drafts on paper before typing them on a keyboard. Others write directly on the computer, making changes as they compose. Some make elaborate plans and outlines before they begin to write a draft; some plunge straight into the task and organize their work as they produce it.

Although the product of this work is more or less public, the process is usually private. For this reason, writing teachers knew very little about the ways in which students and other writers actually worked until the 1970s, when they began to investigate this question. Through interviews, observations, and other methods, they discovered that writers are engaged in a complicated assortment of activities. In a study called "The Dynamics of Composing" (1980), Linda Flower and John Hayes observed that a writer at work is not like "a cook baking a cake or a CPA preparing an income tax return." Instead, they found that "a writer caught in the act looks much more like a very busy switchboard operator trying to juggle a number of demands on her attention and constraints on what she can do" (33).

Although individuals move through the writing process in different ways, the scholars who studied this process found that they could sort specific writing activities into categories of thought and behavior. Here is my own version of these categories, drawn from studies that give them a variety of names.

Prewriting or Planning

At certain times writers are not actually producing sentences and passages of text but are *preparing* to do so: gathering information and ideas from readings, thinking about the task, making notes or outlines. Walking or driving somewhere, pausing for lunch, or talking with someone about the project can also be prewriting activities if they engage our intention to write.

Composing

At other times writers are composing new sentences and passages, either on paper or on the computer, with the idea that these sentences might, at least, appear in the finished product.

Revising or Rewriting

Revision literally means "to see again," from a somewhat different perspective, and *rewriting* means changing what you have previously written, according to this new way of envisioning the task. Some writers revise entire drafts of complete chapters or essays. Others interrupt the composing phase to revise smaller sections, such as paragraphs, before they move on.

Editing or Proofreading

The boundary between revision and editing is not sharp, and in the publishing industry *editing* refers to all changes in a manuscript, including broad revisions. For the writing process, however, *editing* means highly focused attention to specific words or phrases or to the structure of a sentence. This local attention (which includes proofreading for errors and typos) differs from revising: reconsidering the organization of a whole passage or draft.

Release

"Performance, in which the whole fate and terror rests, is another matter," James Agee wrote in his introduction to *Let Us Now Praise Famous Men* after he had described how he *hoped* his book would affect readers. He knew that while he was writing, this outcome was still unpredictable, somewhat beyond his control. So I include this last phase of the writing process to mark that turning point: when we drop a letter into the mail slot or hand a paper to the teacher or send a manuscript off to a publisher.

Some accounts of the writing process describe these kinds of activity as "stages," and you can easily imagine how they could be used to construct a linear prescription for writing — a set of instructions, like a recipe:

1. Figure out what you want to say, and make an outline.
2. Compose a draft according to your outline.
3. Revise your draft.
4. Edit the revised draft.
5. Turn in the finished product.

If you were taught to use the five-paragraph theme or some other essay formula, you were probably also taught sequential methods, similar to these stages, for producing such an essay. And there is a certain amount of sequential logic to the phases of the writing process, especially in retrospect. You can't turn in a paper until it has been written; you can't revise or edit passages until they have been composed; and prewriting, as the term suggests, obviously comes before writing.

In practice, however, writers rarely work in this strictly linear fashion, even when they have been taught to do so. In an early study of writing practices, published in 1971, Janet Emig investigated the actual methods of twenty-five twelfth graders in honors English who had been taught that they should first choose a topic, then construct an outline, follow the outline in composing a draft, and so on. When Emig examined all of the written material these students produced in completing 109 essays for their classes, she found that only 40 essays included written "plans" of any sort and only 9 included formal outlines. When Emig asked experienced English teachers to evaluate only the final copies of these essays, she found no correlation between outlining and the quality or organization of the finished products. In a later study of twelfth graders, Emig found again that the most successful student writers did very little formal, written planning, such as outlining. The high school students in these studies also spent very little time rethinking or revising drafts they had already completed.

My own discussions with college students support Emig's observations. Some students have used outlines and other written plans since high school or earlier and find this preparation valuable, but most do not, and I have noticed no correlation between the use of outlines and the quality of finished work. Many students have told me that when they were asked in high school to turn in outlines and other material with their finished papers, they composed required outlines (sometimes even "rough drafts") *after* they had finished writing.

Does this mean that the students in Emig's study were "just writing" in a linear stream, spending all of their time in the composing phase of the process? Emig found that student writers who did not use written plans were inclined to "compose aloud": rehearsing, thinking ahead, rereading, or speaking about what they were writing while they were composing the paper in a single draft.

With the possible exception of "freewriting" (which I'll describe later in this chapter), writing is never a completely linear process.

It is always somewhat "loopy" or *recursive*, even when we are trying to produce something in a single draft. If you pay close attention to what you are doing, you will probably find that you do not produce sentences continuously for more than a minute or two without pausing to read over what you have previously written, to remind yourself what you have said, to restore a sense of voice and direction, and to gather your thoughts for moving ahead. **[Exercise 3]** When you read back over previous sections you might also pause to edit or even to revise what you have written. Phases of *planning*, *revising*, and *editing* are therefore interwoven with the effort to compose a draft. In a survey of research titled "Understanding Composing," Sondra Perl described these "microloops" in terms of motion and direction. Observation of writers at work revealed

> that throughout the process of writing writers return to substrands of the overall process, or subroutines (short successions of steps that yield results on which the writer draws in taking the next set of steps); writers use these to keep the process moving forward. In other words, recursiveness in writing implies that there is a forward-moving action that exists by virtue of a backward-moving action. (364)

As writers shift among these "substrands" of the process, progress occurs not in a straight line but in overlapping spirals.

The speed with which writers compose a draft therefore depends not just on the number of drafts and revisions they do but also on the amount of time they spend in these microloops. Those who are trying to make the first draft the last often compose very slowly. In their effort to avoid revision, they tend to interrupt the flow of their thoughts frequently to look back and forward, revising, editing, and planning as they compose. In an interview, the anthropologist Clifford Geertz admitted that even though he considered it "a very bad way to do things," he wrote whole articles and books in a single draft:

> I have an outline, especially if it's a book, but I hardly pay attention to it. I just build it up in a sort of craft-like way of going through it carefully, and when it's done it's done. The process is very slow. . . . I usually write about a paragraph a day, but at least it's essentially finished when it's done. (248)

As I'll explain later, college students generally believe that completing a writing assignment in one draft is the fastest, most efficient way to get writing done. For reasons that Geertz illustrates, this is not necessarily true. Because composing itself is almost always a "loopy" process — not a continuous, linear one — writing a three-page paper in one draft might take an hour, six hours, or several days, depending on the amount of time the writer spends pausing to think, reading over what he or she has written, or reconstructing sentences. For the same reasons, producing three drafts of a paper might be faster than writing one.

The Choices Student Writers Make

Timed writing assessments and essay exams severely limit your options for using the writing process. In these situations, when the clock is ticking, you will usually have just a couple of minutes for "prewriting": time just to think about the question and perhaps jot down a quick outline. Then you will have to compose your response in a single draft, reading back and thinking ahead to keep yourself on track.

In other kinds of writing, however, the whole of the writing process is available to you. Between the time you get the assignment and the time it is due, you are free to move among the phases of the process in any way you choose. If one approach doesn't work for you, there are always many other ways of getting writing done. If you experiment, you will probably find that different strategies work best for different kinds of assignments: for informal writing, short essays, longer research papers, or lab reports. In your writing course, specific methods of writing, including revisions, might be built into the assignments. Even with those conditions, however, many choices remain. As long as you have time to work on the assignment prior to the "performance," you have great freedom to choose the best way to "rehearse": to get your work ready for presentation to the reader.

Research tells us, however, that the majority of college students make a very narrow, "Euclidean" range of choices and that they use similar approaches for the many kinds of writing they do. On the basis of this research, including my own, I can therefore predict what most of you will tend to do when you get writing assignments, unless you make deliberate decisions to use different strategies. What I will describe is for the majority of college students the "default mode" for completing papers: the approach they fall into more or less habitually because it was the approach they were taught, because it seems to be most efficient, or because procrastination leaves them with few alternatives. **[Exercise 4]**

I noted that Janet Emig's study in 1971 revealed that high school seniors did not substantially revise assigned writing, and most did not even make formal plans, such as outlines. Instead, they compressed all of the phases of the writing process into a continuous effort to complete the paper in one draft. Often "composing aloud" — as though writing were a very slow, deliberate kind of speech — they planned, rehearsed, and edited sentences one after another from start to finish.

A decade later, Nancy Sommers (who now directs the Expository Writing Program at Harvard) observed similar methods in a study of college freshmen at Boston University and the University of Oklahoma. Sommers gave the same writing tasks to twenty of these student writers and to twenty professional writers: journalists, editors, and scholars. She then examined all of the written material they produced and interviewed them about their methods.

The professional writers in this study used a great variety of "loopy" methods for planning, composing, and revising their work, usually in a series of drafts. For example, one of the writers explained, "I have learned from experience that I need to keep writing a first draft until I figure out what I want to say. Then in a second draft, I begin to see the structure of an argument and how the various sub-arguments which are buried beneath the surface of all those sentences are related." Although the specific methods of these writers differed a great deal — some of them messy and others methodical — a constant theme is that they _expected_ to revise their work extensively from the moment they began a project. As another writer stated,

> My cardinal rule in revising is never to fall in love with what I have written in a first or second draft. An idea, sentence, or even a phrase that looks catchy, I don't trust. Part of this idea is to wait a while. I am much more in love with something after I have written it than I am a day or two later. It is much easier to change anything with time.

I could quote dozens of novelists and poets who just assume that extensive revision will be a necessary part of finding out what they have to say and producing finished writing that works. The whole chapter on revision in John Trimble's book *Writing with Style* consists of one quotation from a *Paris Review* interview with Ernest Hemingway:

Interviewer: *How much rewriting do you do?*
Hemingway: *It depends. I rewrote the ending of* Farewell to
Arms, *the last page of it, thirty-nine times before I was satisfied.*
Interviewer: *Was there some technical problem there? What was
it that had you stumped?*
Hemingway: *Getting the words right. (99)*

By contrast, the college freshmen Sommers interviewed planned to make the first draft the last, and they did not tend to use the term *revision* or *rewriting* to describe changes they made. Instead, they mentioned minor corrections and deletions they made while "reviewing" their papers. In terms of the writing process, once they had planned and composed a paper in one draft, they bypassed revision and simply edited — proofread — what they assumed to be a virtually finished piece of writing. One of these students described both the intention and the practice:

> I don't use the word rewriting *because I only write one draft and the changes that I make are made on top of the draft. The changes that I make are usually just marking out words and putting different ones in.*

Sommers concluded from this research that college freshmen reduced revision to editing, as an "afterthought" to composing a paper, because they confused writing with the linearity of speech. The effort to make the first draft the last also forced them to accept first thoughts as the last thoughts; they therefore believed that good writing resulted primarily from "inspiration," not from rethinking and revising. As one student writer pointed out:

> I throw things out and say they are not good. I like to write like Fitzgerald did by inspiration, and if I feel inspired then I don't need to slash and throw much out.

This student's reference to Fitzgerald is appropriate in an ironic way. When he was an undergraduate at Princeton, and then in the army, F. Scott Fitzgerald did try to write as this student imagines he did: in single "inspired" drafts. In this fashion he produced his first novel, then appropriately called *The Romantic Egoist*, on weekends in three months. But publishers rejected it because, as biographer Robert Sklar noted, "Fitzgerald lacked the time and the patience to do more than a patch-up job." By the end of Fitzgerald's career his approach to writing had completely changed. *Tender Is the Night* went through roughly seventeen drafts over a period of ten years.

Since the 1970s, college writing teachers have tried to persuade students that they should include revision in the process of completing papers. Because typewriters made revision difficult, there was great hope that the flexibility of word processors would encourage students to use the writing process more flexibly as well — especially that they would rethink and revise work in progress. But this revolution in student writing methods did not occur. As a rule, students simply used word processors as very smart typewriters: ones on which they could compose papers directly without worrying about minor mistakes.

In other words, both high school and college students tend to use computers as *composing and editing machines*, not as *revising machines*. Although word processors make it easy to move, add, or delete large sections of text, store multiple drafts, or splice sections of one draft into another, student writers do not tend to use these powers. One reason is that the computer screen conceals most of the document. To reconsider the whole text you need to print out hard copy. It is very easy, however, to make minor revisions on the portion of the text that is visible. The main change I've noticed in writing methods, therefore, is that students are more likely to compose directly on the computer than they were on typewriters, which encouraged them to begin with handwritten drafts to avoid minor typing errors.

To pursue these questions in the present, I often ask my students (at all levels of the university) to interview two of their friends about the specific methods they used to complete their most recent writing assignment. My students then produce reports on these interviews, often with transcriptions of tape recordings. These descriptions correspond very closely with the ones Sommers collected twenty years ago. When they are writing papers or reports *outside* a writing class (where teachers often assign revision), the great majority of college students try to make the first draft the last and avoid substantial revision as much as possible. The linear process my students and their friends typically describe looks something like this:

1. Figure out what you are going to say (with or without an outline).
2. Write the paper.
3. Fix it up.
4. Turn it in.

Although there are many variations within this general routine, the majority of students use some version of this sequence even for long papers. One junior, for example, described the way she wrote a thirteen-page analysis of three films:

> *Right from the beginning I knew that my first draft was going to be my last. The only revisions that I made to the first draft of my paper were typos, and occasionally I would fix awkward sentences. There were absolutely no changes in the ideas, theme, and organization of the paper because they were already determined before I started writing. Part of the reason I did this was time constraints, but most of the time I just didn't feel like it: the sense of completion was so great that I just couldn't bring myself to go back and correct the paper.*

This "sense of completion" — the desire to be finished — is an extremely common theme among the writers my students interview. Some students argue, as this junior initially did, that because they knew exactly what they wanted to say, the structure and content of the paper were "already determined" and did not need to be changed. In their desire to be finished with the task, they convince themselves that their first ideas are also the best or that altering the design of a first draft would ruin it beyond repair. Keeping his own account of his writing practices, another junior captured the moment when he decided not to rethink and revise the paper he was working on:

> *Eight o'clock. I have the sudden urge to go for a walk. Clear my head of all that I have to do by next week. I'll be right back. And as soon as I'm back from wherever it is I'm going, I intend to finish this. Maybe I'll come up with an entirely new presentation. But that would mean I'd have to start the whole thing over again. Forget that idea. I'm going for a stroll.*

In different parts of an interview, we can catch the following freshman in the act of rationalizing a one-draft approach that is actually driven by procrastination and his desire to "get it over with as soon as possible." Asked how he writes the first draft, this student explained:

> *As a procrastinator I usually put it off 'til the night before; I don't know. I hold it off and I usually spend . . . I go into the morning. I go into the night writing papers. You know, as you're writing, you know,*

*when it's late and you're really tired, your paper starts to get worse
and worse, in terms of content. You just want to get it over with. You
type in junk, I guess. That's how you think.*

Later in the interview, when he was asked whether he makes real
changes to the first draft, his viewpoint shifted:

*Well, what I have down is basically what I wanted to put in. It's
exactly like building a wall — you can't take anything out once you've
put it in. I think that each sentence is something I really wanted to
express, and just to take it out is like, like breaking the wall down.*

Along the same lines, a senior confessed that "when I get an idea
on how to approach the subject matter, it is hard for me to let go."
The phrases and sentences she has used get "sticky," she said, and
make it difficult for her to "restructure" what she has already said.
When asked if they ever revised papers, a number of students said
that revision was something they did for writing teachers, when
they were told to turn in rough drafts and then revise. **[Exercise 5]**

Cost/Benefit Analysis

If some version of this linear, one-draft approach is your "default
mode" as you begin your undergraduate studies, I'm not going to
try to convince you that you should just abandon this method. As
with the five-paragraph formula, for one reason, I would seem to be
urging you to trade order for chaos, something for nothing. But
there are a couple of other reasons as well.

I'm arguing for greater *flexibility* in your methods, not that you
should always use one approach or another. There is nothing fundamentally wrong with completing a piece of writing in one draft,
and suggesting that there is would be both misleading and dishonest. I often attempt, at least, to complete short, fairly simple writing tasks (such as letters or brief reports) in a single draft, and
sometimes I can finish longer pieces this way, without much revision.

If the great majority of your fellow students use this approach,
furthermore, they must have reasons. To make informed decisions,
you should know what those reasons are. Other students will prob-

ably have more direct influence on your learning strategies than your teachers will have, simply because you will be in the company of other students, not your teachers, when you are studying, writing papers, and completing other kinds of assignments. But students don't often explain *why* they are using one approach or another, and blindly following the crowd sometimes gets individuals into trouble.

When I asked my students why they and their friends try to make the first draft the last, about 35 percent said that they use methods they learned in high school, but most of these students said they continue to avoid revision because doing so is the most efficient way to complete assignments in college. A few students noted that their high school English teachers had in fact taught them to produce rough drafts and rewrite these drafts at least once but that they had *stopped* revising papers when they entered college. My students and the ones they interviewed, furthermore, were not just freshmen but in many cases juniors or seniors. Most of them — more than 80 percent — had not stopped trying to complete papers in one draft; they had become more skillful at doing so, on more complex assignments.

The most important factor these writers used to explain their strategies was *time*. Unlike their teachers, college students rarely have the luxury of developing an essay over a period of weeks or months. Short papers and reports, of three to six pages, are usually due a week or two after they are assigned, and apart from writing courses, college teachers rarely make rough drafts and revisions a part of the assignment schedule. With four or five courses to maintain, students say, they are often working on more than one writing assignment a week. Given these hectic schedules, if they are managing their time well they need to estimate in advance how many hours they can afford to spend completing a paper and set that time aside. Procrastinators and others who are *not* managing their time well usually need to complete work in the few hours that remain before a paper is due. By that time they feel that they have to "crank out" a paper as quickly as possible.

The main benefit of trying to make your first draft the last, therefore, is a Euclidean kind of efficiency. If Point A is the beginning of the writing process and Point B is the finished paper at the end, the most efficient way to get from one end to the other is a series of stages: *prewriting, composing, revising, editing,* and *release*. It stands to reason that if you can eliminate any of these stages you make the process shorter and more efficient. If you can make the first draft the last, therefore, you can eliminate the revision stage. In theory, if you either knew exactly what you wanted to say or could invent it as you wrote, you could eliminate prewriting as well. And if you could write carefully enough in this draft, you could even dispense with editing. Then the process would be reduced to its most "efficient" form, closest to the linearity of speech: *write the paper and turn it in.*

This logic can sometimes work. But here are the potential costs you should keep in mind, considering the limitations, or "myths," I mentioned at the beginning of this chapter. *The attempt to make the first draft the last works best if you start out with a clear sense of form and direction, if the task is simple, or if your standards are low.* If the opposites are true, the strategy can become inefficient at best. Less linear methods can be more efficient for several reasons:

- If you don't know what form or direction a paper will take, the most efficient way to find out is a quick, exploratory draft that represents thinking on paper.

- Exploratory drafts also work best if the assignment calls for a long, complex paper. If you try to plan the paper in advance to avoid revision, you will be stuck with your first thoughts, which probably won't be the most interesting. If you start from some arbitrary Point A without knowing where the paper will go, you are likely to get lost or change direction.

- If your standards or those of your readers are high, the attempt to avoid revision simply slows down the process of composing to a crawl, even to a halt. For Clifford Geertz, as we've seen, that effort reduces productivity to a paragraph a day. Other writers with high standards feel that to establish control they must have the work planned in detail before they start to compose. To avoid revision, therefore, they spend enormous amounts of time in the prewriting phase. I've known several students who experienced writing blocks because they couldn't meet their standards for complex papers in one draft. Without revision, writing seemed completely impossible.

- The idea that you are producing the finished product, the final performance, will make you more vulnerable to a kind of stage fright. This anxiety produces a writing style I call "gripped": extremely hesitant, tense, cautious, and overly formal. In a book called *Writing without Teachers*, Peter Elbow explained this unfortunate effect on style:

The problem is that editing goes on at the same time *as producing.*
The editor is, as it were, constantly looking over the shoulder of the
producer and constantly fiddling with what he's doing while he's in the
middle of trying to do it. No wonder the producer gets nervous, jumpy,
inhibited, and finally can't be coherent. It's an unnecessary burden to
try to think of words and also worry at the same time whether they're
the right words. (5)

- The same methods don't work to everyone's advantage. Some
  writers become extremely skillful at completing long, complicated papers in one draft the night before they are due. If everyone is using the same strategy, these students will appear to
  be the best writers. But such methods work to the disadvantage
  of many thoughtful, capable writers who need time to consider
  and reconsider what they have to say. If they resist following
  the crowd and develop their own approaches, these students
  often become the best writers in a class.
- For related reasons, if you cling to simple, tidy methods, as
  assignments become more challenging you will eventually become what we might call *methodologically challenged*. In other
  words, you will appear to be a weak writer and might feel that
  you have reached the limits of your ability, when it is really
  your *approach* to writing that has become weak and limited.

All of these limitations relate to the expectations of your teachers, who develop assignments and standards based on their own
writing practices. As writers, however, college students and their
teachers live in rather different worlds. If more than 80 percent of
undergraduates try to make the first draft the last, a similar proportion of their teachers rethink and revise their work extensively — far
more than you probably realize, and far more than they usually
admit. Books and articles commonly go through many whole or
partial drafts, often with advice from colleagues, before scholars send
them off to publishers. Editors then send manuscripts out for "peer
review" from other specialists in the field, who recommend further
changes. Sometimes manuscripts are then rejected or must be extensively rewritten, then sent out again for further reviews and changes
before they are finally published. For most scholars, getting writing
done is a messy, complicated business. Very few of your teachers can
even imagine producing a finished, published article in one draft.

You probably aren't surprised that this is true of English professors, historians, or philosophers, but it is equally true for scientists and social scientists. The highly consistent, formal structure of a lab report or research article (which I'll describe in the next chapter) suggests that writing one, like writing a five-paragraph theme, is a simple matter of filling in the blanks. This is how many undergraduates write lab reports for their science courses. But professional scientists typically produce many drafts of an experimental report, through exchanges with dozens of colleagues, before it is finally published. A biochemist told me he had more than thirty drafts of his most recent article on his computer. In his book *Writing Biology*, Greg Myers observed the long, complex process through which two biologists completed research proposals and articles. With dozens of major revisions before and during the process of submission, one article was rejected three times and the other four times, in different versions, before they were published. As Myers notes, "The authors rewrote the articles each time, so that the published versions are hardly recognizable as related to the first submissions."

College teachers can't expect you to rewrite your papers several times, unless you are taking a writing class that schedules multiple revisions and peer reviews. Otherwise most of your teachers will give you a week or two to complete short papers, perhaps three or four weeks to complete longer ones, in the midst of other assignments. Within these limits, however, teachers will expect that the writing you turn in represents thinking beyond the first ideas and sentences that came to mind while you were composing the first draft. They are routinely disappointed for reasons neither they nor their students fully understand. Students don't always see this disappointment because grades are geared to the general quality of student work, not to the teacher's higher standards. If the majority of students turn in first drafts and first thoughts disguised as finished products, teachers assume that this work represents what students are able to do. When students get decent grades on papers they wrote in one draft, they conclude that their methods work pretty well and that their teachers are satisfied.

But the teachers are less content. The most common view of student writing today is similar to that of Cornell English professor James Morgan Hart about ninety years ago: "Our Cornell experience is that the most difficult thing to overcome is the lack of thought. Most of our freshmen seem to believe that anything patched up in grammatical shape will pass for writing." Hart seemed to recognize that the "lack of thought" resulted less from stupidity than from

writing practices. Because they will not know how you produce writing they assign, when they read "patched up" first drafts many of your teachers will assume they are observing the limits of your ability to write and think, not the weakness of the methods you used.

Alternatives

Because grading standards have adjusted to typical student writing methods, if you are the kind of writer who can become skillful at avoiding revision you can probably get fairly good grades on this kind of writing, perhaps even excellent grades. Your writing teachers can show you alternatives, but they can't supervise your writing in other courses, and neither can I. We can offer you choices, but they remain choices.

If you choose, therefore, you can also read this chapter as a clue that alternative methods offer you great advantages. With the same level of ability as another student who makes the first draft the last, you can produce better writing, closer to the expectations of your teachers, without spending much additional time, if any. You will also get more satisfaction from this work and learn more in the process. Finally, you will have a much wider range of control over your writing in different situations, now and in the future.

How can additional drafts and revisions take the same amount of time as one draft, or in some cases even less? Sounds pretty fishy, I realize.

We've already seen, however, that the effort to make the first draft the last, with high standards, can make writing that draft extremely slow. The pace of writing slows because you are not producing that draft continuously. As Peter Elbow said, "The editor" is "constantly fiddling with what he's doing while he's in the middle of doing it." You frequently interrupt composing to read over and evaluate sentences you have already written, to make changes, to think about the next sentence or paragraph, perhaps even to go for a walk or take a nap if you get tired. If your standards for the finished product are high and you imagine that you are producing that finished work, you might complete a page every two hours or much less.

For the same reason, writing a rough draft with lower standards can allow you to compose very quickly, because there will be less interruption. Students often tell me, "I write very slowly" or "I'm a fast writer," as though writing were a machine that runs at one speed when they turn it on. But you can control the speed of writing as though with a rheostat, not just with a switch.

Here are some strategies for using the whole of the writing process flexibly and efficiently.

Use "freewriting" to generate material quickly. "Freewriting," which Elbow described in *Writing without Teachers*, demonstrates that even "slow writers" can write very quickly, continuously, if they change the rules and standards for what they are doing at the moment. In terms of the writing process, freewriting is *just composing*, without pausing to plan, reconsider, or edit what you are saying. There are no standards for you to meet, and the only rule for freewriting is that you should not stop. Just let thoughts flow directly onto the page, without pausing to read what you have said, to consider what you will say next, or to worry about whether the writing is coherent. **[Exercise 6]**

When I ask my students to do freewriting in class, some of them grumble a bit, but within a minute or two they have become absorbed in this activity and write with gathering speed, getting interested in what they are saying. At the end of fifteen minutes they are still writing intently, filling the second or third page, and I sometimes have trouble getting them to stop. When I ask them if anything seemed difficult, the most common answer is "I couldn't write fast enough to keep up with what I was thinking." And when students show me what they have written in this effortless way, it is often surprisingly fluent and interesting, their voices lively and distinct yet relaxed. Because they are writing quickly, they are more attuned to the sound and rhythms of the sentences.

By definition, freewriting does not produce finished work, except by accident. The purpose of this exercise, instead, is to get language and ideas moving onto the page, where you can work with them. The exercise is completely open: *Write continuously about anything.* When you begin to work on an assignment, of course, you need to think and write about *something* in particular. You can begin to work on that assignment with what Elbow calls "focused freewriting": letting your thoughts and questions about the topic flow freely onto the paper. If you aren't trying to produce the finished product and keep your standards low, in thirty minutes you should be able to produce at least four or five pages of material, in which you will probably find interesting ideas and approaches for the next draft. Many student writers spend more than thirty minutes trying to figure out how to begin their papers and end up with nothing but an assortment of false starts.

You can shift into this rapid flow of writing at any point in the process, not just at the beginning. If the assignment is based on readings, you can write freely for a few minutes before you read, to map out the questions you need to think about. You can also pause to write while you are reading, to explore ideas that occur to you, or after you finish reading. You can shift into freewriting while you are working on a more formal draft, if you find that your writing is becoming laborious and "gripped," or if you run out of ideas. If this happens while you are producing a draft on the computer, you can pause to write more freely on paper and then use those ideas to draft following sections of the document.

You can therefore regulate ease and resistance, continuity and interruption, to the level that seems most productive to you at a particular time in the process of completing an assignment. You can gain this flexibility and control simply by reminding yourself that standards for the finished product are not fixed expectations that you have to live up to immediately. You are still in the process of writing, and until you release your work to the audience, no one can read or judge what you are saying. You can therefore say anything, according to standards that you can raise or lower for your own purposes. In the beginning of the process, especially, "messy" writing, produced with low standards, is often the best, even the fastest, way to end up with polished writing that meets high standards.

Keep "reflective journals" for courses that assign writing. Entries in reflective journals, on lectures or on readings, are essentially locations for focused freewriting — places where you can record and explore ideas while you are having them. Some of your teachers might even require these journals and ask to read them periodically, to find out what you find interesting or confusing or to help you identify paper topics. Some of the most original, promising ideas for papers come from these informal responses to course material, which can give you a head start when you get a writing assignment. Exploratory writing of this kind will also help to prepare you for class discussions.

By writing about her own confusion in this part of a journal entry for her history class, the student has begun to make a transition essential to writing in this field: from the idea that history is a study of the "facts" to recognition that evidence of the past creates problems of interpretation, at once frustrating and fascinating:

> *After reading the various accounts of the Muslim conquest of Iberia in 711, I just want someone to tell me "And here's what really happened" in no uncertain terms. The different versions of the same event are all swimming in my head, and I find it frustrating that I do not know, after all of that, what the truth is! But yes, I also realize that what I am calling "frustration" is, paradoxically, intriguing as well. While it is annoying to keep checking my notes about which text was which, it is at the same time fascinating that these different accounts exist, all claiming to be the "truth."*

Do not wait to compose until you feel "ready."   If you are accustomed to writing papers in a single draft, making room for revision usually means that you need to produce rough drafts before you would normally feel you were "ready" to write. Much of the advantage you gain will result from starting earlier, composing faster, letting ideas and information tumble out so you can make use of them, before you would otherwise even begin to compose.

Start to work on assignments early.   This also means "Don't procrastinate," but a bit more than that as well. If you wait to begin a paper until the night before it is due, you will drastically reduce your range of choices for using the writing process comfortably, efficiently, and successfully. Even at that late hour you could still begin with freewriting, use those ideas to produce a rough draft, then revise and edit the draft, all in the same evening. What you would lose is the kind of fresh perspective writers gain from letting a draft sit for a day or two before coming back to it as a reader. You probably know from experience that your writing looks and sounds different when you read it later, and that delayed reading is more objective. When you have just written something, you are not yet in a position to evaluate and revise it.

Avoid editing, as much as possible, while you are composing.   I find it difficult to keep myself from tinkering with words and sentences while I am composing a draft. Some of that editing is irresistible and perhaps even useful, to clarify ideas and maintain voice. But extensive editing will constantly interrupt the composing phase and break the connection between writing and thinking. Editing, like revision, is also more effective after you let a draft sit for a while. You will be able to see mistakes, think of better words, and improve sentences more accurately if you reserve most of this work for the end of the process.

Try outlining papers between drafts. You might or might not find it useful to make an outline before you start to compose. That preference varies from one writer to another. But outlines are equally useful, if not more so, as aids to revision. For that purpose they will reveal the structure of your draft, the connections and disconnections among points, the logic of an argument, gaps, patches of fog, or contradictions.

Read drafts aloud and listen for flow and cohesion. My students tend to *look* for errors and weaknesses in a draft. But our primary orientation to language is through sound, not vision, and we can *hear* errors, awkward phrasing, and problems of cohesion more accurately than we can see them. **[Exercise 7]**

Do not wait for your teachers to tell you to revise. Some of your teachers, especially in your writing classes, will give you opportunities to revise papers after you have turned them in and after they have made suggestions for improvements. But this kind of revision does not eliminate the need for you to reconsider and rewrite drafts *before* you turn them in or to make changes beyond those a teacher recommends. Most of us teachers are disappointed when students confine revision to the changes we suggest, and we are impressed when students take independent responsibility for improving their work.

When you run into trouble, find help. Most colleges and universities have writing centers, staffed by teachers or advanced students available to help you identify and resolve problems with a draft. If your school does not have a writing center, you should use your teacher's office hours to get advice on problems with an assignment, or ask a friend to read through the draft and make suggestions. None of this help will be possible, of course, if you postpone writing until the night before a paper is due.

As soon as you get an assignment, pause to consider the best method for doing what the assignment asks. Writers fall into "default mode," often inappropriate and inefficient for the task, when they don't stop to think about what they are doing. You can waste lots of time this way.

Another advantage of using rehearsal time flexibly is the opportunity to *relax* while you are composing a draft, when you are not yet onstage. To remind yourself of this advantage, just think of the word *compose* itself. Related to *composure*, the word suggests a calm, patient, creative engagement with the task at hand — the thoughtful development of work in progress. The word *compose* reminds us that writing does not have to be a cramped, high-pressured performance, like a public speech before a critical audience. While you are writing, John Steinbeck advised in a letter to a friend, "Forget your generalized audience. In the first place, the nameless, faceless audience will scare you to death and in the second place, unlike the theatre, it doesn't exist." One of the most anxious writers on earth, even Steinbeck could find a sense of ease and calm — *composure* — in composing, in spite of all the pressure and doubt that surrounded the task, and he knew that this composure was essential to the quality of his work. The following observation comes from Steinbeck's own "reflective journal" (published as *Working Days*), which he kept while he was working on *The Grapes of Wrath*:

> *Worked long and slowly yesterday. Don't know whether it was good, but it was a satisfactory way to work and I wish it would be that way every day. I've lost this rushed feeling finally and can get back to the easy method of day by day — which is as it should be. . . . Today I shall work slowly and try to get that good feeling again. It must be. Just a little bit every day. A little bit every day. And then it will be through. (83)*

EXERCISES

Exercise 1. In two or three pages, describe a process that you thought was going to be linear but didn't turn out that way. What was the goal or product you had in mind at the beginning, and how did you expect to get to it? What happened instead? Did the outcome, or product, change as well? Was this fortunate or unfortunate?

Exercise 2. Describe a "performance" of some kind that required preparation or rehearsal. This could be a musical or dramatic performance, a public speech, or an athletic event. What kinds of preparations did you make before the performance? What would have happened if you *hadn't* made them?

Exercise 3. One way to demonstrate the need to loop back and read over what you have written is to deny yourself the opportunity to do so. If you are composing on a computer, turn off the screen so you can't see what you have written. Keep writing "in the dark." If you are writing on paper simply place a blank sheet over the lines you have written and move it down as you keep writing. What kinds of difficulty does this create? When you have written a number of sentences, turn on the screen or remove the blank sheet and look at your work. Did it suffer in any way from your inability to read it over?

Exercise 4. It will be useful for you to describe your own "default mode" in writing, to make it a conscious choice among others. When you have a writing assignment to complete, how do you "naturally" go about completing it, if you don't stop to consider alternatives? In as much detail as you can, explain exactly what you tend to do.

Exercise 5. Try this research on your own or with other members of your class: Interview two undergraduates separately about the methods they used in writing the most recent papers they completed in their courses. Assure them that this is an anonymous interview.

Use the phases of the writing process to structure your questions. First, ask about the assignment and the amount of time they had to complete it. In that time frame, when did they actually start to work on the paper? What kinds of reading or planning did they do in preparation for writing? Did they use formal outlines? Did they compose a draft all at once, or did they write the draft in pieces, stopping to rewrite sections? When the draft was complete, did they substantially revise it, or did they simply edit and run it through a spell checker? How much time did they spend on this work, and how long before the deadline did they finish? Are these methods typical of their writing strategies? Why do they use them? Are they successful?

Take careful notes during the interview (or, with permission, a tape recording) and write up the results. What differences and similarities do you notice between the two writers? To what extent do these methods correspond to yours? To what extent do they conform to the "norm" I described for student writers?

Exercise 6. Your writing teacher might ask you to do freewriting in class, but if he or she does not, try the exercise at home or during a study break somewhere else. Just start writing, and don't stop for ten or fifteen minutes. To get my students started, I sometimes give them a little nudge, such as "What's most on your mind right now?" or "What do you think of this place so far?" But you can write about anything that occurs to you. If you can't think of anything, just write "I can't think of anything" until you start to think of something else.

Elbow recommends that you do freewriting for a few minutes every day, to keep your writing "muscle" in shape, to keep your voice working naturally, and to remind yourself that writing is always possible — even easy.

Exercise 7.   In *One Writer's Beginnings*, Eudora Welty had this to say about the sound of writing for her as a reader and as a writer:

> *Ever since I was first read to, then started reading to myself, there has never been a line that I didn't hear. As my eyes followed the sentence, a voice was saying it silently to me. It isn't my mother's voice, or the voice of any person I can identify, certainly not my own. It is human, but inward, and it is inwardly that I listen to it. It is to me the voice of the story or poem itself. The cadence, whatever it is that asks you to believe, the feeling that resides in the printed word, reaches me through the reader-voice. I have supposed, but never found out, that this is the case with all readers — to read as listeners — and with all writers, to write as listeners. It may be part of the desire to write. The sound of what falls on the page begins the process of testing it for truth, for me. . . .*
>
> *My own words, when I am at work on a story, I hear too as they go, in the same voice that I hear when I read in books. When I write and the sound of it comes back to my ears, then I act to make my changes. I have always trusted this voice. (13)*

Does this account of reading and listening correspond with your own experience? What do you think Welty meant when she said that her "reader-voice" is not that "of any person I can identify, certainly not my own," but that it is "the voice of the story or poem itself"? When you read over your own work, especially after putting it aside for a day or more, do you have that sense that you are hearing the voice of the writing itself? If your writing has become, in some ways, an object in itself, does that make changing it easier or harder?

4 What Do College Teachers Expect?

The biggest change that occurred in my experience with college writing was learning how to write for a variety of subjects. In high school the majority of the papers that I had to write were for English classes. This normally involved writing analytical papers on novels. In college, I had to learn how to change my writing style according to the different types of subject matter. College writing allows the writer a chance to be versatile. Becoming a versatile writer was a big adjustment for me.

— A college sophomore

Variations

Now we enter the furniture factory. What kinds of objects are apprentice writers supposed to build in its many departments? I'll begin with some examples of writing projects assigned in freshman courses in a few departments.

Comparative Literature

Analyze the role that illusion plays in Virgil's *Aeneid* in leading such characters as Hector, Anchises, Dido, Turnus, and Aeneas to a misplaced faith in the happy outcomes of events. In a world where human free will rather than Absolute Fate determines the outcome of events, how do ambiguity, misperception, confusion, and misunderstanding complicate the course of human action?

Film Studies

One of the themes of the film *Citizen Kane* is Kane's isolation. How do settings, sound, framing, camera angles, and other technical devices emphasize that Kane is cut off from others? Judging from these cues as well as from the film's narrative elements, would you say that Kane becomes isolated only in old age, or would you say that he is always alone?

Philosophy

Define "free will" philosophically. In particular, say whether, to act freely, a person doing something must be able to do otherwise. Here you must explain just what the expression "able to do otherwise" means.

　　Then address two questions: First, is "free will" under your definition compatible with determinism? Second, would Daniel Dennett endorse your definition? Say *why* you think Dennett would (or would not) endorse your definition of free will.

History

Between the early 1900s and the mid-1930s, American Indian people struggled in several different ways both to participate in the national society of the United States and to preserve their distinctive tribal identities. Evaluate the overall success of these efforts.

Linguistics

Pretend that you are an elementary school teacher and that your principal has just written a memo telling all teachers to discipline students caught speaking any language other than English. Write a two-to-three page essay arguing against her decision.

Political Science

Both Rosencrance ("American Influence in World Politics") and Oye ("International Systems Structure and American Foreign Policy") argue that the structure of the international system creates basic constraints that U.S. policy makers must adjust to. However, Rosencrance's argument rests on a logic of system polarity (the transition from bipolar to multipolar), whereas Oye's argument relies on the logic of declining hegemony.

　　In a three-page essay, compare and contrast Rosencrance's and Oye's central arguments. What is the logic of each argument? How comparable are each author's assumptions? Do both use the same kinds of evidence? Which of these two views do you find more persuasive? Why?

Business

Read the case study on the declining values of real estate investments held by Woods Development Corporation. Assume that the

Board of Directors has decided to cut its losses and, over the past year, has sold 46% of this property. Your supervisor in the Accounting Department at Woods has asked you and your two colleagues to draft a five-hundred-word section of the company's annual report to stockholders, explaining this decision and its effects on company earnings, both over the past year and in projections for the future. Your goal is to provide accurate information and analysis that will also reassure investors that these are calculated losses in the long-term interests of a financially healthy corporation.

Biology

The editors of *Science* have asked you to write a short piece for one of their boxes describing the process of genetic drift. Your assignment is to describe genetic drift in a way that may be grasped by the unfamiliar reader and used as a background for the other articles in the issue. Strict page limits apply, so your description must not exceed two double-spaced pages.

Astronomy

Astronomers have big plans to move various ground-based observatories into space (either in orbit or onto the surface of the moon). Choose a proposed space-based observatory, describe why one would want to carry out the work off the earth's surface, and what one could hope to accomplish.

Chemistry

For your lab section on March 30, complete a report for your experiment on the entropy of a solution of potassium nitrate. Your report should include the usual Abstract, Introduction, Experimental Section, and Results and Discussion according to guidelines in your Lab Manual.

You can see from these examples why I've emphasized flexibility in your approaches to writing in college, as "apprentice" writers in a variety of departments. In another year or two you will begin to concentrate your studies in a particular field, and the variety of courses you take will gradually diminish. To the extent that writing is assigned in these courses, its variety will probably diminish as well. You will gradually become a particular kind of writer, increasingly skillful at producing analyses and interpretations of literature, historical narratives and arguments, discussions of social theory, case studies, or scientific reports.

In your first year or two, however, you will probably take courses in four or five different departments each semester, to complete distribution or "breadth" requirements. This is why students often tell me that college work gets easier from one year to the next even though their courses get harder: *While seniors have to complete the most difficult assignments in specific fields, freshmen have to adapt to the greatest variety of assignments.*

You can also see from these examples why I argued that high schools cannot fully prepare their students for college. Even if you went to the best high school in the country, I doubt that the knowledge and skills you bring to college would prepare you to complete all of these assignments, or perhaps any of them. This does not mean that your academic background is weak. I don't know any college professors who could write all of these papers and reports successfully, without further preparation. Each of these assignments requires particular kinds of knowledge and thought, emphasized in a particular course and field of study. Each of these courses provides background readings, lectures, and discussions that help you figure out what teachers expect, and I've condensed some of these assignments from longer versions that include further instructions and suggestions, including guidance on organization and style. Even if you studied genetic drift in high school biology or saw the film *Citizen Kane,* you would have difficulty completing the assignments on these topics without knowledge of the courses and teachers — the specific circumstances in which the assignments become meaningful.

Some General Expectations

This variety among departments and assignments often leads undergraduates to conclude that there is no general rhyme or reason to academic writing: that writing well is a matter of figuring out what individual teachers want. It is certainly true, as I've pointed out, that there is no single formula for Good Writing in college — no single form or style that would work for all of the assignments listed at the beginning of this chapter. It is also true that you will become a good writer by paying close attention to what specific teachers ask you to do and by adapting to those varying expectations. Many unsuccessful papers certainly result from failure to read and think about assignments carefully in the context of the course.

While all of this is true, there are some fairly consistent features of academic writing assigned to undergraduates. I'll describe these general purposes and expectations before I move on to more specific patterns of variation. In some cases I'll risk stating the obvious, because the most general patterns are the ones teachers most often fail to mention.

Purpose

Why do teachers assign essays or reports in their classes? Individual assignments have specific purposes within a course, but writing assignments also have general functions that differ from the goals of writing outside undergraduate studies, even when the forms are similar. Professional writers write to convey ideas and information to large audiences, to make a living, or perhaps to enhance their reputations, but student writing rarely serves these purposes. Instead, writing assignments usually have two functions in higher education:

1. To contribute to the process of learning in a course and field of study
2. To serve as a basis for evaluation

Some assignments are primarily learning tools; others are primarily forms of evaluation — written examinations. In most courses in the humanities, in many of the social sciences, and more rarely in the sciences, writing assignments might be the *only* basis for grading, apart from participation in class discussions. In the comparative literature course called Great Books, for example, the question on the *Aeneid* was one of several optional topics for one of three five-to-seven-page papers required in the course. Students in the class also wrote a one-page "position statement" on each of the eight books studied in the course. Because there were no examinations, grades on these eleven writing assignments constituted the entire grade for the course. In the general chemistry course, by contrast, the five lab reports made up only about 25 percent of the final grade. Examinations, quizzes, and other types of evaluation made up the rest.

In these courses and most others, however, teachers assign writing for both of the reasons I mentioned. In other words, writing serves as a way for you to learn the course material and as a way for teachers to find out what you have learned. To write well, you need to keep both of these purposes in mind: to write not just to do what teachers ask, but also to get more out of the course as a learning experience, which is part of what they expect.

These two motives are built into the original meanings of the word *essay,* the form of most student writing. This word is rooted in the Old French noun *essai,* which means "a test or trial," and the verb *essayer,* "to try something out." *Essay* is also linked with the Latin verb *exagiare,* "to weigh or measure something."

All of these words — whether in French, Latin, or English — have dual meanings. On one hand we use writing to *test* ideas, *try* them out, *weigh* their validity, and *examine* them. On the other hand, the product of this effort becomes a *test* or *trial,* a *measurement* of our knowledge, an *examination.* The dimension of *learning* in academic writing is embedded in the first set of meanings, which apply especially to the writing process. The element of *performance* relates to the second set of meanings, which refer to evaluation of the product. Knowing what you are doing when you write an essay requires awareness of both dimensions of writing: *to examine* the subject you are writing about and *to be examined.*

Style and Tone

Although there are many variations of form and style in academic writing, almost all of these variations occur within a consistent range of style and tone of voice: a tone of *rational explanation and discussion.*

Academic writers are trying to make something clear, and although the specific language they use to establish clarity varies, the tone of an essay in political philosophy or literary studies does not differ very much from the tone of a scientific report.

This tone of rational discussion holds steady even in forms of argument. Personal bias, animosity, and investment in a position should not *appear* to be relevant to an academic argument, and emotional reactions to an issue are usually veiled. In their writing, scholars "attack" each other's positions with counterarguments, alternative theories, or new forms of evidence, and the tone of their writing rarely becomes more heated than the assertion that another scholar has used "faulty reasoning" or "misconstrued the facts."

To describe this style or voice in academic writing we often use the term *objective,* which simply means that the "object" of discussion (whether a character in a novel, a theory, an event, or a molecule) is the main focus of attention. Academic writing is about some dimension of the world — the physical world or the worlds of ideas, perceptions, and imagination. Scholarly emphases on reason, inquiry, and clear explanation favor a voice that sounds relaxed, engaged with the subject, directive, and neither formal nor informal. We should sense that writers are trying to help us understand the subject without calling much attention to themselves.

This "objective" quality of academic writing does not mean that you should avoid all uses of the first person (*I* or *we*) or that your writing must be extremely formal, impersonal, and *dry* to become credible. Some assignments will ask you to link course material to your own experience, and scholars often use the first person to refer to their own research or perspectives. One student, Amber Roche, used the first person to distinguish her own views on genetic testing and health insurance in a paragraph that captures the appropriate style of rational discussion in academic writing:

> *The current system of using risk management seems outdated given the technological advances that have occurred since its implementation. What began as a method of using actual previous claims to determine appropriate premiums (Kass, 1992) has turned into a mess of complicated predictions. Consider also that most genetic disorders cannot be detected through testing; does it seem fair that some people should pay more just because their genetic risk is detectable while others of potential risk pay low rates? As Kevin Goddard of the Vermont Blue Cross said, "Insurance is assuming risk, spreading risk, and managing risk" (Murray, 1992). Since not all risks can be equally determined for the purpose of setting premiums, I suggest a return to community rating as a way to spread and manage risk.*
> **[Exercise 1]**

In an article called "Battling the Six Evil Geniuses of Essay Writing," political scientist Charles King illustrated the work of writers who err on both sides of this ideal of relaxed, rational discussion. On one side, King observed, students attempt to impress their professors with dense, abstract writing, laden with jargon they have picked up from readings and lectures, on the assumption that smart, impressive work is terribly difficult to understand:

> *Rationality is an exogenous component of selective incentives. As such, and in direct contradiction to the concept of endogenizing*

*preferences, actors cannot be truly rational unless they have engaged in
side-payments to rotating credit organizations. This gives Mancur Olson
a collective action problem from which he cannot easily recover. (60)*

At the opposite extreme, King observed, writers sometimes interpret "relaxed discussion" to call for a breezy, offhand, conversational style, in the effort to establish rapport with the professor:

*Well, as I was thinking the other night, modernization and
dependency are really two sides of the same coin. I mean, after all,
who can say who is more modern than someone else? But seriously (is
this a trick question?), there are a couple of ways that one differs from
the other. Modernizationists think that the world is linear and ordered
(they should see my dorm room!). (60)*

"This style is guaranteed to turn off any professor," King said.
What he wants from students, instead, is "a clear and accessible
argument." He recognizes that the specialized language of political
science, as in other fields, provides some useful tools toward this
end, and "learning to wield these terms effectively is part of doing
political science well." Efforts to impress teachers with dense jargon
or chatty informality undermine the clarity and accessibility of an
essay.

Organization

The goal of producing a "clear and accessible argument" presumes
first *that you have a clear argument* or, if the assignment does not call
for one, that you have some other clear objective: to explain something to the reader, perhaps, or to summarize or compare readings.
This goal also presumes *that you will select and organize information
in a logical, sequential order the reader can easily follow.* Those of us
who assign writing usually have thick piles of papers to read and
evaluate, and I don't know anyone who enjoys the struggle to figure out what a paper is trying to say.

Among college teachers in all fields, these values of organization
are universal. This is why I explained in Chapter 2 that all of the
writing you produce in college — from a one-paragraph response to
an essay exam question to a long paper — should have a clear *beginning, middle,* and *end,* with connections that carry the reader
smoothly from one place to another. Because your teachers will

have limited time to read your papers, they appreciate writing they can read through once without getting lost or confused. They want to know from the beginning what you are writing about and why. When they begin to read, they want to know the direction the paper will take, and they hope that you will pursue this course to a clear destination, through a logical sequence of well-organized paragraphs. These principles therefore apply to whole compositions and to individual paragraphs, which should have their own beginnings, middles, and ends, as little compositions. **[Exercise 2]**

If these expectations for organization are so universal, why do student papers so often fail to meet them? Here are some of the most common causes of weak organization in student writing.

Memory dump. This is the term my students often use when they "download" into papers or essay exams everything they can remember about the topic, more or less at random, in the hope that the right answers are in there somewhere and their teacher will find them. Among his "six evil geniuses," Charles King described such a writer as "The Sanitary Engineer":

> *He has crammed a huge amount of facts, terms, typologies, and other information into his short-term memory, and nothing — not even the essay question itself — will prevent him from getting it all down on paper. (60)*

This kind of writer views an essay not as a logical, continuous sequence but as a container.

Categorical sorting. Students often believe that they have completed the task of organizing a paper when they have sorted ideas and information into categories they can list in an outline and use as topics for paragraphs or sections.

Without further attention to the organization and flow of writing within paragraphs and to the connections between them, an orderly outline will not yield a "clear and accessible" essay. The sections of an outline can also be used as separate containers in which the writer dumps categories of information. This weakness is especially common in research papers, which I'll discuss in Chapter 6.

Avoidance of revision. As I explained in Chapter 3, the majority of the papers undergraduates turn in are actually first drafts, "fixed up" more or less to pass as finished writing. This is probably the main reason teachers receive papers that fail to meet their expectations for focus, organization, clarity, and originality.

Interest

Just as no reader wants to be confused by a piece of writing, no reader wants to be bored. All teachers hope that your papers will be interesting to read and that you will be interested in what you are saying.

Because it is difficult to predict the kinds of ideas, arguments, or explanations a teacher will appreciate, the best guide for generating interest is for you to *become* interested in the subject and in the challenge of communicating your interest to the reader. I don't believe that topics for writing are essentially interesting or boring. They can become either, depending upon the ways in which writers approach them. If you approach the subject with an attitude of boredom and disengagement, your writing will probably sound boring and disengaged. The key to producing writing that seems engaged and engaging to readers, therefore, is to let yourself become intrigued by the subject while you are writing. Knowing that you must sound interested in order to write well can stimulate that engagement.

Presentation

Unless you are given other instructions, the work you turn in should be "typed" (which now means "printed out"), double-spaced, with standard margins, on white paper. Most assignments will require titles, and papers longer than four or five pages usually have title pages that include your name, the course name and number, and the date, which is especially useful for identifying drafts of work you might revise. Pages should be numbered (either at the upper right corner or the bottom) and securely stapled together at the upper left corner — not dog-eared or fastened with paper clips. Unless you are asked to do so, you should *not* submit papers in commercial folders or binders. These simply get in the way when teachers read and comment on your work.

Take the trouble to find printers that are working well. Most of us teachers read too much and worry about eyestrain. Even if I don't mention it, I'm irritated when students turn in faint or blurred print that is hard to read. I'm grateful, in turn, when papers are sharply printed, in legible fonts.

"Correctness"

All of the teachers I know are annoyed by what appear to be careless errors in student writing, such as errors of grammar and sentence structure, spelling mistakes, and "typos." If they do not mark these errors on the papers they return to you, the reason is not that they don't notice or don't care. Instead, minor errors are so common in student writing that most teachers don't have time to mark them and do not view this editorial work as their responsibility.

They consider it to be your responsibility, and there are some very good reasons for carefully proofreading papers before you turn them in. Papers that contain several typos, spelling errors, and other mistakes rarely receive high grades. Even if the writing is strong in other respects, minor errors and typos will make it seem sloppy, unpolished, undeserving of an A. Errors also disrupt the flow of the writing and distract the reader's attention from the central themes of an essay or report. Numerous errors sometimes lead teachers to imagine that a solid, fluent paper is "disorganized" or "chaotic," even if it is not.

"The Writing" Always Counts

You might imagine that your writing teacher is the only instructor who really pays attention to "the writing" in your papers. Or you might imagine that this kind of attention is concentrated in the humanities and fades as you move through the social sciences into the sciences and engineering, where teachers are interested only in "the content," "the science," or "the facts."

But these notions are hazardous and in some respects wrong. Teachers in English and in the humanities are more likely to *comment* on sentence structure, organization, and clarity when they evaluate your work. Teachers in other fields might say they are primarily interested in "the content" or "the ideas" and might not comment on your papers as pieces of writing, sometimes because they don't feel confident about this kind of response. Regardless of these variations, the quality of "the writing" always counts because the reader has no other basis for evaluation, unless mathematical formulas, charts, or illustrations are included. Most papers consist only of writing, and a grade represents the teacher's assessment of the quality of that writing, even if he or she calls it something else.

Pay Close Attention to the Assignment!

The preceding generalizations do not allow me to predict in detail what teachers will ask you to do, even in a particular field of study. I will describe some common patterns, but teachers in any field might give you assignments that defy prediction, and some of them will be the most valuable learning experiences you encounter. Failure to read and follow the assignment carefully will defeat its purpose and undermine your performance.

For example, several students misread the following assignment from a first-year astronomy course. Because the whole assignment was very long and detailed, I'll only present some relevant sections:

> This assignment places you in the role of a scientifically knowledgeable staff adviser to an influential member of the Senate Appropriations Committee whom we shall refer to as Senator Wisdom. In particular, Senator Wisdom's opinion is especially valuable when it comes to considering "big science" projects, funding for the NSF, NIH, NASA, etc. In times of fiscal constraint, tough decisions have to be made. Many proposals for science projects are made, but few are chosen to be presented to the politicians. Of those, only a few can actually be funded. How are the politicians to decide?

The assignment goes on to describe Senator Wisdom's academic background and integrity, along with the case at hand: Project Gemini, a proposal "to build two eight-meter optical-infrared telescopes, one in Hawaii and one in Chile," in a joint venture between the United States and several other countries. The assignment lists a number of specific questions the senator has about the proposed design, locations, cost, and potential value of these telescopes. Why, for example, are there two in these locations, and "Why should the telescope be useful at both optical and infrared wavelengths?" The assignment was to answer these questions in a two-to-four-page report:

> Senator Wisdom needs you to explain to her what the Gemini project is supposed to do and why it is important. However, since she is the lawmaker and you are the staffer, she wants from you

only the objective facts and not your opinions. Keep this ⟨
in mind as you write for her, your boss.

Failure to keep this last instruction in mind is what got several
students into trouble and would have gotten them into trouble with
Senator Wisdom as well. Asked to *explain* the features of this science
proposal to the senator, they tried to *persuade* her that she should
promote the project. As explanation drifted into argument, their
grades on the papers fell.

If you find an assignment confusing, ask for clarification!

Because the Gemini project assignment was detailed and clear,
misinterpretations resulted from careless reading. When they construct assignments, however, teachers cannot always predict what
will be clear to their students, and they count on you to let them
know when their instructions are incomplete or confusing.

Ambiguous assignments make procrastination especially hazardous. Teachers will not be very sympathetic if you tell them that you
didn't understand the assignment but couldn't get help because you
didn't read it until the night before the paper was due. If you read
the assignment carefully when you receive it and do not understand
what it asks you to do, they will be happy to offer advice — in class,
after class, or during their office hours. If you are uncomfortable
about admitting confusion, first ask other students if they understand what the assignment requires.

What Assignments Ask You to Do

If you read an assignment carefully, you will be able to understand
the teacher's expectations most successfully if you also recognize the
most common goals of academic writing. Assignments sometimes
state these goals clearly, but in some cases teachers will just assume
that you can figure out the type of writing the assignment requires.
Here are some of the main forms and purposes of assignments, with
the key term in italic type:

- A *summary* provides a condensed explanation of the substance
  of another text.
- Some assignments will ask you to *compare* two or more texts,
  usually on the basis of a particular theme or issue.
- Others might ask you to *analyze* a reading or issue: to identify
  its constituent elements.

- Analysis is the opposite of *synthesis,* which involves putting together or associating elements that were separate — identifying common themes, for example, among different texts.
- An *argument* explains and supports your position on an issue.
- Some assignments will ask you to *criticize* another text or perhaps a painting, a film, or a performance. In academic writing this term does not mean "attack"; it means *evaluate* — to weigh strengths and weaknesses.
- You might be asked to *interpret* texts, performances, or events — to give the reader some new, deeper way of understanding them.
- A *proposal* is an explanation of what you intend to do in a project — usually in some kind of research.
- A *report* explains the purpose, design, and results of an experiment or project.

These goals and forms are weakly connected with fields of study. Because scholars in the humanities study "texts" of various kinds, assignments in their classes usually ask you to write about other writing or about films, theater, music, or works of art and architecture. *Summary, comparison, analysis, synthesis, argument, criticism,* and *interpretation* are common features of these assignments.

Most social scientists apply principles of scientific investigation to structures and phenomena that are difficult to study "objectively," such as the workings of the human mind, political and economic systems, or the fabric of social relations. Because approaches to these subjects raise considerable debate over theory and methods, teachers in the social sciences usually assign papers based on readings of theory and case studies. For example, they might ask you to *compare* two theories of poverty, to *argue* for one or the other on the basis of evidence from published research, or to *evaluate* theories and methods in this research.

Because scientists attempt to understand specific physical, chemical, or biological structures and phenomena, they are most likely to assign research *proposals* and *reports* based on these kinds of investigation, along with *analysis* or *synthesis* of published research.

I said that these connections are weak, however, because college teachers are free to assign any kind of writing they consider useful, and the forms of their assignments, especially for freshmen, do not always correspond with the kinds of writing they do as scholars.

Your English teacher might ask you to write on the basis of your own observation and experience or about issues raised in social research. A science teacher might assign readings and writing on the ethical or legal implications of biomedical research, on environmental issues, or on the teaching of evolution in public schools.

It would be misleading, therefore, to suggest that writing in the sciences is one distinct category of writing, separate from writing in the humanities and writing in the social sciences. The boundaries between disciplines and clusters of disciplines are not so distinct, for students or for scholars. Emerging fields, such as environmental studies and cognitive studies, include perspectives from the sciences, social sciences, and humanities.

Each of the forms and purposes just discussed might be the central goal of an assignment, but in many cases you will need to combine these forms. For example, teachers will occasionally ask you *only* to summarize assigned readings. More often, summary will serve other purposes. You will probably need to summarize the positions authors take in order to compare these positions or take sides in a debate. Every assignment implicitly asks you to devise a strategy appropriate for that occasion. **[Exercise 3]**

In the next sections I describe some of these forms in greater detail.

Summaries, Voiced and Unvoiced

Because most of the assignments you receive in college will refer to readings, the ability to summarize the work of other writers accurately and clearly is an essential skill. Some assignments will call entirely for summary, even if they do not use the word:

> How does Michael Lind, in his article "To Have and Have Not," explain increasing inequality in the American economy? Who are the members of the "new oligarchy," and how do they differ from older generations of elites?

This assignment might have gone on to ask you to *compare* Lind's argument with another view of the American economy, to *evaluate* his analysis, or to *reply* to Lind with an argument of your own. All of these assignments would still require a coherent, accurate summary of Lind's article and possibly of other readings as well. Summary is therefore both a type of essay and a type of writing used in essays of great variety, including research papers.

The most common misconceptions about summaries result from the breadth of this term, which teachers, writing texts, and dictionaries often use to describe *explanations, paraphrases,* and *synopses.* To reduce this confusion, I'll try to make one distinction clear, between *voiced* and *unvoiced* summaries.

Writing assignments almost invariably call for *voiced summaries,* not unvoiced ones. When assignments ask you to summarize a reading or to explain an author's position, they are asking you to summarize the text *in your own voice,* using quotations from the text — the author's voice — when these are useful for your purposes. In a voiced summary you are explaining to the reader in your own words what another writer has said, referring directly to the author and usually to the name of the work. A voiced summary usually begins with an explanation of the central theme or argument of the reading, even if that theme appears in the middle of the text or near the end:

> In his article "To Have and Have Not," Michael Lind argues that the growing power of the "new oligarchy" results largely from its invisibility.

For further illustration, read the following excerpt from a chapter of Elizabeth Wayland Barber's book *Women's Work: The First 20,000 Years* (1994). Subtitled *Women, Cloth, and Society in Early Times,* this book might be assigned in courses on gender roles, the history of textiles and apparel, labor history, or cultural anthropology.

A Tradition with a Reason

Elizabeth Wayland Barber

For millennia women have sat together spinning, weaving, and sewing. Why should textiles have become *their* craft par excellence, rather than the work of men? Was it always thus, and if so, why?

Twenty years ago Judith Brown wrote a little five-page "Note on the Division of Labor by Sex" that holds a simple key to these questions. She was interested in how much women contributed to obtaining the food for a preindustrial community. But in answering that question, she came upon a model of much wider applicability. She found that the issue of whether or not the community *relies* upon women as the chief providers of a given type of labor depends upon "the compatibility of this pursuit with the demands of child care." If only because of the exigencies of breast feeding (which until recently was typically continued for two or three years per child), "nowhere in the world is the rearing of children primarily the responsibility of men. . . ." Thus, if the productive labor of women is not to be lost to the society during the childbearing years, the jobs regularly assigned to women must be carefully chosen to be "compatible with simultaneous child watching." From empirical observation Brown gleans that "such activities have the following characteristics: they do not require rapt concentration and are relatively dull and repetitive; they are easily interruptible [I see a rueful smile on every care giver's face!] and easily resumed once interrupted; they do not place the child in potential danger; and they do not require the participant to range very far from home."[1]

Just such are the crafts of spinning, weaving, and sewing: repetitive, easy to pick up at any point, reasonably child-safe, and easily done at home. (Contrast the idea of swinging a pick in a dark, cramped, and dusty mine shaft with a baby on one's back or being interrupted by a child's crisis while trying to pour molten metal into a set of molds.) The only other occupation that fits the criteria even half so well is that of preparing the daily food. Food and clothing: These are what societies worldwide have come to see as the core of women's work (although other tasks may be added to the load, depending upon the circumstances of the particular society).

Readers of this book live in a different world. The Industrial Revolution has moved basic textile work out of the home and into large (inherently dangerous) factories; we buy our clothing ready-made. It is a rare person in our cities who has ever spun thread or woven cloth, although a quick look into a fabric store will show that many women still sew. As a result, most of us are unaware of how time-consuming the task of making the cloth for a family used to be.

In Denmark fifty years ago young women bought their yarns ready-made but still expected to weave the basic cloth for their households. If they went to a weaving school rather than being taught at home, they began with a dozen plain cotton dish towels.

---

[1]Notice Brown's stipulation that this particular division of labor revolves around *reliance*, not around *ability* (other than the ability to breast-feed), within a community in which specialization is desirable. Thus females are quite able to hunt, and often do (as she points out); males are quite able to cook and sew, and often do, among the cultures of the world. The question is whether the society can afford to *rely* on the women as a group for all of the hunting or all of the sewing. The answer to "hunting" (and smithing, and deep-sea fishing) is no. The answer to "sewing" (and cooking, and weaving) is yes.

My mother, being a foreigner not in need of a trousseau, and with less than a year at her disposal to study Danish weaving, consented to weave half of *one* towel to get started. The next assignment was to weave three waffle-weave bath mats. (Indeed, the three were nicely gauged to last a lifetime. The second wore out when I was in college, and we still have the third.) Next came the weaving of woolen scarves and blankets, linen tablecloths, and so forth. Most complicated were the elaborate aprons for Sunday best.

Thirty years ago in rural Greece, much had changed but not all. People wore store-bought, factory-made clothing of cotton for daily wear, at least in summer. But traditional festive outfits and all the household woolens were still made from scratch. It takes several hours to spin with a hand spindle the amount of yarn one can weave up in an hour, so women spun as they watched the children, girls spun as they watched the sheep, both spun as they trudged or rode muleback from one village to another on errands. The tools and materials were light and portable, and the double use of the time made both the spinning and the trudging or watching more interesting. In fact, if we reckon up the cleaning, spinning, dyeing, weaving, and embroidering of the wool, the villagers appeared to spend at least as many labor hours on making cloth as on producing the food to be eaten — and these people bought half their clothing ready-made!

Records show that, before the invention of the steam engine and the great factory machines that it could run, this sort of distribution of time and labor was quite normal. Most of the hours of the woman's day, and occasionally of the man's, were spent on textile-related activities. (In Europe men typically helped tend and shear the sheep, plant and harvest the flax, and market any extra textiles available for cash income.)

"So why is it, if women were so enslaved by textile work for all those centuries, that the spinning jenny and power loom were invented by a man and not a woman?" A young woman accosted me with this question after a lecture recently.

"Th[e] reason," to quote George Foster, writing about problems in pottery making, "lies in the nature of the productive process itself which places a premium on strict adherence to tried and proven ways as a means of avoiding economic catastrophe." Put another way, women of all but the top social and economic classes were so busy just trying to get through what had to be done each day that they didn't have excess time or materials to experiment with new ways of doing things. (My husband bought and learned to use a new word-processing program two years before I began to use it, for exactly these reasons. I was in the middle of writing a book using the old system and couldn't afford to take the time out both to learn the new one and to convert everything. I was already too deep into "production.") Elise Boulding elaborates: "[T]he general situation of little margin for error leading to conservatism might apply to the whole range of activities carried out by women. Because they had so much to do, slight variations in care of farm or dairy products or pottery could lead to food spoilage, production failure, and a consequent increase in already heavy burdens." The rich women, on the other hand, didn't have the incentive to invent laborsaving machinery since the work was done for them.

And so for millennia women devoted their lives to making the cloth and clothing while they tended the children and the cooking pot. Or at least that was the case in the broad zone of temperate climates, where cloth was spun and woven (rather than made of skins, as in the Arctic) and where the weather was too cold for part or all of the year to go without a warming wrap (as one could in the tropics). Consequently it was in the temperate zone that the Industrial Revolution eventually began.

The Industrial Revolution was a time of steam engines. Along with the locomotive to solve transportation problems, the first major applications of the new engines were mechanizations of the making of cloth: the power loom, the spinning jenny, the cotton gin. The consequences of yanking women and children out of the home to tend these huge, dangerous, and implacable machines in the mills caused the devastating social problems which writers like Charles Dickens, Charlotte Brontë, and Elizabeth Gaskell (all of whom knew each other) portrayed so vividly. Such a factory is the antithesis of being "compatible with child rearing" on every point in Judith Brown's list.

Western industrial society has evolved so far that most of us don't recognize Dickens's picture now (although it still does exist in some parts of the world). We are looking forward into a new age, when women who so desire can rear their children quietly at home while they pursue a career on their child-safe, relatively interruptible-and-resumable home computers, linked to the world not by muleback or the steam locomotive, or even a car, but by the telephone and the modem. For their part, the handloom, the needle, and the other fiber crafts can still form satisfying hobbies, as they, too, remain compatible with child watching.

Here is a brief *unvoiced* summary, or paraphrase, of the passage. Notice that this paraphrase is written as though Barber had been asked to condense her own chapter to a single paragraph.

> *Why have women, rather than men, been responsible for the production of cloth and clothing over millennia and across cultures? The answer to this question is linked with women's primary responsibility for child care. Time-consuming tasks such as spinning, weaving, and sewing could be performed at home, while caring for children, and were easily interrupted. Although the Industrial Revolution moved mass production of textiles from the home into factories, in this century women in many societies, including Denmark and Greece, have continued to weave and sew cloth while caring for children. Men invented the machines that industrialized this work because women of all but the leisure class had no time to invent alternative methods. Making cloth and clothing while caring for children and cooking have consumed most of women's time throughout temperate zones, where people need cloth for warmth, and many social problems following the industrial revolution resulted from the removal of women from the home to the factory. Although few women in the electronic era know how to spin or weave, sewing remains a women's hobby, still associated with raising children.*

This condensation follows the order of the original, and because I did not establish a voice of my own, distinct from Barber's, quotations would have seemed odd, as though Barber were quoting herself. If I can't quote Barber, I must struggle to avoid repeating her phrases and sentences in my paraphrase. Paraphrasing therefore pulls us toward plagiarism, which I will discuss in Chapter 6.

For these reasons, unvoiced summary has limited value in academic writing. Because the writer of such a summary has no voice independent of the text, he cannot easily go on to amplify, analyze, or evaluate what he has summarized.

Now consider the features of a *voiced* summary of the same passage:

> *In the chapter called "A Tradition with a Reason" in her book* Women's Work: The First 20,000 Years, *Elizabeth Wayland Barber argues that over the millennia prior to the Industrial Revolution,*

women throughout temperate zones produced cloth and clothing because their responsibility for child care favored tasks that were "repetitive, easy to pick up at any point, reasonably child-safe, and easily done at home." Citing George Foster, an expert on the social dimensions of pottery production, Barber suggests that traditional methods of making cloth were so labor-intensive that women had no time for innovation. Men invented the "huge, dangerous, and implacable machines" that removed this industry from the home to the factory and removed women and children from the home as well, as factory workers. Barber claims that the industrialization of women's work "caused the devastating social problems" described by Dickens and other nineteenth-century novelists. During and after the Industrial Revolution, however, women in countries such as Denmark and Greece continued to spin, weave, and sew at home, and today, as women's hobbies, "fiber crafts . . . remain compatible with child watching."

In the voiced summary, I describe Barber's chapter to a third party, the reader. Once I have established my voice for this purpose, viewing the text as an object of description or explanation, I have considerable freedom to determine what is important, how I should organize the explanation, and when I should let Barber speak for herself, in quotation marks. As the reader, you can clearly distinguish my voice from Barber's, my summary from her chapter. I am not trapped in her text, and I can easily move from an explanation of what she said to other perspectives and forms, other purposes for writing. For comparison or argument, I could compose my summary to emphasize the features I intended to question, challenge, or compare with another text. You can easily imagine that my summary might be a part of a longer essay, with further objectives.

Summaries can vary greatly in length, depending more on their purpose than on the length of the text they describe. Mentioned in passing, a summary of an entire book might consist of a sentence or two; exam questions might also require very brief accounts of whole books or articles. In these brief summaries you should capture the main idea or argument of the text, not necessarily what the author says first. (The first sentence of the voiced summary of Barber serves this purpose.) Longer summaries, from a paragraph to several pages, then describe supporting arguments, main categories of information, or important examples. **[Exercise 4]**

Comparison, Using Analysis and Interpretation

Assignments will often ask you to compare the views of two or more authors, and this task will require some very basic, predictable decisions about organization. Apart from scientific reports, which follow a conventional format, writing assignments in college rarely tell you how your paper should be organized — where you should start, what you should say next, and how your paper should end.

Although you will need to figure out how to organize every essay you write, these choices are not entirely open, especially when your purpose is comparison. Here your main goal is to avoid confusion between the objects of comparison while making points of correspondence and difference clear. If you have to compare two texts (or two buildings, paintings, or organizations), A and B, you have two basic choices. One choice is to describe A entirely and then describe B, concluding perhaps with a discussion of the similarities and differences you have observed. If analysis of the two texts reveals that they address a common set of issues, in each section you can discuss these issues in the same order. A crude outline might look like this:

Introduction to the texts and issues

  I. Text A
    A. Issue 1
    B. Issue 2
    C. Issue 3

  II. Text B
    A. Issue 1
    B. Issue 2
    C. Issue 3

Conclusion

The second choice is to use the issues running through the two texts as the main sections of your paper, comparing the two texts in each section in a framework such as this:

Introduction to the texts and issues

  I. Issue 1
    A. Text A
    B. Text B

II. Issue 2
   A. Text A
   B. Text B

III. Issue 3
   A. Text A
   B. Text B

Conclusion

Which strategy should you use? In some cases either would work, and the choice is therefore a matter of preference. As a rule, however, the first approach works best when the paper is fairly short, two to three pages, or when separate accounts of the texts represent them best because they raise slightly different issues. In a short paper the reader can keep your full discussion of A in mind as you discuss B. Continually shifting back and forth between A and B will fragment the discussion and make the paper sound choppy.

The second approach usually works best in longer papers and in those that emphasize specific issues more than the whole of the author's perspective. If you spend three or four pages discussing A before you turn your attention to B, the reader might have trouble remembering points of comparison or contrast, especially if there are several.

You can vary these basic schemes in many ways, and the numbers I've used are only examples. An assignment might ask you to compare three texts, not two, and you might decide to emphasize two, four, or eight points rather than three. Or you might see one central issue with several implications. One common variant of the second approach begins with summary introductions to the texts and then discusses similarities (points of correspondence or agreement), then differences (points of divergence or conflict), followed by conclusions. This strategy can work for short papers or for very long ones.

I should emphasize, however, that *choosing a skeletal framework for organization does not replace thought about the texts and will not in itself produce a fluent, cohesive, interesting paper.* To make an essay work, you need to think about the assignment, read the texts carefully, consider the sequence of points you wish to make, establish connections between them, and write fluently within sections.

This thought and effort will be essential because the readings teachers ask you to compare will not tell you what to say about them. Nor are they likely to correspond as neatly as the idealized outlines I have sketched. Unless authors directly address one another, in ongoing arguments, their books and articles rarely parallel each other, point for point. It is more likely that teachers will ask you to compare readings that offer different perspectives on related topics. Points of comparison might not be immediately obvious, or there might be only one central point of comparison among readings that are otherwise only marginally related. Writers with different perspectives, furthermore, might *not* disagree.

Imagine, for example, that an assignment asks you to compare Barber's "A Tradition with a Reason" with the following passages from Jessie Bernard's article "The Good-Provider Role: Its Rise and Fall," published in *American Psychologist* in 1981.

The Good-Provider Role:
Its Rise and Fall

Jessie Bernard

Abstract

The general structure of the "traditional" American family, in which the husband-father is the provider and the wife-mother the housewife, began to take shape early in the 19th century. This structure lasted about 150 years, from the 1830s to 1980, when the U.S. Census no longer automatically denominated the male as head of the household. As "providing" became increasingly mediated by cash derived from participation in the labor force or from commercial enterprises, the powers and prerogatives of the provider role augmented, and those of the housewife, who lacked a cash income, declined. Gender identity became associated with work site as well as with work. As affluence spread, the provider role became more and more competitive and escalated into the good-provider role. There were always defectors from the good-provider role, and in recent years expressed dissatisfaction with it increased. As more and more married women entered the labor force and thus assumed a share of the provider role, the powers and prerogatives of the good-provider role became diluted. At the present time a process that Ralph Smith calls "the subtle revolution" is realigning family roles. A host of social-psychological obstacles related to gender identity have to be overcome before a new social-psychological structure can be achieved.

Whatever the date of the virtuous woman described in the Old Testament (Proverbs 31:10–27), she was the very model of a good provider. She was, in fact, a highly productive conglomerate. She woke up in the middle of the night to tend to her business; she oversaw a multiple-industry household; *her* candles did not go out at night; there was a ready market for the high-quality linen girdles she made and sold to the merchants in town; and she kept track of the real estate market and bought good land when it became available, cultivating vineyards quite profitably. All this time her husband sat at the gates talking with his cronies.

A recent counterpart to the virtuous woman was the busy and industrious shtetl woman:

> The earning of a livelihood is sexless, and the large majority of women . . . participate in some gainful occupation if they do not carry the chief burden of support. The wife of a "perennial student" is very apt to be the sole support of the family. The problem of managing both a business and a home is so common that no one recognizes it as special. . . . To bustle about in search of a livelihood is merely another form of bustling about managing a home; both are aspects of . . . health and livelihood. (Zborowski & Herzog, 1952, p. 131)

In a subsistence economy in which husbands and wives ran farms, shops, or businesses together, a man might be a good, steady worker, but the idea that he was *the* provider would hardly ring true. Even the youth in the folk song who listed all the gifts he would bestow on his love if she would marry him — a golden comb, a paper of pins, and all the rest — was not necessarily promising to be a good provider. . . .

In our country in Colonial times women were still viewed as performing a providing role, and they pursued a variety of occupations. Abigail Adams managed the family estate, which provided the wherewithal for John to spend so much time in Philadelphia. In the 18th century "many women were active in business and professional pursuits. They ran inns and taverns; they managed a wide variety of stores and shops; and, at least occasionally, they worked in careers like publishing, journalism and medicine" (Demos, 1974, p. 430). Women sometimes even "joined the menfolk for work in the fields" (p. 430). Like the household of the proverbial virtuous woman, the Colonial household was a little factory that produced clothing, furniture, bedding, candles, and other accessories, and again, as in the case of the virtuous woman, the female role was central. It was taken for granted that women provided for the family along with men.

The good provider as a specialized male role seems to have arisen in the transition from subsistence to market — especially money — economies that accelerated with the industrial revolution. The good-provider role for males emerged in this country roughly, say, from the 1830s, when de Tocqueville was observing it, to the late 1970s, when the 1980 census declared that a male was not automatically to be assumed to be head of the household. This gives the role a life span of about a century and a half. Although relatively short-lived, while it lasted the role was a seemingly rock-like feature of the national landscape.

As a psychological and sociological phenomenon, the good-provider role had wide ramifications for all of our thinking about families. It marked a new kind of marriage. It did not have good effects on women: The role deprived them of many chips by placing them in a peculiarly vulnerable position. Because she was not reimbursed for her contribution to the family in either products or services, a wife was stripped to a considerable extent of her access to cash-mediated markets. By discouraging labor force participation, it deprived many women, especially affluent ones, of opportunities to achieve strength and competence. It deterred young women from acquiring productive skills. They dedicated themselves instead to winning a good provider who would "take care of" them. The wife of a more successful provider became for all intents and purposes a parasite, with little to do except indulge or pamper herself. The psychology of such dependence could become all but crippling. There were other concomitants of the good-provider role.

Expressivity and the Good-Provider Role

The new industrial order that produced the good provider changed not so much the division of labor between the sexes as it did the site of the work they engaged in. Only two of the concomitants of this change in work site are selected for comment here, namely, (a) the identification of gender with work site as well as with work itself and (b) the reduction of time for personal interaction and intimacy within the family.

It is not so much the specific kinds of work men and women do — they have always varied from time to time and place to place — but the simple fact that the sexes do different kinds of work, whatever it is, which is in and of itself important. The division of labor by sex means that the work group becomes also a sex group. The very nature of maleness and femaleness becomes embedded in the sexual division of labor. One's sex and one's work are part of one another. One's work defines one's gender.

Any division of labor implies that people doing different kinds of work will occupy different work sites. When the division is based on sex, men and women will necessarily have different work sites. Even within the home itself, men and women had different work spaces. The woman's spinning wheel occupied a different area from the man's anvil. When the factory took over much of the work formerly done in the house, the separation of work space became especially marked. Not only did the separation of the sexes become spatially extended, but it came to relate work and gender in a special way. The work site as well as the work itself became associated with gender; each sex had its own turf. This sexual "territoriality" has had complicating effects on efforts to change any sexual division of labor. The good provider worked primarily in the outside male world of business and industry. The homemaker worked primarily in the home. . . .

Women and the Provider Role

The present discussion began with the woman's part in the provider role. We saw how as more and more of the provisioning of the family came to be by way of monetary exchange, the woman's part shrank. A woman could still provide services, but could furnish little in the way of food, clothing, and shelter. But now that she is entering the labor force in large numbers, she can once more resume her ancient role, this time, like her male counterpart the provider, by way of a monetary contribution. More and more women are doing just this.

The assault on the good-provider role in the Depression was traumatic. But a modified version began to appear in the 1970s as a single income became inadequate for more and more families. Husbands have remained the major providers, but in an increasing number of cases the wife has begun to share this role. Thus, the proportion of married women aged 15 to 54 (living with their husbands) in the labor force more than doubled between 1950 and 1978, from 25.2% to 55.4%. The proportion for 1990 is estimated to reach 66.7% (Smith, 1979, p. 14). Fewer women are now full-time housewives.

For some men the relief from the strain of sole responsibility for the provider role has been welcome. But for others the feeling of degradation resembles the feelings reported 40 years earlier in the Great Depression. It is not that they are no longer providing for the family but that the role-sharing wife now feels justified in making demands on them. The good-provider role with all its prerogatives and perquisites has undergone profound changes. It will never be the same again.[1] Its death knell was sounded when, as noted above, the 1980 census no longer automatically assumed that the male member of the household was its head.

The Current Scene

Among the new demands being made on the good-provider role, two deserve special consideration, namely, (1) more intimacy, expressivity, and nurturance — specifications never included in it as it originally took shape — and (b) more sharing of household responsibility and child care.

As the pampered wife in an affluent household came often to be an economic parasite, so also the good provider was often, in a way, a kind of emotional parasite. Implicit in the definition of the role was that he provided goods and material things. Tender loving care was not one of the requirements. Emotional ministrations from the family were his right; providing them was not a corresponding obligation. Therefore, as de Tocqueville had already noted by 1840, women suffered a kind of emotional deprivation labeled by Robert Weiss "relational deficit" (cited in Bernard, 1976). Only recently has this male rejection of emotional expression come to be challenged. Today, even blue-collar women are imposing "a host of new role expectations upon their husbands or lovers. . . . A new role set asks the blue-collar male to strive for . . . deep-coursing intimacy" (Shostak, Note 1). It was not only vis-à-vis his family that the good provider was lacking in expressivity. This lack was built into the whole male role script. Today not only women but also men are beginning to protest the repudiation of expressivity prescribed in male roles (Davis & Brannon 1976; Farrell, 1974; Fasteau, 1974; Pleck & Sawyer, 1974). . . .

[1]Among the indices of the waning of the good-provider role are the increasing number of married women in the labor force; the growth in the number of female-headed families; the growing trend toward egalitarian norms in marriage; the need for two earners in so many middle-class families; and the recognition of these trends in the abandonment of the identification of head of household as a male.

Pleck and Lang (1979) tell us that men are now beginning to change in the direction of greater involvement in family life. "Men's family behavior is beginning to change, becoming increasingly congruent with the long-standing psychological significance of the family in their lives" (p. 1). They measure this greater involvement by way of the help they offer with homemaking chores. Scanzoni (1975), on the basis of a survey of over 3,000 husbands and wives, concludes that at least in households in which wives are in the labor force, there is the "possibility of a different pattern in which responsibility for households would unequivocally fall equally on husbands as well as wives" (p. 38). A brave new world indeed. Still, when we look at the reality around us, the pace seems intolerably slow. The responsibilities of the old good-provider role have attenuated far faster than have its prerogatives and privileges.

A considerable amount of thought has been devoted to studying the effects of the large influx of women into the work force. An equally interesting question is what the effect will be if a large number of men actually do increase their participation in the family and the household. Will men find the apron shameful? What if we were to ask fathers to alternate with mothers in being in the home when youngsters come home from school? Would fighting adolescent drug abuse be more successful if fathers and mothers were equally engaged in it? If the school could confer with fathers as often as with mothers? If the father accompanied children when they went shopping for clothes? If fathers spent as much time with children as do mothers?

Even as husbands, let alone as fathers, the new pattern is not without trauma. Hall and Hall (1979), in their study of two-career couples, report that the most serious fights among such couples occur not in the bedroom, but in the kitchen, between couples who profess a commitment to equality but who find actually implementing it difficult. A young professional reports that he is philosophically committed to egalitarianism in marriage and tries hard to practice it, but it does not work. He even feels guilty about this. The stresses involved in reworking roles may have an impact on health. A study of engineers and accountants finds poorer health among those with employed wives than among those with nonemployed wives (Burke & Weir, 1976). The processes involved in role change have been compared with those involved in deprogramming a cult member. Are they part of the increasing sense of marriage and parenthood as "all burdens and restrictions"?

The demise of the good-provider role also calls for consideration of other questions: What does the demotion of the good provider to the status of senior provider or even mere coprovider do to him? To marriage? To gender identity? What does expanding the role of housewife to that of junior provider or even coprovider do to her? To marriage? To gender identity? Much will of course depend on the social and psychological ambiance in which changes take place.

A Parable

I began this essay with a proverbial woman. I close it with a modern parable by William H. Chafe (Note 2), a historian who also keeps his eye on the current scene. Jack and Jill, both planning professional careers, he as doctor, she as lawyer, marry at age 24. She works to put him through medical school in the expectation that he will then finance her through law school. A child is born during the husband's internship, as planned. But in order for him to support her through professional training as planned, he will have to take time out from his career. After two years, they decide that both will continue their training on a part-time basis, sharing household responsibilities and using day-care services. Both find part-time positions and work out flexible work schedules that leave both of them time for child care and companionship with one another. They live happily ever after.

That's the end? you ask incredulously. Well, not exactly. For, as Chafe (Note 2) points out, as usual the personal is also political:

> Obviously such a scenario presumes a radical transformation of the personal values that today's young people bring to their relationships as well as a readiness on the part of social and economic institutions to encourage, or at least make possible, the development of equality between men and women. (p. 28)

The good-provider role may be on its way out, but its legitimate successor has not yet appeared on the scene.

Reference Notes

1. Shostak, A. *Working class Americans at home: Changing expectations of manhood.* Unpublished manuscript, 1973.
2. Chafe, W. *The challenge of sex equality: A new culture or old values revisited?* Paper presented at the Radcliffe Pre-Centennial Conference, Cambridge, Massachusetts, April 2–4, 1978.

References

Bernard, J. Homosociality and female depression. *Journal of Social Issues,* 1976, *32,* 207–224.

Burke, R., & Weir, T. Relationship of wives' employment status to husband, wife and pair satisfaction and performance. *Journal of Marriage and the Family,* 1976, *38,* 279–287.

David, D. S., & Brannon, R. (Eds). *The forty-nine percent majority: The male sex role.* Reading, Mass.: Addison-Wesley, 1976.

Demos, J. The American family in past time. *American Scholar,* 1974, *43,* 422–446.

Farrell, W. *The liberated man.* New York: Random House, 1974.

Fasteau, M. F. *The male machine.* New York: McGraw-Hall, 1974.

Hall, D., & Hall, F. *The two-career couple.* Reading, Mass.: Addison-Wesley, 1979.

Pleck, J. H., & Lang, L. Men's family work: Three perspectives and some new data. *Family Coordinator,* 1979, *28,* 481–488.

Pleck, J. H., & Sawyer, J. (Eds.) *Men and masculinity.* Englewood Cliffs, N.J.: Prentice-Hall, 1974.

Scanzoni, J. H. *Sex roles, life styles, and childbearing: Changing patterns in marriage and the family.* New York: Free Press, 1975.

Smith, R. E. (Ed.). *The subtle revolution.* Washington, D.C.: Urban Institute, 1979.

Tocqueville, A. de. *Democracy in America.* New York: J. & H. G. Langley, 1840.

Zborowski, M., & Herzog, E. *Life is with people.* New York: Schocken Books, 1952.

Bernard's article is not about clothing production or specifically about women's work in preindustrial societies. Bernard argues, instead, that the notion that men should provide all essentials for their families is a fairly recent and short-lived feature of the industrial revolution. In the sections excerpted here, Bernard suggests that the old roles of women as providers for the family extended well beyond the home itself, into agriculture, the gathering of food, and commercial activity. And while the male "good-provider role" now fails to characterize divisions of labor between women and men, because both are now likely to work outside the home, a new, clear conception of gender roles has yet to arise.

An assignment that asked you to compare these texts would probably focus on specific questions about them. Here is one example:

> Barber suggests that the removal of women and women's work from the home "caused the devastating social problems" associated with the Industrial Revolution. Would Jessie Bernard entirely agree with this view of women's work and of the social problems accompanying industrialization?

Answering such a question requires more than simply knowing what each author said and comparing their work point for point. Because relevant perspectives are embedded in essays with very different designs and purposes, you will need to read *analytically* to locate passages that refer to the issues in the assignment. Because Bernard does not directly refer to Barber's views on women's work and the textile industry, you will also need to construct an *interpretation* of her essay: to imagine how she would respond to Barber, using evidence from her work to support your interpretation. For this purpose, as in a voiced summary, you will need to integrate quotations from these authors with your own explanation of their arguments. **[Exercise 5]**

Critical Reading and Argument

The ability to summarize a text in your own voice is essential to the task of comparing texts. In other words, *summary* is usually a part of *comparison*. Summary and comparison, in turn, often provide a basis for *argument*. Assignments like the one suggested on Barber and Bernard might go on to ask you to explain your own viewpoint on these issues or to answer a specific question from your own perspective:

> At the end of her article, Bernard concludes, "The good-provider role may be on its way out, but its legitimate successor has not yet appeared on the scene." What do you consider to be the ideal roles of women and men today? To what extent have we resolved the issues that Bernard considered unresolved in 1981?

The following is another example of an assignment from a political science course that calls for *comparison* (including summary) of readings, for *interpretation*, and for an *argument* from your own perspective:

> In a five-page essay, compare Hobbes, Locke, and Rousseau on the idea of "human nature." What are their views of it, and how does it operate in their theories? What follows from these views in terms of each theorist's vision of politics and the state? Which of these conceptions of "human nature" do you find most convincing and why? **[Exercise 6]**

Students often imagine that assignments such as this ask for their "opinion," and they sometimes begin to respond to the question with the phrase "In my opinion." This word *opinion* annoys many college teachers, for reasons I'll explain, and I recommend that you delete it from your vocabulary in academic work. To call an idea your opinion suggests that it is simply an arbitrary, personal matter of preference that requires no justification and invites no further discussion.

> In my opinion, San Francisco is more interesting than Seattle.
>
> I think *Pulp Fiction* is a great movie.
>
> Economics is boring.

We often express opinions of this sort in conversation, and most of them pass quietly as matters of individual preference or taste. In the language of argument, these opinions are "uncontested assertions," and as long as they remain uncontested you don't need to defend them or even to think about them further.

Now and then, however, someone will *challenge* these opinions from a different perspective.

> I think Seattle is a fascinating place, and much nicer than San Francisco.
>
> *Pulp Fiction* is just stylish and shallow. In another ten years no one will watch it.
>
> Economics is my favorite course this term, and my major.

If you stick with your opinions in the conversations that follow, you will need to support and defend them as *positions*. Now engaged in an argument, or at least in a discussion, you will have to think about your preferences or aversions and explain why you have them. In doing so, you will need to take the other person's views into account and either refute them or change your own perspective, to reach some kind of understanding.

When teachers ask you to *take a position, present an argument*, or *explain your views*, therefore, they are not just asking for your "opinion" on the issues at hand. They expect you to engage in a discussion of these issues, acknowledge alternative viewpoints, and explain with reasoning and evidence how you arrived at the position you put forth. Even if teachers disagree with your position, they will iate an argument that is thoughtful, well supported, and interesting.

How can you find a position? What makes an argument interesting?

Interesting arguments result from critical reading and thinking, but the meaning of this term *critical* differs in academic work from common usage. When teachers say (as they frequently do) that they want their students to "think and read critically," they do not mean that you should try to find something *wrong* with every reading, every theory, design, or system. They mean instead that you should think beyond the surface of readings and issues, remain open to alternative perspectives, and, above all, *ask questions*. Thinking and reading critically in college does not mean rushing to judgment, opposing every position you encounter, but just the opposite: *suspending judgment, delving into the complexity of issues, examining the way arguments work, and considering questions that remain unanswered.*

For this purpose, the adage "There are two sides to every argument" is false. There are many sides to every argument, and the most interesting ones will result from the questions you ask about the most obvious, polar positions in a debate.

Should we limit "greenhouse gas" emissions that cause global warming?

If you leap too quickly, uncritically, to the "yes" or "no" side of this debate, you will miss the complex issues it raises and your argument will not be very interesting. If you pause to ask further questions, your perspectives will become increasingly deep and rich — open to positions that reflect the intricate problems this central question poses:

Is global warming actually occurring?

Do gas emissions cause this phenomenon?

Which gases cause it?

How and where are these gases produced?

How can they be limited, and at what costs?

What levels of emission are acceptable?

Who should establish and enforce these limits?

What further information do we need?

Some readings and assignments delineate such critical issues very clearly and raise explicit questions you should answer. Other readings and assignments pose greater challenges for critical thinking, because they are very open or appear to be closed, the arguments self-evident and unquestionable. For example, consider Barber's "A Tradition with a Reason" once again. As she carries us across millennia and cultures, with a relaxed tone of authoritative explanation, Barber does not invite critical inquiry. And as you read this and other material you can benefit from what Peter Elbow calls "the believing game": letting yourself assume that what an author says is valuable, plausible, perhaps even true.

If a teacher asks you to evaluate Barber's work, however, you must also play what Elbow calls "the doubting game": considering the possibility that Barber's arguments and information are misleading, incomplete, perhaps even false.

As a college freshman reading the work of scholars who have spent years studying subjects you know little about, you might find "the doubting game" intimidating. Your first response to an assignment that calls for evaluation or argument might be "Who am I to question what she says?" Believing appears to be the safest alternative, and once you have chosen it, asking further questions will seem very difficult.

At the beginning of the writing process, however, asking questions of any text is fairly easy and quite safe, even if you know little about the subject. The only danger is that these questions will carry you more deeply into the subject than you intended to go, toward writing that will be more complex and interesting than you first imagined. Without trying to take a position immediately, just register questions, observations, or points of confusion while you read; write them down, in the margins or in a notebook. Here are four questions you might ask while reading Barber's chapter:

1. Barber seems to be generalizing about women throughout the world over the past twenty thousand years, yet on the last page she limits these generalizations to "the broad zone of temperate climates." What do women do in tropical and arctic climates, or among nomadic people?

2. Barber quotes Judith Brown that "nowhere in the world is the rearing of children primarily the responsibility of men." Is this true? If so, must it remain true in the future, given the changes she describes in the last paragraph?

3. She says, "Consequently" the industrial revolution began in the temperate zone. As a consequence of what? The conclusion doesn't seem to follow from her preceding comments.
4. Is Barber suggesting that time-consuming domestic work is the norm for women everywhere, always?

With these questions and others you might begin to assemble a critical perspective on Barber's essay. Are there connections among these questions? Among them is there a central question or theme you could use to evaluate the reading? **[Exercise 7]**

Scientific Reports

The basic form of the scientific report is fairly consistent throughout the sciences and most of the social sciences — whenever you are asked to report on a lab experiment, a field study (conducted in a natural habitat), or a social research project (based on interviews or questionnaires, for example). This kind of writing typically consists of a series of sections in a certain order:

Introduction

Methods

Results

Discussion/Conclusions

The predictable form of a scientific report makes writing one seem deceptively simple and very different from the essays assigned in many other courses. Undergraduates have told me that lab reports at first seemed a mysterious, alien form of writing and gradually became a routine task of putting information in the right places, according to a prescribed format described in their laboratory manuals. They often conclude that scientific writing isn't *really* writing at all — only a matter of "getting the facts straight": making sure that introductory facts are somewhere in the introduction, methodological facts are in the methods section, and so on. Science teachers sometimes encourage this attitude by using grading methods that assign points for the accuracy and placement of individual pieces of information, not for the organization and clarity of the writer's explanations.

Such grading schemes might lead you to believe that the order and flow of writing within the sections will not matter. In practice, however, disorganized, poorly written reports typically receive low grades, even if they include most of the necessary information. In a research report titled "Students and Professionals Writing Biology: Disciplinary Work and Apprentice Storytellers," Sharon Stockton found that the standards biology teachers use to grade lab reports often differ from the standards described in course guidelines. As the title of Stockton's study suggests, scientific reports are not just containers for facts; they are also "stories" about the experiment, and teachers evaluate the way those stories are told, even if they seem to be just scanning for points.

If you think of the scientific report as a particular kind of story, the challenge of writing one effectively will seem less mysterious and more directly related to other kinds of writing you do. Although scientific research has become increasingly specialized and its language increasingly technical, scientists have been telling essentially the same kinds of stories about their research for more than two hundred years. Early scientific reports were first-person narratives, often published as "letters," describing particular discoveries the authors made in the laboratory, on expeditions, or through simple observation.

By the end of the eighteenth century, frequent challenges to their claims had forced authors to *explain their intentions, describe experiments* in ways that could be tested, and *substantiate results.* With or without formal headings, the sections of a report fell into a consistent order that is still used in professional articles and student reports. You can think of the sections of a scientific report as answers to a logical series of questions about your experiment:

Introduction: What were you doing and why?

Methods: How did you do it?

Results: What did you find out?

Discussion/Conclusions: What do the results mean?

Most reports also begin with an *abstract:* a brief *synopsis* of the entire project, including a sentence or two each about the research problem, the experimental methods, the major findings, and their importance. The abstract is essentially a brief, *unvoiced summary* of the entire report. Although the abstract appears at the beginning of the report, authors usually write it last, when the rest is finished.

Guidelines in some lab courses will ask you to combine *results* and *discussion* or to add *conclusions* at the end, but these variations do not alter the sequence in which you describe your research. Scientists tell these stories about investigation in a certain order because altering this order makes no sense. Good storytellers would not explain the meaning of results before they had presented the results; they would not describe the results of an experiment before they described that experiment; and they would not describe their methods before they explained what they were doing and why.

Although students often believe that lab reports have little to do with anything they learned about writing in English classes, the structure of a scientific report conforms very closely to the shape of the keyhole essay or five-paragraph theme taught in many high school English classes.

Introductions usually begin with explanations of the general type of research the experiment represents and end with a specific statement of the research problem or question — a topic statement, or hypothesis. Professional scientists use the typical funnel shape of the introduction (see p. 117) first to define their area of research, then to summarize previous research in that area, and finally to identify the specific research problem they have tried to solve.

Introductions should take the same shape in your undergraduate lab reports, with some adaptations to your circumstances. You probably will not be making original contributions to a body of research literature, as a member of a professional community. The experiments you report on will demonstrate known principles and procedures or will create occasions for you to develop experimental questions and methods. As a consequence, your introductions will begin with a brief discussion of the general principles your experiment demonstrates or of the category of questions you tried to answer. It will move, then, to the specific form and purpose of your experiment. Here is an example of the introduction to a freshman lab report written for the general chemistry assignment at the beginning of this chapter.

Introduction

The second law of thermodynamics states that for any process, including spontaneous processes, the total entropy of the system and its surrounding increases. A process such as solution is marked by changes in entropy, so a value called the standard entropy of solution can be obtained. The entropy of solution is related to free energy: a higher entropy leads to a more negative free energy.

In this experiment, solid potassium nitrate was converted to aqueous potassium and nitrate ions. This caused an increase in entropy because the ordered KNO_3 crystals broke up in solution to produce randomly ordered ions. The equation for this reaction is summarized below:

$$KNO_3(s) + H_2O(1) \rightleftharpoons K^+(aq) + NO_3^-(aq).$$

This reaction is reversible because the aqueous ions can come back together (under the right condtions) to form potassium nitrate molecules.

The purpose of this experiment was to determine the entropy of solution of potassium nitrate. The entropy was determined by using the equation in $K_{sp} = \Delta H^0/RT + \Delta S^0/R$, which takes the form $y = mx + b$. Values of K_{sp} were determined at different temperatures and were plotted against $1/T$. The y-intercept multiplied by the universal gas constant R is the entropy.

The *body* of a lab report consists of specific experimental procedures and results. Sometimes called the "Experimental" section of a report, or "Materials and Methods," the *methods* section is a narrative account of the research procedures you used, in chronological order, including specifications of equipment, methods of measurement, and relevant times and quantities. You should record this information in your laboratory or field notebook. Using this section as a set of instructions, readers should be able to repeat your experiment with the same results.

You should present the *results* of your experiments in sequences and forms that readers can easily correlate with the methods previously described. When these results are entirely quantitative, students often simply include tables, graphs, or equations, without explanation, on the assumption that numbers speak for themselves. But this is not standard practice in scientific articles. In all sections, scientists use language to guide the readers through the report. At the beginning of the Results section of her chemistry lab report, this student explains to the reader how results presented in her table correspond with experimental procedures and variables (Table 1):

Results

We calculated the solubility product constant of KNO_3 at various temperatures. Table 1 presents the amount of KNO_3 used in each trial, with the corresponding molarity and solubility product of each solution. As predicted, the K_{sp} increased with temperature.

TABLE 1

Sample Number	Mass of KNO_3 (g)	Molarity K^+ = Molarity NO_3	Ksp (M^2)	Temperature (Kelvin)
1	2.532	5.009 M	25.09	305
2	4.024	7.960 M	63.36	324
3	5.255	10.40 M	108.2	334
4	6.537	12.93 M	167.2	341
5	8.014	15.85 M	251.2	353

The *conclusion* of a scientific report includes discussion of the results, conclusions that can be drawn from the research, and error analysis: your attempts to account for results that deviate from predictions or to explain procedural errors recorded in your research notes. In addition to answering *What do the results mean?*, this section might discuss *What went wrong?* and *What should we do next?* Because science teachers view experiments and reports as learning exercises, they are impressed by demonstrations that you understand principles and errors, through clear explanation. Statements such as "I probably didn't wash the beaker carefully" do not constitute error analysis.

When I asked a group of chemistry graduate students to describe the shape of a typical experimental report, in general and in specific terms, they settled on the shape of a martini glass because the methods and results sections are very specific in comparison with the introduction and conclusion (Figure 2). The olive in their diagram represents the research question or hypothesis, which, like the thesis statement in the keyhole essay, lands at the bottom of the introduction.

Teachers of freshman science courses will not assume that you already know how to perform experiments or write scientific reports. Laboratory manuals usually include detailed instructions for procedures and guidelines for writing reports. Beyond the general advice I've provided, therefore, you should read the instructions for writing in your science courses very carefully. More often than not, poor grades on scientific reports result from lack of attention to these guidelines.

There are a couple of factors, however, that laboratory manuals often fail to make clear to students: how to handle quantitative data in tables, equations, and so on, and how to decide when to use active or passive voice.

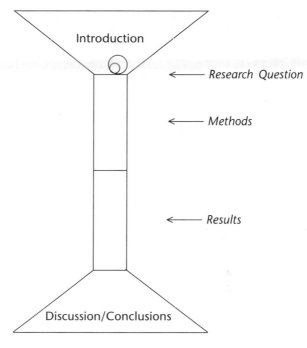

FIGURE 2

Tables, Figures, and Equations.   Like many other kinds of literature, the stories scientists tell about their research are usually illustrated, and in some cases these tables and figures — graphs,
drawings, or photographs — are extremely important parts of the
text. For every student who underestimates the importance of writing in a lab report, another will underestimate the importance of
clear, accurate figures.

In practice grading exercises with chemistry teachers, I found
that evaluation of tables and figures was the greatest cause of variation when several teachers were grading the same report. Some
teachers are not very concerned about the appearance of a graph or
chart as long as it contains the necessary information. Others become extremely annoyed when figures are sloppily drawn, poorly
labeled, and difficult to read. These differing standards often
accounted for a difference of a full letter grade on the report. Most
of these teachers had not conveyed their preferences to students because they assumed everyone shared their views.

Because you can't predict your teacher's attitude, it makes sense to put thought and care into graphs, charts, and tables. These illustrations should be centered at logical places in relation to the text, with numbers (*Figure 1, Table 3*) and accurate labels. On graphs, axes should be labeled as well, with clear lines and data points. The bars in bar graphs should also be clearly distinguished with labels and shading or color. Most undergraduates have access to software for drawing figures and tabulating data in highly legible forms. If you do not, draw figures and tables neatly on graph paper, trace them onto the text pages of your report with a good black pen, and type the labels.

Chemistry, physics, and engineering reports, especially, will often include mathematical or chemical equations in the text, and all science writers have to learn how to integrate these symbolic expressions within the flow of their writing. In some respects mathematical and chemical symbols represent distinct languages, but in other ways they function as sentences or as parts of speech and sentences. The famous equation $E = mc^2$ serves as the subject of this sentence — as the subject of the verb *serves*. Yet the equation is also a sentence that you can write or read in words: *Energy equals mass times the speed of light squared.*

Science journals and style manuals have worked out elaborate guidelines for the use of symbols and equations — far too many rules for me to list here. You can find them in books such as the *ACS Style Guide*, published by the American Chemical Society. In general, you should keep in mind that symbols and equations should read as integrated parts of your writing, not as disconnected expressions. In other words, readers should be able to read the entire report, including equations, aloud, the symbolic expressions included as grammatical elements of English sentences, with appropriate punctuation.

Important equations are usually centered on separate lines, with space above and below, and numbered at the right margin. But these equations should also connect with language on either side, as in this sentence from a lab report on thermochemistry:

A reaction of known ΔH can be measured and the heat capacity determined by the relation

$$Cp = qp/\Delta T, \qquad (1)$$

where ΔT is found by graphing the linear curve of heat loss and extrapolating it to $t = 0$ to find the total change in temperature.

Active versus passive voice. The emphasis on "objectivity" explains why scientists use the passive voice more often than other academic writers do: a passive construction places the *object* that a verb acts upon in the emphatic position, as the subject of the clause.

When all *oxygen* was removed from the air, *pressure* in the container was adjusted to its initial value.

The choices of active or passive voice can become very confusing, however, because while science teachers might tell you to use the passive voice in reports, other teachers might tell you to avoid the passive voice when you write. Yet teachers themselves are often confused about the differences between the passive and active voice, and they rarely explain these differences to students. I'll begin, therefore, by explaining the difference.

In the active clause *we poured the solution into a beaker*, the word *solution* is the direct object of the verb *poured*. In the passive form, *the solution was poured into a beaker*, the *solution*, the object of the action, becomes the subject, and the agent of the action *(we)* vanishes. The passive voice therefore allows writers to focus attention on *what was done or was observed*, not on *who did it or observed it*.

Students and teachers often confuse the passive voice with avoidance of the first person (*I* or *we*) and the active voice with use of the first person. But you can form active clauses without the first person, using any noun or pronoun as a subject (*the results supported our hypothesis*), and you can form passive clauses *with* the first person (*we were given a week to complete the report*). Almost any passage you read, in the sciences or in other fields, will include a mixture of active and passive constructions to achieve a variety of effects. As a consequence, "rules" that you should always use or avoid the passive voice are useless.

To gain control over these constructions, you should recognize that the active and passive voices offer a variety of options for composing and revising sentences. *There is nothing fundamentally wrong (or right) about the passive voice*. Like other sentence types, passive constructions become tedious when writers use them habitually, most often to avoid the first person, without pausing to consider options.

The choice between passive constructions and the first person becomes most unavoidable in the Methods sections of scientific reports, where you must describe what you did during the experiment. Lab manuals usually tell you which form instructors prefer, and if they don't, you should ask. But strings of first-person sentences (*I measured. . . . I observed. . . . I calculated. . . .*) become just as monotonous as strings of passives (*. . . was measured . . . was observed . . . was calculated*). Even in the Methods section you can find ways to vary sentence types. In this section of her report "Gravimetric Determination of a Chloride," a freshman consistently used the passive voice to avoid the first person. Here are the last two sentences in the section:

> *The precipitate was dried in the oven for one week until a constant mass was reached. Its final mass was then observed and recorded.*

With the first person, the active choice would sound a bit different, but not necessarily better if it were used throughout the section:

> *I dried the precipitate in the oven for one week until it reached a constant mass. I then observed and recorded its final mass.*

But there is another option. She could have converted the first sentence to a different kind of active construction, with *precipitate* as the subject, and used either the passive or the first person in the second sentence:

> *The precipitate dried in the oven for one week until it reached a constant mass. Its final mass was then observed and recorded. (Or I then observed and recorded its final mass.)*

This type of active construction simply acknowledges that in scientific research, and in the world at large, all sorts of things happen without direct human agency: *precipitates dry, cells divide, chemicals react, turbulence increases, genes determine, results indicate,* and *hypotheses predict.* Recognizing these agents other than yourself is the key to writing sentences that are not only more active, but also more accurate and varied. **[Exercise 8]**

What individual teachers will like or dislike isn't entirely predictable, but all teachers like to read sentences and passages that flow smoothly, in logical sequence, and in a variety of forms. If you keep in mind that a scientific report is a story that needs to be told well, listen to the way your report sounds, and revise sentences and paragraphs that sound rough, you will present your understanding of the experiment more clearly and your report will be easier to read. Teachers who have to evaluate twenty or thirty of these reports will be grateful for your effort.

Informal Writing

Within the writing process, the questions and notes you produce in the prewriting phase and rough drafts are also examples of *informal writing:* written work dedicated to the process of thinking and learning but not, as a rule, graded as finished writing. Lecture notes fall into this category. So do laboratory notebooks and other kinds of research notes used as a basis for writing reports.

Many of your teachers will assign some type of informal writing as a basis for formal writing assignments or discussion, and some of them will grade this work, largely to make sure that you do it and take it seriously. Lab notebooks are standard requirements in science laboratory courses and are usually graded, because thorough, accurate lab notes are essential to experimental science. Some kinds of informal writing might be graded informally as well, with checks or S/U (Satisfactory or Unsatisfactory) marking systems. Other teachers will read and perhaps respond to this work without grading it, to stimulate thought and to find out what their students are thinking.

Here are some types of informal writing that might be assigned in almost any field of study:

Informal papers.   Rarely longer than a page or two, these assignments usually ask students to summarize or comment on specific readings, films, lectures, or issues recently covered in the course. These are often weekly assignments, turned in and graded with checks or S/U, and sometimes exchanged in small-group discussions. One anthropology professor, for example, calls these weekly papers "Argument Notes," in which students first *summarize* an assigned text, then *integrate* these ideas with central themes in the course, and finally respond to the text with *questions and reactions.*

Study questions.   Teachers will often assign responses to study questions in preparation for discussion in lecture periods or in separate discussion sections, to make sure you have done the assigned reading and are ready to discuss current topics in the course. Some teachers will ask you to respond to these questions on index cards, which they will collect at the end of the period.

Written problem sets.   Problem sets in math, science, and engineering courses usually require mathematical calculations or diagrams, but teachers will sometimes ask you to explain concepts or reasoning in full sentences and paragraphs. They want to know how well you understand the concept, how you thought through the problem, and how well you can convey your understanding.

Course journals.   Lecture notes represent one kind of informal course journal, but other kinds — sometimes called *reflective journals* or *double-entry notebooks* — have become increasingly popular among college teachers over the past ten years. In such a journal you do not just record what the teacher or texts say; you also record your own observations or questions about lectures and readings. In a double-entry notebook, for example, you might be asked to use one side for conventional notes and the other side for your own thoughts, questions, or counterarguments. Teachers rarely grade these journals, but they often require, collect, and read them, responding to points of debate or confusion. Many teachers also help their students use journal entries to generate ideas for papers.

Five-minute essays.   In lecture courses, teachers will sometimes give you a few minutes at the end of the period to summarize what you have learned, raise questions, and register arguments. Like study questions, these brief comments are often completed on notecards and turned in, but rarely graded. These teachers know that when lectures end abruptly you will not pause to consider what you have heard and that you will forget lingering questions if you don't write them down. Teachers occasionally pause for this brief, informal writing in the middle of a lecture as well.

Teachers assign informal writing because they know that the most valuable kinds of learning result from active engagement with the course material, not from passive reading and listening. They also know that students who write papers and enter class discussions without prior reflection rarely come up with interesting ideas.

Furthermore, teachers assign informal writing because they enjoy reading it. Many professors and teaching assistants have told me that their students' best ideas and often their best writing appear in their informal papers and journals, when they are thinking freely and writing in relaxed voices. The fact that you can say almost anything that comes to mind allows interesting, unpredictable things to surface. And when you are just thinking on paper, without trying to adopt a formal structure and tone, your writing will tend to sound more naturally voiced and relaxed, with inflections of humor, perplexity, conviction, fascination, and other tones that you might exclude from formal papers. In the following example of an informal "thought paragraph" written for a biology course, the student has connected concepts of time in the study of evolution with questions raised in other fields, such as cultural anthropology, philosophy, and agricultural economics:

> The concept of time is so casually taken for granted. I had never really thought about it until the professor explored the subject. The three principles mentioned in lecture: irreversible process, periodic process, and the use of known events, are logical and sit well with the brain. Upon deeper introspection, however, I found the concept of irreversible time to be deeply ingrained in my western mind. How do our individual concepts of time enlighten or cloud, or benignly affect our perception of the world? I see westerners as "progress-oriented" beings; changes are made in constant effort to progress to bigger and better things in an irreversible time scheme. But an agricultural society is more "cycle-oriented"; planting is done with the known result of growth and harvest in the periodic time scheme. Evolution makes sense in the light of the irreversible time scheme. Can evolution be explained periodically? Would an agricultural society have more difficulty with the idea of evolution than westerners would?

This example represents the kind of lively inquiry teachers hope their students will bring to a course. The themes that emerge when you simply let yourself "think on paper" are usually more interesting, both to the writer and to the reader, than the ones you might choose when you deliberately "think of a topic" as you begin to work on a paper.

Even if teachers do not assign these types of informal writing, therefore, I recommend that you use them on your own. If you set aside a few minutes to write down your thoughts and questions about course material, several benefits will result:

• You will learn more.

• You will find the course more interesting.

• You will be better prepared to raise and answer questions.

• You will generate more complex, rich topics for writing assignments.

A Brief Summary

Although there are some very general expectations that will apply to almost all of the writing you do in college, a survey of actual assignments across the curriculum reveals a great variety of specific forms, purposes, and standards that differ widely even within a field of study. In other words, there are no reliable formulas for writing essays in college; nor can you reliably predict what a history teacher or a biology teacher will ask you to do in an assignment. Even lab reports, the most uniform of all types of academic writing, can vary considerably according to specific teachers' goals in a course.

The main challenge you will face, therefore, is to do what particular assignments and teachers have actually asked you to do, within the larger context of a specific course.

I emphasize the obvious because undergraduates so often do *not* do what the assignment asked them to do, but something else that they thought they should do, something they were once taught to do, or something they always do when writing essays.

Because assignments will not tell you exactly what you should write, responding to them effectively is not a simple or slavish matter of following instructions. Good assignments provide a structure — a set of constraints — within which you can write freely, demonstrating your knowledge, creative intelligence, and skill. If you misinterpret that structure of expectations, you will not know where your freedom lies. If you spend five or ten minutes just reading and thinking about an assignment, registering what it asks you to do and trying to imagine the kind of paper that would meet those expectations, you can use that freedom with a stronger, more accurate sense of composure.

EXERCISES

Exercise 1. Specific uses of language create qualities of tone in writing, but these specifics can be hard to identify. While reading and listening carefully to the paragraph on health insurance (p. 83), can you identify specific language that makes it sound like a relaxed, rational discussion with the reader?

Exercise 2. Read the paragraph on health insurance again (p. 83), this time thinking about its organization. Does it read as a "little composition" in itself, with a beginning, middle, and end? Does it flow smoothly, in a logical sequence of sentences? To test this logical sequence, try moving any of the sentences to a different place. If the paragraph is well organized, moving sentences will damage the logic and flow.

Exercise 3. With the typical terms and purposes of assignments in mind (pp. 89–90), look over the examples of assignments at the beginning of this chapter and, in a sentence or two for each, explain what they ask students to do. Note that not all of the terms are represented among these assignments, and some assignments have more than one purpose.

Exercise 4. Choose an essay or textbook section of at least five pages from your course readings or from other sources, such as a magazine or newspaper. Write three *voiced summaries* of this selection: the first in two sentences, the second in one paragraph, and the third in two pages.

Exercise 5. Write a three-page paper in response to the assignment on Barber and Bernard (p. 108). Begin with a *voiced summary* of Barber's chapter, emphasizing the points most relevant to the question. Then explain how Bernard would respond, according to your own interpretation, using specific quotations and explanations to support your views.

Exercise 6. From analysis of the political science assignment (p. 108), without reading the texts, can you imagine how you might organize such a paper? Where would you begin, where would you go from there, and where would you end up? Construct an outline of the way such a paper might be organized.

Exercise 7. Beginning with a brief, general summary, write a two-to-three-page evaluation of Barber's chapter, using the questions raised on pages 111–12 or questions of your own. As I suggested, pause to consider whether one of these questions is central, whether connections or a theme runs through them, and write about that central question or theme. Otherwise you will end up with a simple list of disconnected points.

If you prefer, use another article or essay, beginning with a list of questions you compile as you read and considering themes or connections among them.

Exercise 8.   Here is a passage from the Methods section of a freshman biology report on the effects of cold on human pulse rate and blood pressure:

> For each subject, (a bath) of cold <u>water was drawn</u> from the tap, filling the tub to the point where (the subject) <u>could be submerged</u> to the chest. The subject was then tested for heart rate and blood pressure before entering the water. The subject was then immersed in the cold bath, and measurements of blood pressure and heart rate were taken in one-minute intervals for five minutes. Five minutes, it was reasoned, would be enough for the body to recover from its initial shock and make the cardiopulmonary adjustments necessary. It was expected that reasonable comparisons might be drawn based upon sex, age, body size, and health.

First identify the passive verbs in this passage and their grammatical subjects by underlining the verbs and circling the subjects as in the first sentence.

Now rewrite the passage using the first person, *I* or *we,* and the active voice, as in the sentence *For each subject, we drew a bath of cold water from the tap, filling the tub to the point where we could submerge the subject to the chest.*

Does this passage sound any better in the active voice?

Now vary actives and passives in ways that make the passage sound best to you. Look for active subjects other than *I* or *we.*

5 | Reading: How to Stay on Top of It

> Reading involves a fair measure of push and shove. You make your mark on a book and it makes its mark on you. Reading is not simply a matter of hanging back and waiting for a piece, or its author, to tell you what the writing has to say. In fact, one of the difficult things about reading is that the pages before you will begin to speak only when the authors are silent and you begin to speak in their place, sometimes for them, doing their work, continuing their projects, and sometimes for yourself, following your own agenda.
>
> — David Bartholomae and Anthony Petrosky,
> *Ways of Reading*

Amanda's Question

A couple of years ago Amanda, a freshman in my fall-term writing class, announced a piece of advice she had picked up from a junior she had met:

"She told me the most important thing you need to learn here is what *not* to read!"

I thought about this for a moment and said, hesitantly, "Well, that's *sort of* true." But Amanda looked more distressed than enlightened. "What's the matter?" I asked.

"She didn't tell me *how you know* what not to read," Amanda replied.

Amanda was in the School of Industrial and Labor Relations (ILR), which students say means "I Love Reading." Her teachers in labor history, economics, human resources, and organizational behavior assigned whole books, articles, and chapters of textbooks each week, in preparation for writing assignments and essay exams. Just getting through all of this reading was difficult. Understanding and remembering what she had read, figuring out what was important and unimportant, seemed impossible. And this challenge is not confined to students in ILR, to English majors, or to this university. Science teachers assign dense chapters of textbooks and lab manuals, and freshmen in these courses are also completing distribution requirements in the social sciences and humanities, along with writing courses that often require extensive reading. Performance on examinations, problem sets, labs, research projects, and writing assignments depends heavily on knowledge acquired from texts of many kinds. As a consequence, effective reading probably represents the most crucial set of skills you can develop in college, where reading everything thoroughly, from beginning to end, might be impossible.

This was what troubled Amanda and the other freshmen in my class. They sensed that there was something wrong with their approaches to the great volume of reading in their courses. They had begun to realize that more advanced students often spent less time on assigned readings with better results on exams and papers. Perhaps these juniors and seniors had figured out "what *not* to read," as Amanda's friend suggested, and could focus more attention on important material. Given a particular assignment, however, the question is not simply *Should I read this?* If the answer is "yes," there are some further, related questions you need to ask:

- What am I reading?
- Why am I reading it?
- How can I read it most efficiently?
- How can I remember what I will need to know about it?

These questions acknowledge that reading is not a single kind of activity. There are diverse styles of reading, different approaches and strategies, used for specific purposes and for particular kinds of texts. And when I refer to "texts" I mean written documents of all kinds — not only textbooks, but other books, essays, articles, or reports. *Reading for pleasure, for general understanding, to prepare for exams, to write papers on the subject, or to find specific information —* these reasons for reading require different kinds of attention and engage different kinds of cognition and memory.

Texts are also structured in ways that facilitate certain kinds of reading. Some are meant to be read from beginning to end; others, including most textbooks, present information schematically, with many potential points of entry and direction. If you fall into the task of reading without pausing to consider *what, why,* and *how* you are going to read, you might be wasting almost all of the time you spend.

Becoming a Predatory Reader

In my freshman classes I often call this strategic approach *predatory reading* or *reading from the top of the food chain.*

A colleague once objected to this language because it sounds so aggressive, even violent. She wanted her students to feel that reading was a peaceful, pleasurable activity that transports them to other times and places, other ways of viewing the world. My colleague was describing a wonderful kind of reading experience that I hope all of you have had and will continue to have: letting yourself become absorbed in a good book, drawn into the lives of characters, the chain of events, or the flow of information in the world the author creates.

But this is only one way of reading — for pleasure — and, for reasons I'll explain, it will have very limited uses in your academic work. To describe alternatives, I use aggressive terms such as *predatory reading* to counteract the passive approaches you might bring with you to college or fall into once you arrive. In most academic work, you can't afford to become absorbed, consumed, by the great volume of reading you must do. Nor can you afford to let your reasons for reading become secondary to the author's reasons for writing. If you do, you won't stay on top of your work; you will just fall into it and become lost. More specifically, just falling into assigned reading in a passive, linear fashion will have several unfortunate results:

- You probably won't finish all of the reading assigned.
- You won't remember most of what you read.
- You will have no coherent record to remind you of what you once understood, while you were reading.
- If writing assignments then ask you to respond to this material — with arguments, interpretations, or new questions of your own — you will have no immediate response.

The alternative is to read always with some conscious *intention*, a deliberate strategy. Staying on top of your reading requires awareness that texts are not just linear streams of words but constructed objects. Like other constructed objects — such as a table or a car engine — they are composed of parts, assembled in a particular order for particular purposes. Understanding them is in large part a matter of knowing how they are constructed. If you know how they are constructed, you can also take them apart, rearrange the pieces in ways that are most useful to you, or pull out the parts you want to consume. Predatory reading simply acknowledges that books are, as people say, "food for thought."

For survival, every entering student must learn these strategies for staying on top of assigned reading; every scholar has already learned them. After visits to faculty offices, undergraduates sometimes express wonder at the vast amounts of knowledge these scholars have consumed. They have seen walls lined floor to ceiling with shelves of books and periodicals. "I can't believe they've read all those books!" students tell me, and I reply, "Well, you're right not to believe it."

The truth, of course, is more complex than a question of having read or not read something. Having a "mastery" of books and articles does not necessarily mean you have read them from cover to cover. Sometimes it means much more, sometimes much less, and almost always something different. More accurately, "mastery" of published material means knowing

what it is,

why it was written,

how to find information within it,

and how to use this material for your own purposes.

Scholars use some books entirely as references, for looking up specific information when they need it. They selectively read certain portions of books or articles and ignore others. In some cases they have only glanced through a work, looking for the main idea or for specific kinds of information. And they have read some of the books, articles, selected passages, or poems on their shelves many times with intense care, underlining sentences and making extensive notes.

When teachers assign reading in their courses, therefore, they do not expect you to read everything once from beginning to end. They assume that you will develop a range of reading strategies similar to their own and choose the methods most appropriate for particular assignments. To understand the functions of these methods, you should first consider how your mind and memory work.

Reading and Memory

Why are you reading?

While you are reading something for one of your courses, your first goal is to understand what the writer is saying. Although this immediate goal of "reading comprehension" is a necessary part of learning, this does not, in itself, constitute learning or *working knowledge* of the material, of the sort that you can use in the future to pass exams, write papers, or participate in discussions. Your understanding does not become useful unless you can remember the material and the way you made sense of it, including critical responses, questions, or points of confusion you need to clarify later.

Not remembering is actually the norm, and forgetting occurs very rapidly unless you take some active measures to retain information. Psychological studies indicate that after reading or listening people typically forget more than half of what they learned within one hour. Their memory then continues to deteriorate more gradually, to about 30 percent after nine hours and about 20 percent after a week. And these are proportions of what you once knew. If you are tired or distracted, not "taking in" what you read or hear, your retention will be much lower. Without some strategy for controlling memory, what you remember will also be unpredictable. The 20 percent that you recall after a week might not be the information you need most to remember.

This massive loss of memory is normal because we don't want or need to recall most of what occurs to us for more than a few seconds. Some crucial kinds of learning, such as motor skills, are very tenacious. If you learned to ice-skate one winter, you did not forget how to do this over the next summer; the same kind of memory applies to riding a bicycle, typing, or throwing a ball. In general, however, we register a very small proportion of the sensory information available to us, and we retain most of this registered information only momentarily — just long enough to steer ourselves through immediate experience.

While you are reading, therefore, you will normally recall what you previously read just long enough to maintain a sense of connection with the sentences you are currently reading. This brief storage period is called *short-term memory*. Unless you take deliberate measures to shift important information into *long-term memory* — measures comparable to using the Save command on your computer — the bulk of what you read will simply evaporate. Even if the material seemed perfectly clear to you at the time, an hour, day, or week later you won't be able to retrieve most of it, and what you do recall probably will have meshed with some prior framework or association you brought to the reading. You might remember an example involving cats simply because you love animals or miss your pet at home, not because this example was central to the text. Otherwise you will be left with very general, long-term *impressions* of reading: a vague recollection that the subject was interesting or uninteresting, that you disagreed with the author but not why, or that it made you sleepy.

Continuous streams of information will not end up in long-term memory unless you actively construct a framework for remembering and retrieving what is important: some kind of *mnemonic*, or aid to memory. In other words, you need to break up the stream and repackage it somehow. On average, for example, people can't store memory of more than seven random numbers, which explains the standard length of telephone numbers, why we can remember them, and why most of us can't remember the numbers on our credit cards. But we can recall longer sequences of numbers if we cluster them into logical units or create some other mnemonic. We "package" the long-distance area code separately and attach it to local numbers, or we locate logical sequences, repetitions, multiples, and sound patterns. For example, the number 321-1428 is easier to remember than an unpatterned string (such as 738-4192) if you register the fact that 321 is an inverted sequence and that *one four* times *two* equals *eight*. What we initially remember, then, is not the whole but the mnemonic: *the framework for remembering*.

This is why you take notes in lectures. You know you won't remember much of the stream of spoken words unless you make a record of what the teacher said. And because you can't record everything, you need to identify important information and write it down in some kind of logical framework that will later remind you of the whole. You will remember the lecture initially by referring to your notes, the mnemonic you constructed for the purpose of remembering. Good lecture notes repackage the material more efficiently than the lecture itself, by clustering the information into memorable categories, subcategories, and lists. For the purpose of studying or writing a paper on the topic, reading effective notes can be *more* useful and efficient than listening to the entire lecture again, because the notes have already digested the material in ways you can understand and therefore reconstitute your own comprehension. For the purpose of taking exams or writing papers, *your* comprehension, not your teacher's, is most essential.

The streams of words you read are equally unmemorable, but students are much less likely to repackage what they read, with outlines or notes. The main reason, I suppose, is that a text is objectively *there* when you finish reading it. You can always go back to it, as to a transcript of a lecture, and read it over. But rereading a text is no more efficient than passively listening to a lecture again. You are still left with no record, no mnemonic, to shift your short-term comprehension into lasting memory: into real learning and working knowledge.

To accomplish this transfer, for specific purposes, you need a repertoire of reading strategies.

Passive, Linear Reading

You are in a linear mode of reading when you begin with the first word of a text and continue to the last word, letting the linear sequence of words dictate the order in which you encounter information. This way of reading is entirely passive if you don't bring any goals or strategies to the task — if you simply follow the linear flow of the sentences, with your eyes and mind, and let the writing act upon you, happen to you.

What actually happens to you, in this passive mode of reading, will depend on many variables over which you have little control, such as your level of alertness, the qualities of the writing, and your interest in the subject. How much you understand and remember a week later will also depend on these variables. If you are tired, if the writing is abstract and tedious, and if the subject doesn't engage your interest, the drone of words might become a sedative or you might get to the end of a chapter and have no recollection of what you just read. Even if you are alert and interested, your memory of the text a week later might be very sketchy, because passive reading stimulates long-term memory more or less at random, if at all. In this mode, which I call *falling into the text,* readers are vulnerable to the writing and to other factors that surround the act of reading, such as preoccupations, distractions, and patterns of association (or disassociation) with the content.

This is the way you *want* to read a really good novel, simply for pleasure. Just open it to the first page, start reading, and let the flow of language carry you off on a literary journey. If it's a compelling book, you will become absorbed in it, and that's where the pleasure lies. The events and characters might become so real in your imagination that you forget you are reading — forget that they are inventions, constructed out of language on the page. The effect is essentially like watching a wonderful movie and forgetting that you are in a theater watching actors performing a script under direction and on constructed sets, all on film projected on a flat screen.

But this kind of intense absorption, this surrender to the medium, does not necessarily create memory. The most immediately gripping novels, such as thrillers and mysteries, often leave very little lasting recollection beyond a vague memory of fear or suspense. Becoming passively engrossed in a book doesn't leave you in a very good position to take an examination on it a week later or to write a summary or critical review. **[Exercise 1]**

This is why passive, linear reading isn't very useful in academic work. Apart from the fact that this way of reading doesn't reliably engage long-term memory, most of the reading you do in college won't capture and hold your attention like a good novel. If you surrender to it, allow yourself to become absorbed, it will probably put you to sleep.

Unfortunately, passive, linear reading is for most people the default mode, when they haven't decided to read in some other way or aren't aware that there are options. More than half of the freshmen in my classes initially try to read their textbooks and other assignments in this fashion: starting with the first word of a chapter and continuing to the end, trying to stay alert and receptive, hoping they will remember what they have read. Unless they deliberately read in a different way, however, they won't remember very much.

Highlighting

Those of you who have tried to study textbooks by reading them passively, hoping that you will absorb what you need to know, have probably realized that you need to be *doing something* to make important material soak in. This activity on your part is what distinguishes reading from *studying* — *examining* something in the effort to understand it. But to *study* a text, what exactly should you be doing?

When they reach the end of a textbook chapter and can't remember what they read at the beginning, students typically resort to highlighting passages that seem important. This use of transparent markers has largely replaced its older counterpart, underlining. If you buy used textbooks you might find that someone has already performed this task, sometimes in two or three colors to distinguish categories or levels of importance. I've seen used textbooks that were almost completely highlighted. Apparently everything turned out to be important.

As a learning tool, highlighting has some values and limitations that you should consider before you fall into the practice. I'll start with the advantages:

- Because you are doing something with and to the text, highlighting keeps you more alert and allows you to read longer without becoming distracted and fatigued.

- Figuring out what you should highlight helps you understand what you are reading and determine whether you understand it. If you don't know what is important enough to highlight, you probably don't yet understand the material or why it was assigned.

- Highlighting creates the beginning of an analytical understanding of texts, of the way they are structured. When pulled out of the text, highlighted passages should resemble an outline or summary of the work.

- Perhaps the main advantage of highlighting is the reduction of study time later, when you need to read through the material again in preparation for an exam or a writing assignment and remember almost nothing. If you have left a textbook chapter unmarked, you will have to spend almost as much time reading it again as you did the first time. If you have effectively marked the most important parts, you can sometimes review only those highlighted portions and reduce your study time by more than half.

For some purposes, however, highlighting is a waste of time or an insufficient aid to learning. Here are some of the limitations:

- Highlighting (or underlining) alone simply emphasizes the authority of the text — what its author says, believes, or knows. The practice therefore leads you toward memorization and repetition, not toward interpretation, inquiry, or criticism. As a consequence, highlighting works best as a preparation for "objective" examinations of your knowledge or for writing summaries. It is *not* sufficient preparation for raising questions, for participating in discussions, or for writing arguments, analyses, and interpretations based on readings.

- While it can lead you toward a systematic understanding of the text, highlighting does not effectively *represent* systematic understanding of the material as a structure of information and ideas, even if you use several colors. Highlighting usually emphasizes a linear series of important points, not the connections among them.

- If you need only to grasp and retain the general idea or a few specifics, highlighting while you read is an inefficient, sometimes pointless activity. For these purposes there are much better strategies, which I'll describe later.

- Highlighting doesn't create long-term memory. When the practice becomes routine, as a way of marking in passing what you need to study later, it can even reduce your memory.

- While thoughtful, effective highlighting can make studying more efficient, inaccurate highlighting can get you into trouble. If you highlight in a linear fashion while you read, you might not recognize important passages the first time through. If you miss them and study only the highlighted portions later, this practice can actually lower your performance on exams.

The most effective highlighting does not simply flag all of the passages you should read again when exams approach; it also creates a framework for understanding and remembering what you have read. That framework is usually built into the text, as a logical structure of ideas and information. Highlighting should help to make that structure visible, and observing the ways in which texts are structured can also help you write more effectively. As a consequence, highlighting works best when paired with a nonlinear reading strategy such as *analytical scanning* (see p. 146).

At every level of organization, from the structure of a paragraph to the design of an entire book, there is usually a *main idea* followed by *supporting points*, often leading to *conclusions*. In a book this structure consists of several layers. There is a main idea or topic for the entire volume. Subtopics of this general theme are also the main topics of individual chapters, which are often subdivided into sections, each with its own theme. A paragraph, the smallest unit of organization, will also have a topic, supporting points, and sometimes a conclusion.

As a rule (though one with many exceptions) *main ideas appear at beginnings, conclusions at ends, and supporting points in between*. Authors usually present the central theme of a book in the introduction — usually toward the beginning of the introduction — and present their conclusions at the end. The theme of a chapter also tends to appear at the beginning, as does the topic sentence of a paragraph. Textbooks (and sometimes other books and articles) usually provide summaries at the ends of chapters.

If you are aware of this conventional structure, you can locate main points more easily and recognize the supporting points that follow. For this purpose, two colors of highlighter are useful: one to mark the main ideas and the other to indicate supporting points within a section. Double and single underlining can serve the same purpose.

For example, consider this passage from Edward O. Wilson's book *The Diversity of Life* (1992):

> *Evolution is blinkered still more by the fact that the frequency of genes and chromosomes can be shifted by pure chance. The process, an alternative to natural selection called genetic drift, occurs most rapidly in very small populations. It proceeds faster when the genes are neutral, having little or no effect on survival and reproduction. Genetic drift is a game of chance. Suppose that a population of organisms contained 50 percent A genes and 50 percent B genes at a particular chromosome site, and that in each generation it reproduced itself by passing on A and B genes at random. Imagine that the population comprises only five individuals and hence 10 genes on the chromosome site. Draw out 10 genes to make the next generation. They can all come from one pair of adults or from as many as five pairs of adults. The new population could end up with exatly 5 A and 5 B genes, duplicating the parental population, but there is a high probability that in such a tiny sample the result instead will be 6 A and 4 B, or 3 A and 7 B, or something else again. Thus in very small populations the percentages of alleles can change significantly in one generation by the workings of chance alone. That in a nutshell is genetic drift, about which mathematicians have published volumes of sophisticated and usually incomprehensible calculations.*

But let us go on. Population size is critical in genetic drift. If the population were 500,000 individuals with 500,000 A genes and 500,000 B genes respectively, the picture would be entirely different. At this large number, and given that even a small percentage of the adults reproduced — say 1 percent reproduced — the sample of genes drawn would remain very close to 50 percent A and 50 percent B in each generation. In such large populations genetic drift is therefore a relatively minor factor in evolution, meaning that it is weak if opposed by natural selection. The stronger the selection, the more quickly the perturbation caused by drift will be corrected. If drift leads to a high percentage of B genes but A genes are superior in nature to B genes, the selection will tend to return the B genes to a lower frequency. (81)

This is a clear, concise explanation of genetic drift as a factor in evolution, and while you were reading it you probably felt that you understood what Wilson was saying. If I ask you to write a brief explanation of genetic drift two weeks from now, however, your memory of the passage will have faded considerably, perhaps to oblivion. If *The Diversity of Life* is assigned reading in a biology or environmental studies course (and it often is), your immediate understanding will be of little value unless you take measures to recall this knowledge and study efficiently when you face an exam or writing assignment.

Highlighting can serve this purpose if you imagine what would most efficiently stimulate understanding after short-term memory has faded. If you highlight the main structure of the explanation, this process will also strengthen your immediate understanding and enhance memory when you look at the passage again.

What should you highlight? As in most explanations and arguments, Wilson introduces central topics toward the beginnings of paragraphs, devotes the middle portions to examples, and ends paragraphs with conclusions. Highlighting should underscore this structure; *highlighted material should read, ideally, as a brief summary or outline of the entire passage.* Here is one way to highlight the structure of Wilson's explanation:

Evolution is blinkered still more by the fact that the frequency of genes and chromosomes can be shifted by pure chance. The process, <u>an alternative to natural selection called genetic drift,</u> occurs most <u>rapidly in very small populations</u>. It proceeds <u>faster when the genes are</u>

neutral, having little or no effect on survival and reproduction. Genetic drift is a game of chance. Suppose that a population of organisms contained 50 percent A genes and 50 percent B genes at a particular chromosome site, and that in each generation it reproduced itself by passing on A and B genes at random. Imagine that the population comprises only five individuals and hence 10 genes on the chromosome site. Draw out 10 genes to make the next generation. They can all come from one pair of adults or from as many as five pairs of adults. The new population could end up with exactly 5 A and 5 B genes, duplicating the parental population, but there is a high probability that in such a tiny sample the result instead will be 6 A and 4 B, or 3 A and 7 B, or something else again. _Thus in very small populations the percentages of alleles can change significantly in one generation by the workings of chance alone._ That in a nutshell is genetic drift, about which mathematicians have published volumes of sophisticated and usually incomprehensible calculations.

But let us go on. _Population size is critical in genetic drift._ If the population were 500,000 individuals with 500,000 A genes and 500,000 B genes respectively, the picture would be entirely different. At this large number, and given that even a small percentage of the adults reproduced — say 1 percent reproduced — the sample of genes drawn would remain very close to 50 percent A and 50 percent B in each generation. _In such large populations genetic drift is therefore a relatively minor factor in evolution, meaning that it is weak if opposed by natural selection._ _The stronger the selection, the more quickly the perturbation caused by drift will be corrected._ If drift leads to a high percentage of B genes but A genes are superior in nature to B genes, the selection will tend to return the B genes to a lower frequency.

Here I've used a single underline to highlight the most central points and double underlining to indicate supporting points. A quick glance at the examples between would be sufficient to remind you of the details used to illustrate these central statements.

Note that although you can look for important statements _toward_ the beginning and end of paragraphs (or sections or chapters), those statements are not necessarily the first or last sentences. To highlight effectively you need to read analytically and locate structural features. **[Exercise 2]**

Again, highlighting is most effective as an aid to studying the text later, if you need only to understand and remember important information. If you want to avoid reading the text again or if you are supposed to read and respond to it critically, other approaches to reading will be more effective.

Notes, Outlines, and Summaries

Students are often surprised that weeks or months later I can still remember papers they wrote for my class, sometimes more vividly than they can. They say, "You must have a really good memory." But I don't. The reason, instead, is that I don't just read those papers; I also write extensive comments, both at the margins and at the end. In those comments I try to explain what I got out of the paper and what I thought the writer was trying to do, along with evaluations of the work. *I remember their writing as the object of my own active attention and response.*

You will notice the same kind of enhanced recollection if you discuss a book with a friend shortly after you read it, describe it to someone in a letter, or write a book report. These active responses will stimulate lasting memory of the book much more effectively than just reading or highlighting. Much later you will remember what *you* said — the way you described the book and what you liked or disliked about it — more vividly than the aspects you did not describe. Writing and speaking are in themselves *mnemonics*: they help to create long-term memory.

A sense of urgency, a desire to get the reading done, might convince you that pausing to make notes, construct outlines, or write summaries would be a waste of your time, since the author has already written what you need to know. Why rewrite it or write about it? Most textbook chapters are already outlined, in a sense. The material is usually broken down into sections, with headings and subheadings, often with numbered lists of points and boldface indications of important terms. Textbooks often include chapter summaries that digest the material for you, along with study questions to help you make sure you understand it.

Until you make this structure meaningful in your own terms, however, it will remain the structure of the text and will represent the author's knowledge, not yours. If you can explain the material to someone else, summarize it in your own words, or outline the structure, the knowledge is yours in two ways:

1. This linguistic processing will engage long-term me
2. In a summary or outline you will have a record of understanding — something you can read quickly late your memory.

The framework of a good outline will also stimulate recollection of details, examples, or supporting arguments. Even if you can't recall these specifics without reading the material again, the structure of your outline will allow you to scan the text quickly, filling in the pieces you have forgotten. If it is sufficiently clear, a brief outline or diagram can even *eliminate* the need to read the text again. Without rereading, the following outline would recall the substance of Wilson's explanation of genetic drift, including the examples:

Genetic drift

— *alt. to nat. selection*
— *rapid in small pop.*
— *if not working against nat. selection*
— *"game of chance"*

ex: *5 A & 5 B = 6 A & 4 B or 3 A & 7 B*
500,000 A & 500,000 B = about 50/50%
[Exercise 3]

Like highlighting, however, an outline reaffirms the structure and substance of the text, not your own position in relation to the text. For this reason, notes — either in the margins or in a separate notebook — are especially important if writing assignments or essay exams ask you to respond to readings. If you make notes while you read, you will have a record of your responses to the text: points of agreement or disagreement, alternative interpretations, correspondence or contrast with other readings, or unanswered questions. These notes on your thoughts about the text will put you in a stronger position to develop arguments, interpretations, or comparisons than you would be if you had only read the work passively, without paying attention to the way it struck you. Passive reading reaffirms the authority of the text and can actually put you at a disadvantage if you need to take a position, to establish your own authority.

All of these active strategies become essential if assigned readings are badly written or otherwise difficult to understand. If a text does not make sense, you must *make sense of it* somehow, and what

you need to remember is what you understand, not literally what
the author said. When readings do not directly communicate what
you need to know, you want to avoid getting "trapped in the text."
Your own notes, outlines, and paraphrases can help you escape
writing that you hope never to read again.

Here is an example of reading you would not want to get
trapped in — one you would want to escape at all costs. It is a
passage on contractual relations from *The Structure of Social Action*
(1949), by the sociologist Talcott Parsons. Try just reading it passively, from beginning to end, to see what happens to you.

*Spencer's contractual relation is the type case of a social relation-
ship in which only the elements formulated in "utilitarian" theory are
involved. Its prototype is the economic exchange relationship where
the determinant elements are the demand and supply schedules of the
parties concerned. At least implicit in the conception of a system of
such relationships is the conception that it is the mutual advantage
derived by the parties from the various exchanges which constitutes
the principle binding, cohesive force in the system. It is as a direct
antithesis to this deeply imbedded conception of a system of "relations
of contract" that Durkheim wishes his own "organic solidarity" to be
understood.*

*The line which Durkheim's criticism takes is that the Spencerian,
or more generally utilitarian, formulation fails to exhaust, even for the
case of what are the purely "interested" transactions of the market-
place, the elements which actually are both to be found in the existing
system of such transactions, and which, it can be shown, must exist, if
the system is to function at all. What is omitted is the fact that these
transactions are actually entered into in accordance with a body of
binding rules which are not part of the ad hoc agreement of the
parties. The elements included in the utilitarian conception are, on the
contrary, all taken account of in the terms of the agreement. What
may, however, be called the "institution" of contract — the rules
regulating relations of contract — has not been agreed to by the
parties but exists prior to and independently of any such agreement.*

*The content of the rules is various. They regulate what contracts
are and are not recognized as valid. A man cannot, for instance, sell
himself or others into slavery. They regulate the means by which the
other party's assent to a contract may be obtained; an agreement*

secured by fraud or under duress is void. They regulate various consequences of a contract once made, both to the parties themselves and to third persons. (311)

I think everyone will agree that this is difficult reading, partly because it is an abstract discussion of social and economic philosophy, with few concrete examples to help us apply the concepts to the real world. Most readers would also agree that this passage is poorly written — much less clear and coherent than it might have been. If you are having trouble understanding academic writing, be sure to consider the possibility that the author is at least partly to blame. Someone described Parsons's writing as "ink of dust on pages of lead," and you can see why if you look at the terribly convoluted third sentence in the first paragraph:

At least implicit in the conception of a system of such relationships is the conception that it is the mutual advantage derived by the parties from the various exchanges which constitutes the principle binding, cohesive force in the system.

Even the shortest sentence in the passage — *The content of the rules is various* — can be condensed more effectively to three words: *The rules vary.* I can't imagine anyone reading *The Structure of Social Action* for pleasure.

Still, this is an important book in the field of sociology, by a well-known sociologist, and a teacher might assign it or something equally impenetrable in one of your courses. What will you do if you have to read this passage and are expected to understand it to take an exam or write a paper?

Passive readers would read the passage over and over, beginning to end, in the hope that they would eventually understand it. Trying to highlight the "important parts" wouldn't help much. Even if you did understand what Parsons was trying to say, which of these obscure sentences or phrases would you highlight? **[Exercise 4]** None of them captures the essential distinction the passage is about.

You can understand and remember this distinction only by building your own framework, using your own language. And this is possible if you examine the passage analytically and record what you figure out, even if you have very little background knowledge of the subject. Even this dense, murky passage has some obvious structure:

1. A paragraph on Spencer, with a transition to Durkheim in the last sentence of that paragraph
2. A general explanation of Durkheim's theory
3. Illustrations of the "rules" Durkheim had in mind, introduced by the transition sentence *The content of the rules is various.*

Analysis of this structure offers your only hope of understanding writing that, when read as a continuous stream of words, makes little sense at all. Because this is a very abstract text, about "contractual relations," it might make sense to imagine a more concrete example, such as the sale of a car: The central question is *How do we reach agreement on the sale of this car?* And then *What holds this deal together?* How would Spencer and Durkheim answer these questions?

To construct an understanding I can later remember, I could write a brief summary in my own words:

> *Parsons distinguishes the views of Spencer and Durkheim concerning the bases for "contractual relations": economic transactions and other kinds of agreements. Spencer's "utilitarian" position limits these factors to the individual interests, or "demand and supply schedules," of the parties involved in the agreement. Durkheim argues that all sorts of other "rules," such as laws and customs, govern the terms of contractual relations. Durkheim calls this "organic solidarity."*

If you were about to write a paper or take an essay exam on this material, which would you prefer to have before you: this voiced summary or Parsons's original passage? **[Exercise 5]**

For a similar purpose, I could also create a "mnemonic diagram" of the passage (Figure 3):

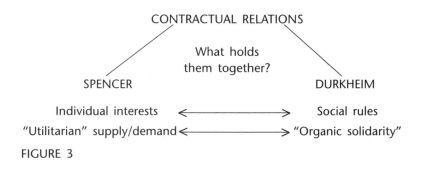

FIGURE 3

Some Other Ways of Reading

When using the methods of reading described in the previous sections, you will probably need to go through the text at least once, pausing to highlight material, take notes, or construct outlines. But there are other ways of moving through a text and getting what you need to get out of it — ways that are more or less linear, much faster or much slower, depending on your reasons for reading.

Reference

We think of "reference books" as volumes such as dictionaries or encyclopedias, but almost any book can be used primarily as a reference: a source of specific pieces of information you can look up when you need them, without reading anything else. When you pull such a book off the shelf, you probably turn straight to the index or table of contents. In a volume on the premodern history of China, for example, you might be interested only in the Shang dynasty or only in the art or religion of this period because you are investigating these narrow topics. Every book with an index is potentially an "encyclopedia" on its own subject.

Supplementary readings on a course syllabus are often intended for use as references, and you will also use books and articles as references when you write research papers, as I will explain in the next chapter. The list of works cited in a bibliography does not necessarily mean that the writer has read all of this material from beginning to end.

Selective Reading

In some cases only certain portions of a book or particular articles in a journal are immediately important. Scholars therefore might have read these sections very closely while ignoring or only glancing at everything else. Scientists and social scientists selectively read many research articles, looking only at the abstract or introduction, perhaps, to see what an article is about or at the methods, figures, specific results, or conclusions, depending on their interest. We also read selectively while looking through magazines: reading only the first paragraph or the sidebars or just looking at the pictures and captions.

Analytical Scanning

You might imagine that this kind of reading is the same as "skimming," but in some respects it is the opposite. Skimming is cruising quickly over the surface, to get a general sense for the content. The effect resembles the view you get through the window of an airplane or high-speed train: a stream of blurred, general impressions. Analytical scanning is more like examining a topographical map or aerial photograph of a whole area: studying the structure of the landscape and noting high points or centers of importance. Not bound to any linear path, your vision can move in any direction, focus closely, or widen to encompass the whole.

When scanning a book, you might begin by examining the table of contents, to see how the work is organized and, in a very general way, what it contains. Then, to figure out what the author is trying to do — the purpose of the book — you might scan the introduction, focusing especially on the beginning and end, where authors are most likely to state their intentions. Then you might skip to the last chapter, where you are likely to find conclusions or summaries of the entire work. With this knowledge of what the author was setting out to do and then claimed to have done, you can turn back to the beginnings of particular chapters to determine how this goal was accomplished. In these chapters, as in the entire volume, you will usually find the most central points at the beginning and end. This method is especially useful for studying textbook chapters, which are often designed for nonlinear, analytical reading.

If you become adept at scanning in this way, you can "read" an entire book in twenty or thirty minutes. If you take notes in the process, you will end up with a more useful understanding of its content than you would have if you had spent several hours reading it from cover to cover in a passive, linear fashion. **[Exercise 6]**

Close Reading

While selective reading and analytical scanning are much faster than reading through a text from beginning to end, word by word, some assignments will require much more time and attention. Extremely difficult texts, extremely important ones, an essay you will discuss in class, or a poem you must interpret in a writing assignment might require several readings and careful analysis.

As a consequence, the length of a reading assignment bears little relation to the time you might spend on it. While it is possible to pick up the central themes of an entire book in thirty minutes, you might need to spend an hour reading two pages of an important essay or one short poem. Students often tell me fatalistically that they *have* to spend a certain amount of time reading a certain number of pages, as though this pace was unalterable. From my perspective, this simply means they are stuck in a certain way of reading.

In some respects, close reading and analytical scanning are related strategies, not opposites. In both cases you are analyzing the structure of the text, moving back and forth through it, not bound to follow its linear order. **[Exercise 7]**

Overcoming Resistance to Strategic Reading

If the reading strategies I've described are so effective, why are the majority of the students you will observe in study lounges still reading their textbooks from beginning to end, a highlighter poised over the page, waiting for the chance to mark something worth remembering?

As I noted previously, a passive, linear approach to reading is the default mode — the easiest way of reading to fall into *without thinking*. And that, of course, is the problem. If you aren't actively thinking about *what* you are reading, *why* you are reading it, and *how* you are reading it, you aren't going to get much of lasting value out of the time you spend.

But there are some other reasons students cling to reading methods that don't actually work very well in undergraduate studies. Students have told me that if they don't read every word in the order in which it appears they are afraid they "will miss something." What if something really important lies in one of those parts you skipped over? It seems illogical that you could learn more by reading less or that you could understand something better by spending less time reading it.

The flaw in this reasoning lies in the assumption that you will learn and remember written material simply because your eyes happened to pass over it, following the linear trail of words from beginning to end, or because you covered it with transparent marker. Having read something in this way offers no reliable assurance that you have learned and will remember what you read. In your effort not to miss anything, you might, in the long run, miss almost everything. By the next day you might be left with nothing but a warm sense of virtue for having completed your homework. **[Exercise 8]**

I've also known people who have a kind of aesthetic objection to reading something "out of order" or selectively — an attitude akin to the moral outrage some people feel toward readers who skip to the end of a novel to find out what happens. From this perspective, the linearity of a book or essay represents its integrity, and reading in a linear fashion demonstrates respect for that integrity. Analytical or selective reading, out of order, therefore violates the integrity of the text, much as dissecting a frog does violence to the living creature.

While analytical reading bears some resemblance to dissection, texts are not like living creatures. You can read them in any order you like, dismantle them, examine their structural elements, take what you want from them in notes, and still be left with an undamaged whole. Then you can return to them, if you like, and read them over in a different way. The same can't be said for highlighting, which really does alter (even damage) the text. By contrast, the Grand Masters of Strategic Reading would be so skillful and efficient that they could buy all of their textbooks for the term, extract everything they needed from them before the bookstore's full refund deadline expired, and return them unmarked, like new.

Answering Amanda

To summarize what I've said in this chapter, I'll return to Amanda's lingering question: How do you know what *not* to read?

To answer this question I had to invert it: How do you know *what* to read? And knowing *what* to read means knowing *how* to read a particular text for a particular purpose.

A number of Web sites provide detailed guidance on reading and study skills in college. Here are two that give you links to other sites and materials:

- Gray, Greg. *Learning to Learn.* Centre for Academif and Adaptive Technology, University of Toronto. **http://snow.utoronto.ca/ Learn2/tools.html**

- Learning Assistance Center, South Mountain Community College. **http://www.smc.maricopa.edu/sub1/lac/r_rdg.html**

EXERCISES

Exercise 1. Think of the last novel you read for pleasure or the last movie you saw. Try to write a review of this book or movie, including a summary of the plot, with the names of main characters and places, and evaluate its literary or cinematic qualities.

If this is difficult (as I suspect it is), how would you need to read the book or watch the movie differently to prepare to write such a review later?

Exercise 2. Choose a section of about two pages or a brief essay from your course readings and practice highlighting analytically, to emphasize the structure of the text. If you then read only the highlighted portions, do they constitute a brief, coherent, unvoiced summary of the whole? If you are highlighting effectively, they should.

Exercise 3. Now make an outline or diagram to represent the structure of the same reading you chose for Exercise 2. Set this material aside for two or three days and return only to your outline. Using this outline, could you explain the content of the reading in a two-paragraph essay exam?

Exercise 4. To experience the limitations of highlighting, try to highlight the important parts of the Talcott Parsons passage (pp. 142–43) — the sentences or phrases that would remind you of its meaning in a week or two.

Exercise 5. Here is another difficult text — not because it is badly written but because it was written so long ago, in the seventeenth century, in language very different from the English we now use. This is the beginning of *Leviathan*, by the political philosopher Thomas Hobbes, a book frequently assigned in philosophy, political science, and other fields.

Read this passage two or three times, and while you are reading try to "translate" what Hobbes said into language that is easier for you to understand and remember. Now write a one-paragraph, voiced summary of the passage in your own language, quoting Hobbes when it would be useful to remember his terms. The question your paragraph should answer is *How does Hobbes describe the "State" or "Commonwealth"?*

From *Leviathan*

Thomas Hobbes

The Introduction

Nature (the Art whereby God hath made and governes the World) is by the *Art* of man, as in many other things, so in this also imitated, that it can make an Artificial Animal. For seeing life is but a motion of Limbs, the beginning whereof is in some principall part within; why may we not say, that all *Automata* (Engines that move themselves by spring and wheeles as doth a watch) have an artificiall life? For what is the *Heart*, but a *Spring;* and the *Nerves*, but so many *Strings;* and the *Joynts*, but so many *Wheeles*, giving motion to the whole Body, such as was intended by the Artificer? *Art* goes yet further, imitating that Rationall and most excellent worke of Nature, *Man.* For by Art is created that great LEVIATHAN called a COMMON-WEALTH, or STATE, (in latine CIVITAS) which is but an Artificiall Man; though of greater stature and strength than the Naturall, for whose protection and defence it was intended; and in which, the *Soveraignty* is an Artificiall *soul,* as giving life and motion to the whole body; The *Magistrates*, and other *Officers* of Judicature and Execution, artificiall *Joynts; Reward* and *Punishment* (by which fastned to the seate of the Soveraignty, every joynt and member is moved to performe his duty) are the *Nerves,* that do the same in the Body Naturall; The *Wealth* and *Riches* of all the particular members, are the *Strength; Salus Populi* (the *peoples safety*) its *Businesse; Counsellors,* by whom all things needfull for it to know, are suggested unto it, are the *Memory; Equity* and *Lawes,* an artificiall *Reason* and *Will; Concord, Health; Sedition, Sicknesse;* and *Civill war, Death.* Lastly, the *Pacts* and *Covenants,* by which the parts of this Body Politique were at first made, set together, and united, resemble that *Fiat,* or the *Let us make man,* pronounced by God in the Creation. (81–82)

Exercise 6. The best way to teach yourself effective analytical scanning is to give yourself far too little time to figure out what a book or chapter says — a time so brief that linear, continuous reading is impossible.

Choose an article of about ten pages or an entire book. For the article, give yourself only *ten minutes* to figure out what the author is saying and to write a one-paragraph summary. For a book, give yourself only *thirty minutes* to grasp its main ideas and organization and write a one-page summary.

Exercise 7. Try using analytical scanning and close reading on the same text. Give yourself only fifteen minutes to scan a whole chapter of one of your textbooks, to figure out the overall structure and content. Then spend fifteen minutes closely studying a specific section of less than one page, examining the way this information is presented, and outlining or summarizing the content.

Neither strategy is always the "right" way to read a textbook. Instead, they allow you to cover different amounts of material in the same time, with different qualities of understanding. The strategy you use therefore depends on the amount of time you have and the kind of understanding you need.

Exercise 8. You can test the arguments I've made by reading two different chapters of the same textbook in two different ways, and then find out how much you remember later. Scan one chapter analytically and outline its content in a few minutes, deliberately searching for important points and structural elements. Spend at least twice as much time reading another chapter from beginning to end, trying simply to absorb the material, without taking notes.

Wait at least one day and then try to summarize both chapters from memory, each in a paragraph or two, without looking at the chapters or at the notes you kept on the first. Which one do you remember best?

6 Investigative Writing

Strategic knowledge is the ability to put old strengths to new purposes. Imagine the writer as a ballet dancer who has spent the last twelve years perfecting the basic movements of ballet — the first, second, third positions, the grand plié, the arabesque, and so on. Eventually these movements are combined into exercises at the barre and across the room (like the "school exercises" in figure skating) — basic movements requiring skill and dedication, which are never abandoned. However, when the dancer walks onto the stage as a performer in his or her own right, we expect a new thing. Those basic movements are *transformed* into dance and they are used, not for themselves, but to carry out the expressive, interpretive *purpose* of the dancer and the dance.

— Linda Flower, "Negotiating Academic Discourse"

What Is a Research Paper?

Running from ten to thirty pages or more, research papers are the longest writing projects you will complete in college, unless you write a senior honors thesis (which is also a type of research paper). College teachers might assign research papers in any field of study, but they are especially common in the social sciences (sociology, psychology, anthropology) and related fields (history, environmental studies). In some cases a research paper will be the *only* formal writing assignment in a course, and because it will count for a large proportion of your final grade — typically 30 to 60 percent — knowing how to complete this kind of project successfully is especially important. Although teachers usually assign research papers early in the term, they are typically due at the end, and for this reason they are often called *term papers*.

Although all research papers are based on investigation, they do not represent a specific type of writing in other respects. Some teachers will simply ask you to report on your investigations. Others will ask you to compare or interpret the views of other writers, answer specific questions, or take clear positions on the issues you have studied. Like shorter essays, therefore, research papers have a variety of functions, including most of the purposes for writing I described in Chapter 4. They are distinguished from other types of college writing only by their length and by the fact that they include references to a number of other texts.

This problem of handling references to several sources does require a few special skills and conformity to particular systems of citation and documentation. In this chapter I'll offer some advice about handling multiple references, citing sources appropriately, and avoiding the hazards of plagiarism in research-based writing. Detailed formats for documentation are widely available in handbooks for college writing, which also include sample research papers and guidelines for quotation and citation. Because you should own one of these handbooks for college writing (one will probably be assigned in your freshman writing course), I haven't included complete formats for documentation. Nor have I included a full sample research paper.

Instead, this chapter will emphasize the *intellectual* challenges and rewards college teachers have in mind when they assign investigative writing. For reasons I'll explain, these intellectual goals will probably require changes in the way you approach and complete research papers for your college courses.

Motives and Methods

I assume that most of you have written at least one research paper in high school, probably in English but perhaps in other subjects such as history. High school teachers often assign research papers to prepare you for investigative writing in college — to make sure that you know how to find, use, and document information from published sources. This emphasis on the handling and documentation of source material might lead you to think of a research paper as a single kind of writing that you complete by following a routine series of procedures. Here are the most common procedures college freshmen have been taught or have developed on their own:

1. Choose a topic.
2. Using subject files in the library catalogue or in other references (such as the *Readers' Guide to Periodical Literature* or Internet search tools), locate sources of information on the topic.
3. Read through this material, taking notes and recording useful quotations on large note cards.
4. Construct an outline from the categories of information you have gathered.
5. Following your outline and notes, write the sections of the paper, incorporating source material in appropriate sections.
6. Document references and add a bibliography (or list of works cited).
7. Check the paper over for errors and typos, and turn it in. **[Exercise 1]**

If your goal is simply to demonstrate that you can find information on a subject and explain what you have found to a reader, these methods will get the job done.

From the perspective of most college professors, however, this approach, like standard formulas for writing shorter essays, yields disappointing results. In most cases, college teachers do not understand what went wrong in the *process*, but their complaints about the *product* are fairly consistent:

- The topic is too broad and unfocused.
- The writer doesn't pose a real question, take a real position, or write with a sense of purpose.
- The body of the paper consists of clumps of information from sources, roughly sorted into categories.
- Sources are inappropriate or out of date.
- The writer doesn't clearly distinguish his or her voice and viewpoint from those of cited authors, or he or she depends too heavily on these sources.
- The paper is disorganized, the most promising ideas buried in body paragraphs or raised only in the conclusion.

If they assign research papers, your freshman writing teachers will help you avert these problems and meet the expectations of teachers in other courses. They will introduce you to library systems and research methods on your campus, and they will probably guide you through stages of work on a research project, including attention to focus, organization, and revision. Some of your other teachers who assign research papers might also review proposals and outlines, suggest good sources of information on the topic, and give you advice for revising a rough draft. With this kind of support, students are more likely to produce work that meets their teachers' expectations.

Outside the writing class, however, professors will frequently assign a research paper toward the beginning of the term and leave you to your own devices, with the assumption that you understand how to produce the kind of paper they assigned. When they read and grade these term papers several weeks later, they will have no idea how you got them written — what you did in the process or what you thought you were supposed to do. When students receive critical comments like those I just listed, they are often mystified, because they thought they were doing exactly what they were supposed to do and can't think of a better strategy.

What is the problem?

Professors do not assign research papers just to make sure you can find and document references on a topic. They want to give you a taste of real scholarship in their fields of study, based on your own investigations. All of your professors are scholars who conduct research for the purpose of raising and answering *questions* in ways that will contribute to knowledge in their fields. These questions become significant within a larger *frame of reference* that includes the work of other scholars; for this reason scholarly writing is always part of an *ongoing discussion*. Academic writers use quotation and citation not just to tell readers where they got their information, but more often to acknowledge the previous research, ideas, and arguments of other participants in the discussion.

The most common educational goal of a research paper, therefore, is *to give you the experience of identifying and trying to answer specific questions.* When they assign research papers, professors give you the chance to explore some corner of the subject on your own. They hope you will share some of their own curiosity and fascination with this kind of investigation, along with the satisfaction they get from exchanging the results of their research with others. They also hope that when they read your paper they will learn something new — information they haven't encountered or ideas they haven't considered. Some will expect you to interpret source material from a new angle or to develop a cohesive argument. Most of these teachers will be disappointed, therefore, if you simply repackage information recorded on your note cards, without identifying and pursuing a significant question from your own perspective.

If you think of this process as a real investigation, a research paper can be the most rewarding learning experience you will have in college. I still vividly recall some of the independent research projects I completed as an undergraduate, even when I've forgotten almost everything else about the courses in which they were assigned. These projects stand out in my memory because I was not just reporting what the "real" authorities said; through the process of research and writing I *became* an authority on very specific questions. This is the kind of learning experience your professors hope you will have.

While these are noble motives and goals, professors often underestimate the difficulty of finding a position of authority for writing about significant questions in their fields of research. They forget that for scholars like themselves, research questions emerge from a broad frame of reference based on years of study. How can undergraduates like you, who have just begun to study the subject, figure out what is important or interesting?

To some extent, the course itself provides this frame of reference. In a course called International Environmental Issues, for example, lectures and readings build the foundations for understanding key environmental problems and recognizing the "actors" (such as government agencies and interest groups) most involved. With this background, students can identify an issue or case they would like to investigate more deeply toward the development of a clear position. To make sure topics are in focus, the professor requires a brief proposal and list of references early in the process, and he also comments on rough drafts before the final deadline.

Even with this background and guidance, however, students in this course often turn in unfocused papers that simply rehash a loose assortment of references. In the most general terms, these research papers don't seem to have a real *author*, with a particular voice and viewpoint, engaged in the discussion surrounding the topic.

I believe that this problem usually results from the sequence of procedures I listed at the beginning of the chapter. Used as a linear formula for completing research papers, these procedures undermine the process of inquiry through which writers find a sense of authority and become authors: writers who have something in particular to say. All of the benefits I described for flexible, exploratory movement through the writing process apply especially to research papers, partly because they are longer and more complex than other assignments.

Revising Your Strategies

Because all of the steps I listed in the typical sequence are in some respects necessary, most of your teachers will have trouble explaining what you should do differently. Of course you need to choose a topic, find sources of information, take notes from those sources, organize your material, write the paper, and document references. With the expectations of college teachers in mind, I'll briefly explain what goes wrong at each stage and offer alternative approaches. For reasons that will become obvious, problems and alternatives at one stage will affect others as well.

Choose a Topic

The problem. You will get into trouble from the very beginning of the process if you imagine that "choosing a topic" completes the task of deciding what the paper will be about. The kind of topic you choose at this point simply represents a category of information you intend to explore: a point of departure for your investigation, *not* for the paper you will eventually write. In other words, you might confuse an initial *research topic* with a *research question, thesis,* or *position.*

This is why professors so often complain that research papers are too broad and unfocused: the writers have simply chosen a topic, gathered information on that topic, and written the paper from that information without locating a focused question or viewpoint. At best, then, the paper will look like a good encyclopedia entry. For reasons that will become apparent at the next stage, most of the topics students initially choose embody hundreds if not thousands of potential research questions. Over many years of teaching and collaboration with other teachers, I can't recall a single research paper topic that was too narrow.

Solutions. When you have chosen a topic for research, continue to remind yourself that this is only a point of departure in the process of identifying a real question or developing a real viewpoint from which you can write. This process should continue throughout your research and even into the phase of writing a first draft.

The whole process of research and writing should be one of figuring out specifically what *you* want to say about the topic.

For example, an American history professor once complained that a student in her class had written a research paper on the topic "slavery in South Carolina." For a student who knew very little about the subject, this was a reasonable point of departure. While gathering information, however, he had not continued to narrow the topic or ask further questions. In response to the paper, therefore, his professor *did* ask questions:

> What about slavery in South Carolina?
>
> Why are you writing this paper?
>
> Why should I want to read it?

In the process of reading general information on this subject, the student should have begun immediately to look for a narrower topic and for specific questions to pursue. He would quickly discover, for example, that Charleston, South Carolina, was the main port for the slave trade to the Americas in the eighteenth century and that plantation economies and crops along the coast differed from those farther inland. This information might have led him to ask some questions that would have narrowed his topic:

> What were the differences between coastal and inland agriculture, and how did they affect living and working conditions for slaves in these areas?
>
> What do the narratives of former slaves tell us about life on a South Carolina plantation, and how reliable are these accounts?
>
> How did the development of rice cultivation affect the slave trade to Charleston?
>
> How did the slave trade affect the economy of the city?
>
> How and why did this trade change from the eighteenth century to the beginning of the Civil War?
>
> What were the roles and living conditions of urban slaves?
>
> How were slaves distributed from the port of entry to other regions of the South?
>
> How did this distribution affect slave families?
>
> How and how frequently did slaves escape from plantations in this region?

What were the connections between plantation owners and the state and federal governments? **[Exercise 2]**

These are just a few of the questions embedded in the broad topic "slavery in South Carolina," which contains enough material for thousands of research papers. If your assignment calls for an argument, through the process of research you will need first to identify a question and then to gradually develop a position on the issue. You won't be able to do this at the beginning, when you know little about the subject, so the task of refining your topic must continue throughout your research.

In other words, a purely linear, "Euclidean" approach will not work.

Locate Sources of Information on the Topic

The problem. General topics are easier to handle if you are using a small high school or public library, where a subject index will locate only a few sources. Because university library systems often contain more than three million books and thousands of periodicals, a subject search on a broad topic will locate too much material, most of it outdated or inappropriate in other ways. If you try to use high school search methods in a large library, you can spend many hours sifting through references to find only a few that are useful.

Even if you have narrowed your topic, subject searches will turn up many sources you won't want to use and will exclude some of the best material on a topic. One reason is that subject listings include work devoted primarily to that topic, while the best sources might be on related topics listed under different headings. As a consequence, this strategy will rarely lead you directly to the information you need.

In the Cornell online catalogue, for example, a search under "slavery" produced five thousand titles listed by subheadings. The great majority of those books were on slavery in the United States — about forty under the subheading "South Carolina." These forty books, however, are not necessarily the best sources on the subject. Most of the three or four thousand titles on slavery in America contain extensive references to South Carolina, and thousands of other books and articles on related topics (such as the political and social history of the South) might be useful.

Internet searches are even more random, shotgun approaches that turn up huge numbers of useless references and miss most of the useful ones. This unreliability led philosophy professor David Rothenberg (in a *Chronicle of Higher Education* article called "How the Web Destroys the Quality of Students' Research Papers") to charge that Internet search engines "are closer to slot machines than to library catalogues." A Web search on "slavery in South Carolina" first listed nearly 5 million sites containing references to these words, and further searches within this list produced an odd assortment of 602 sites (such as "Are Gun Control Laws Discriminatory?") almost entirely irrelevant to the topic. More focused topics — such as "rice plantations on the South Carolina coast" or "the slave trade into Charleston" — would not necessarily produce better results. **[Exercise 3]**

Even if you enjoy browsing, you can't afford to spend hours sorting through such material; nor can you afford to use references uncritically — a problem especially serious on the Internet where there are no screening standards. *Remember that you are writing a research paper for scholars concerned about the quality of information used to support arguments and explanations.* Ideas and information are not necessarily valid just because they appeared in print or on a Web site. Biased and outdated sources can seriously undermine the quality of your paper, even if your own ideas are sound.

Solutions.   *First aim for quality rather than quantity, and use good references to find others.* If you can find one authoritative, recent reference in the debris of a subject search, stop browsing and turn immediately to this source. Good books, scholarly articles, and some Internet sites have bibliographies of related material, usually of similar quality. Use these bibliographies as search tools, locating the most promising titles they list. The literature cited in a good reference will also contain bibliographies, and these chains of reference will efficiently locate material of consistent quality and focus, already related as pieces of a "conversation" among scholars. The best references will also help you identify the central questions the topic raises.

The syllabus for your course might list references of this sort among supplementary readings, allowing you to avoid messy library searches altogether. When you have identified a general topic, it is also a good idea to ask your professor for a couple of central sources and for help finding a focus. Teachers usually recommend research questions they find interesting, increasing the chances that your papers will meet expectations unstated in the assignment.

When you do search for library material, consult the reference librarians, who can recommend resources and strategies that might save you hours of research time. Reference librarians are hired and trained to give you this kind of assistance, so you don't need to worry that you are bothering them with naive questions.

Read Sources and Take Notes

The problem. The methods students develop in high school often encourage them to assemble a pile of reference material without reading, then to do all of the reading and note taking, and only then begin to plan and compose a draft. Completing these tasks in separate stages might seem to be the most efficient, orderly way to get the paper written, but it is not. If you gather all of your references before you read them, you will have no way of evaluating the material, yet your paper will depend on its quality. Separating these procedures will also discourage you from narrowing and focusing your topic during your research, since the pile of references you accumulated will represent your first thoughts, and specific questions you want to pursue will require further trips to the library, further searches for different types of information.

In turn, if you try to complete your reading and note taking before you begin to develop a plan for writing and a viewpoint of your own, at the end of the reading stage you will be left with notes on what other writers have said. Then you will tend to base your outline on these categories of information, not on your own perspective. Instead, gathering and reading research material should gradually give you a sense of authority on the subject, a particular viewpoint, and a voice with which you can explain this viewpoint to the reader. *When you begin to write you should not feel that all you have to say is what other writers have said in the references you cite or that you are writing the paper directly from your notes.* Aimless, passive reading through piles of references can waste enormous amounts of time and leave you with a collection of random notes of uncertain value.

Solutions. A research paper assignment is the ideal occasion for you to practice predatory reading: deliberately searching for and extracting the information you need through a variety of reading strategies (see Chapter 5). And you should use these strategies throughout your research and writing, not just in a single stage of the process.

Start with one or two of the best sources you can find. Read them first, using this reading both to focus your topic and to identify other sources. You might want to read some sections of a book thoroughly for background information and take extensive notes but scan or completely ignore sections less relevant to your work. In other words, you should always read with a purpose in mind — to find specific information, to acquire background knowledge, to identify research questions, or to understand an author's position — and choose a reading strategy that serves this purpose. If you always read with a specific purpose you will also know what to write in your notes, and these notes will differ according to your goals: detailed information, broad perspectives, questions the source raises, summaries of an author's position, or relevant quotations.

The research methods taught in many high schools and textbooks give note cards a kind of emphasis they don't deserve and can't live up to, as though research, thinking, and writing can be reduced to tidy bookkeeping or a sort of card trick. It really doesn't matter what you write your notes on, as long as you can find the information again when you need it. For this purpose note cards are fine, but no better than a bound notebook or a legal pad.

Whether you use note cards, notebooks, or loose sheets of paper, it is important to keep notes on particular sources separate, with full bibliographical references recorded at the top. You will need the following information about each source later, when you compile your bibliography at the end of your paper:

- Author's full name
- Full title of the work
- Publisher's name and city
- Year of publication
- Volume, issue, and page numbers for articles in periodicals
- Page numbers, editor's name, and volume title for essays within a book

Also remember to record specific page numbers for quotations, paraphrases, and other material you might cite in the text. Be sure to put quotation marks around direct quotations, so that you can later distinguish the author's words from your own paraphrases and observations. This careful, bibliographical record keeping will save you from annoying returns to the library when you are documenting sources.

Your notes should include not only what references say but also what *you* are thinking about what they say. What questions come to mind? How are your references related? How are your plans for the paper taking shape?

I recommend that you keep notes on your own perspectives on cards or pages separate from quotations and other direct references to sources or that you enclose your own thoughts in parentheses as I did in the sample note cards below. In other words, while you are doing research you should think of yourself as an author, with your own emerging ideas and voice, separate from those of the authors you read. If your thoughts are scattered among references to others, it will be difficult to keep track of them as a cohesive whole, to distinguish them from references, or perhaps even to find them when you begin to write.

Brumberg, Joan Jacobs. *Fasting Girls: The History of Anorexia Nervosa.* New York: New American Library, 1989.

Brumberg's view of eating disorders includes historical and cultural perspectives. The development of anorexia as "addiction to starvation" involves a combination of cultural, biological, and psychological factors that determine which individuals are vulnerable in a particular time (38). But the terms and meanings change from one period to another. (Contrast with Chernin)

"Simply put, when and where people become obesophobic and dieting becomes pervasive, we can expect to see an escalating number of individuals with anorexia nervosa and other eating disorders" (40).

Brumberg — 2

Wealth and class are also factors, because food must represent something beyond nutritional needs.

"In affluent societies the human appetite is unequivocally misused in the service of a multitude of nonnutritional needs. As a result, both anorexia nervosa and obesity are characteristic of modern life and will continue to remain so" (269).

(Is this completely true? Affluence is not just modern. Check for other periods and cultures where food had other meanings — obesity and thinness valued?)

Writers who are studying several sources at once sometimes prefer to record bibliographical information on separate note cards or on a master list of references and code these references on their notes by number or letter. Then you can simply write "8" or "G" above notes on that source, along with specific page numbers, and the code will refer you to your index of sources when you are writing the paper. That index will also be a handy resource for writing the bibliography.

Construct an Outline

The problem. Writers often imagine that if they can sort their research notes into categories and construct an outline, the task of organization is complete. All they need to do is follow the outline. They are often bewildered, then, when a teacher says the paper is disorganized, without real direction or focus. In fact, clustering reference material under the subheadings of an outline won't ensure that the paper will be cohesive, even if the outline lists a logical series of topics. Because it represents your initial thoughts about the structure of the paper, an outline can even *prevent* you from seeing new connections and directions while you write, if you follow the outline too strictly.

Solutions. As I noted in Chapter 3, the use of formal outlines is really a matter of preference, and maybe of personality. Good writing (and bad writing) can occur with or without outlines, and this is true even for long research papers.

Whether you use a formal outline or do not, you should begin to develop plans for writing *while* you do research, as I have suggested, not after. When you have finished most of your reading, therefore, you should have a clear question you intend to address — a point of departure, a direction, and a destination. Some writers like to make a map of this route before they begin to compose. If you begin with the intention of revising your first draft, however, you will give yourself the freedom to explore the topic further as you write and can substantially reorganize the paper in the second version. While you are writing, your perspective might shift and stronger, more focused viewpoints might emerge toward the end of the paper. For this reason, outlines for research papers, as for other kinds of writing, are often most useful *between* drafts, to help you identify a new thesis, move it toward the beginning of the paper, and restructure what follows.

Write the Paper, Incorporating Source Material

The problem. Research papers written directly from note cards in one draft account for most of professors' complaints that papers are unfocused and carelessly written. The "card trick" approach can undermine your work in two related ways:

1. If you write directly from your notes, you will tend to lose your voice and authority as the author of the paper. The paper will become a collection of references to other writers, other authorities, without the cohesion and direction writers establish from a clear point of view.
2. Without a clear voice and viewpoint of your own, you will have trouble distinguishing your language and ideas from those of other writers. As a consequence, figuring out when you should cite references will be difficult.

The rule of thumb teachers often provide is that you should cite all language and information you got from your sources unless that information represents "common knowledge." If you are writing directly from your research notes, however, almost *all* of the language and ideas in the paper will come from references. And what is "common knowledge" if everything in your notes was news to you?

In effect, the research paper then becomes a collection of unvoiced summaries: paraphrases of source material, with or without citation. Writers in this dilemma tend either to cite almost everything or to cite almost nothing, and in the latter case they often drift into forms of plagiarism I'll describe later. Because they have no voice with which they can easily refer to other writers, they also tend to drop quotations into the middle of their own passages, so the reader has no way of identifying the author without looking up the citation. Here is an example of such "dropped quotations" (which I also call "mysterious voices"):

> Stress is defined as "the pattern of specific and nonspecific responses an organism makes to stimulus events that disturb its equilibrium and tax or exceed its ability to cope" (Zimbardo, 472).

In this sentence the passive verb *is defined* suggests that everyone defines stress in this way and that the particular author of the quotation is irrelevant. In the dropped quotation the writer abdicated her responsibility for choosing to present this particular definition.

Solutions. If you've followed my advice thus far, by the time you begin to compose a full draft you should have thought and learned enough about a focused research question to explain what you have discovered to someone else, without looking at your notes. Obviously you won't recall all of the details, but if you imagine that someone has asked your research question (*How do beavers decide which trees to cut down?* or *Why did rice production create a market for African slaves?*), you should be able to reply with a coherent explanation or argument. In other words, *you have become an authority on the topic,* and if you need to supplement your explanation with references to other authorities, you know where to find them.

This is the best way of making sure that you are approaching the task with authority and voice of your own. If you feel mute on the subject without your research notes, you are not in a position to write, and your paper will probably turn into a bunch of references. If you can explain the subject to a listener in your own words, you can also explain it to a reader. While you are writing, then, you will recognize when you need to refer to other authorities or find specific information that supports your explanation. Information from other writing and the voices of other writers can appear in your paper only because you have *chosen* to include them for your own reasons. You have decided to let the reader know, by paraphrase or quotation, what these other writers have said. You are in charge of this paper and are responsible for its quality.

If you are explaining the subject to the reader primarily in your own words, integrating quotations and other references will also seem more natural. As in a voiced summary, you will be telling the reader what another writer had to say. In her revision, therefore, the writer who used the dropped quotation established her own voice and introduced the definition much more effectively:

> In his book Psychology and Life, *Philip Zimbardo defines stress as "the pattern of specific and nonspecific responses an organism makes to stimulus events that disturb its equilibrium and tax or exceed its ability to cope" (472).* **[Exercise 4]**

Toward the end of this chapter I'll explain more fully how to integrate references with your own writing.

Even if your teacher does not ask you to submit a rough draft, you should begin to write early enough to revise your paper. The most effective research papers are almost always rewritten, because the sharpest focus and the best ideas will usually occur while you are composing a draft, often toward the end. You need to be willing to reorganize the paper around a new viewpoint, and toward that end you need to reserve time.

Document References and Add a Bibliography

The problem. As I have said, a research paper is simply a long form of essay based on readings used to support an explanation or argument. Because you might refer to two or more sources in a single page, however, in a research paper you need a system of documentation: a way for readers to keep track of the sources you mention. The complexities of these systems might make you feel that you don't know what you are doing or that a research paper is an alien form of writing.

Solutions. Don't let the technicalities of documentation intimidate you or distract you from the more important challenges of developing a substantial, cohesive, informative research paper. Although you need to use a format for citation consistently and accurately, your teachers will be more concerned with the quality of your research and writing than with the details of your documentation. Obscure and inconsistent methods of citation can be annoying, especially if readers want to find work the writer mentions, but perfect adherence to a format will not redeem a paper that has little to say.

While you are conducting research and writing, you simply need to keep a record of bibliographical information and page numbers, as I noted on page 162, to avoid time-consuming searches for missing information when you are completing the paper. As you compose you should also note page numbers in the draft when you refer to sources. But the details of citation, like proofreading, are best left for the end of the process, when they will not interfere with the flow of your writing and thinking.

If you can't remember exactly how to cite references and list them in a bibliography, you are certainly not alone. There are several systems of documentation, each so detailed that many experienced writers must consult reference books to recall how they should cite a particular source. Fortunately, these references are readily available, and when you choose a system or your teacher assigns one, you can simply follow it. I'll briefly describe these systems and list some references to them in the next section of this chapter.

Check for Errors and Typos, and Turn It In

The problem. Considering the length and importance of research paper assignments, you might expect that the research papers students turn in would be more polished than their shorter papers, but they frequently contain more errors and typos. Procrastination, I suspect, is the main reason for this carelessness. Students routinely underestimate the time required to finish a long paper and find themselves completing the documentation and bibliography late in the night before the deadline. Under these circumstances it is tempting to assume that careful proofreading is unnecessary beyond a quick spelling check.

Careless errors, however, will create the more general impression of careless writing and thinking. When teachers encounter lots of spelling errors, typos, poor word choice, and other signs that the writer isn't paying attention to detail, they rarely consider a paper to be first-rate, even if the ideas are brilliant. Weak effort at the end of the process, therefore, can undermine your best efforts in other phases of research and writing.

Solutions.   The obvious (and only) solution is to allow sufficient time to read the paper carefully, aloud, preferably a day after you have finished the final draft.

Do not trust spell checkers and proofreading software to do this work for you! These systems can help you identify errors and other local weaknesses in a draft, but no experienced writer trusts them entirely. Spell checkers can identify only words in their internal dictionaries. As a consequence, they will flag words they do not recognize and will ignore misspelled words that accidentally correspond with spellings they recognize, such as *then* used for *than* or *there* used for *their*.

While proofreading software has improved somewhat in recent years, it still cannot really "understand" written English, identify all errors, or offer reliable advice. Electronic proofreaders are especially hazardous for those of you who use English as a second language, because the errors in usage and syntax you are most likely to make are the most difficult for a computer program to identify and correct. At best these systems can help you use your own eyes, ears, and sensibilities. At worst, they will tell you to change correct sentences into incorrect versions.

Documentation Systems

In the past, *citation* was almost synonymous with *footnotes,* inserted at the bottom of each page or listed at the end of a research paper as *endnotes.* Footnotes or endnotes are still acceptable for citation in most courses and are frequently used in publications, but *in-text* (or *parenthetical*) citations have become more common in academic writing and are also more efficient. With these systems you can continue to use footnotes occasionally for their second purpose: to provide comments or information you do not want to include in the text.

Unless they explicitly require footnote citations, almost all of your teachers will accept one of the two most common formats for in-text citation and bibliography: the *Modern Language Association (MLA)* system, used primarily in the humanities, or the *American Psychological Association (APA)* system, used most often in the social sciences. I'll describe these systems very briefly and then tell you where to find the detailed formats.

MLA Format

In the MLA system, if you have introduced the source with the author's name in the text, you can cite the reference at the end of the quotation or paraphrase by simply including the page number in parentheses:

> In an open letter to Ezra Pound that follows the introduction to *A Vision,* Yeats offers the immodest prediction that his book will, "when finished, proclaim a new divinity" (27).

If you have not introduced the author by name in the text, include the author's last name before the page number in the parentheses: (Yeats 27). If your paper includes references to more than one publication by an author and you do not introduce the specific title, you should include a brief title in the parentheses: (*Vision* 27).

All of these parenthetical citations in the text refer your readers to the bibliography, which MLA calls the *list of works cited.* When combined with names or titles in the text of your paper, your parenthetical citations allow readers to find the source easily in your list of works cited. Here is the basic form of a bibliographical entry in an MLA list of works cited:

> Yeats, William Butler. *A Vision*. New York: Collier, 1969.

APA Format

The APA system accomplishes the same task of referring readers to the bibliography (called the *reference list*) with a combination of the author's last name and the date of publication. If you introduce the author in the text, place the publication year in parentheses immediately after the name:

> Bruno Latour and Steve Woolgar (1986) described the motivations of scientists to publish in economic terms, as "cycles of credit," measured in terms of "investment and return" (p. 190).

In this system, page numbers are used primarily after direct quotations, often in separate parentheses from the date of publication. If you have not introduced the authors' names in the text, you should include their last names in parentheses, followed by a comma and the publication date (and, if citing a direct quotation, the page number):

> In interviews about their motivations to publish, scientists often use economic terms such as "credit" or "investment and return" (Latour and Woolgar, 1986, p. 190).

APA bibliographical entries are somewhat different from the MLA form. Note that the APA bibliography lists only the initials of authors' first names, followed by the date of publication:

> Latour, B., & Woolgar, S. (1986). *Laboratory life: The construction of scientific facts*. Princeton: Princeton University Press.

These examples illustrate only the basic forms of reference to books. To use one of these systems accurately, you will need a manual that includes formats for all types of sources.

The *MLA Handbook for Writers of Research Papers*, 5th ed. (New York: MLA, 1999) and the *Publication Manual of the American Psychological Association*, 4th ed. (Washington: APA, 1994) provide detailed instructions and examples for references to almost every kind of source, including newspaper and magazine articles, government documents, public lectures, online sources, and interviews.

The *MLA Handbook* also contains a format for using footnotes or endnotes rather than parenthetical citations, if you prefer or are required to do so. Another standard source for footnote systems is *The Chicago Manual of Style*, 14th ed. (Chicago: University of Chicago Press, 1993). These style manuals are available in most campus bookstores. You can also find them in the library and possibly at your school's writing center.

Handbooks for college writers also contain sufficiently detailed formats for documentation, along with sample research papers that illustrate ways of introducing and integrating references. Your freshman writing teacher might assign one of these handbooks for writers, and there are dozens of them in print. Your campus bookstore is likely to have one of these handbooks that contains similar instructions for documentation.

Internet Sources

Internet sources, like print publicatons, must be documented in full with titles, authors, and dates as well as URLs. It is not sufficient to list a URL or e-mail address without further explanation. You can find up-to-date formats for citing Internet sources on the MLA Web site <www.mla.org/style/sources.htm> and on a Web site created by Xia Li and Nancy Crane for APA online citations <www.uvm.edu/~ncrane/estyles/apa.html>.

Here are examples of MLA and APA formats for listing online sources in your bibliography. (The first date given is the most recent update of the site; the second date is the date the writer accessed the site.)

MLA Format

Citation Style Guides. 30 Jan. 2000. Syracuse U. 11 Aug. 2000 <http://libwww.syr.edu/research/refshelf/style.htm>.

APA Format

Syracuse University. (2000, January 30). *Citation style guides* [Online]. Available: http://libwww.syr.edu/research/refshelf/ style.htm [2000, August 11].

Theft, Fraud, and the Loss of Voice

Derived from the Latin word for kidnapping, *plagiarism* is the theft of someone else's "brainchild" — that person's language, ideas, or research — and the origin of the word conveys the seriousness of such offenses in the view of college teachers and administrators. The reason is that words, ideas, and research are the main forms of currency in academic life. Because they represent the "intellectual property" with which scholars have built their careers, using that property without permission or credit is a form of larceny. Teachers also assume that the writing and other work students turn in is the product of their own effort, and because grades (another form of academic currency) are based on that work, "borrowing" language and ideas from someone else constitutes cheating.

As a consequence, all colleges and universities include warnings against plagiarism among their published rules for academic conduct, along with the procedures and penalties that result from breaking those rules. Because such regulations are usually strict and often unfamiliar to new students, you should read them carefully to make sure you know what practices are prohibited. The most serious forms of plagiarism can lead to failure in a course, notice of misconduct on one's academic record, and even suspension.

Legalistic accounts of plagiarism, however, are also idealistic. In other words, they assume an ideal world in which the boundaries between right and wrong, acceptable and unacceptable practices, one's own language and the language of others, can be clearly defined by regulations. In fact, the term *plagiarism* covers a wide range of deceptions and errors, from serious cases of cheating to minor instances of faulty citation. Plagiarism also includes some types of "unauthorized assistance," and some forms of assistance authorized in one course or assignment might be unauthorized in another. Some of the practices that many students consider acceptable survival strategies are, for their teachers, punishable offenses. In my effort to clarify these boundaries, therefore, I will also be quite frank about the dilemmas and temptations you are likely to face in your college work.

I'll begin with the most obvious violations of academic integrity codes and end with some deeper, more ambiguous questions about authority, acknowledgment, and originality in academic work — questions essential to all writing based upon research.

Theft and Fraud

The great majority of formal plagiarism charges result from deliberate attempts to deceive teachers, avoid work, and gain unfair advantage over other students. While these practices share common motives, they take several forms:

- Using published material verbatim, without citation or quotation marks, as all or part of work submitted as your own. (This category includes not only writing but also quantitative data, graphs, and other published research material.)
- Close, deliberate paraphrase of another author's published or unpublished work without acknowledgment.
- Submitting as your own work papers or portions of papers formerly written by other students or purchased from commercial services.
- Having someone else write a paper for you and turning it in as your own work, or writing a paper for someone else.
- Submitting copies of a single paper (written individually or collaboratively) as the individual work of two or more students.
- Turning in a paper you previously wrote for another course, or one paper for two current courses, without permission from the instructors.

When I identify these kinds of deception I prosecute them without hesitation, as other teachers do, but I've also learned not to jump to hasty conclusions about the motives and characters of students who resort to plagiarism. Heavy workloads and intense competition sometimes encourage students to use any strategy that gives them an edge, and if substantial numbers adopt this survival-of-the-fittest ethos, more scrupulous, responsible students can get drawn into plagiarism and other forms of cheating in order to compete.

In a misdirected fashion, some of these violations are also generous. To counter the effects of competition between individuals, students share work and help one another — behavior that would represent virtue in other circumstances but becomes a violation when students are being graded for individual performance. A very bright, capable senior once explained to me, in a completely matter-of-fact way, that freshmen were disadvantaged in a large science course because they didn't yet have access to the sorority and fraternity files of old lab reports, and had to write their own! These files of old papers, paper-writing and note-taking services, published volumes of student research papers, Cliffs Notes, and other easy routes to completing assignments seem to authorize strategies that campus regulations condemn. Internet services make the purchase of "prewritten" term papers entirely too easy, and although selling papers might be legal, turning them in as your own work can violate campus and course policies.

With these and other opportunities available, and with other students using them, what will you do when you are short on time, energy, or ideas or when you feel that a teacher expects you to write with authority and skills you don't have? What will you do when you find that a published source says exactly what you would like to say on an assigned topic or when your friend has already written a paper on the subject and offers it to you? You don't have to be morally bankrupt to find plagiarism tempting in such situations.

But each year thousands of otherwise honest, fair-minded students are convicted of plagiarism. Setting some real moral issues aside, one very good reason for avoiding *all* forms of plagiarism is that you might get caught. And if you do, you will find yourself in deep trouble. Frequently and unpredictably, these cases come to the attention of teachers for reasons that plagiarists fail to take into account:

- Teachers are often much more familiar with published sources on a subject than their students realize.

- Many teachers are attuned to shifts of voice and style, both within a paper and from one paper to the next. They can tell when the author has changed.

- Teachers talk to one another about student work, more than students realize, and show papers they have received to other teachers, sometimes to get advice.

- If they are suspicious that a paper has been taken from the Internet, some teachers use search tools to locate the sources, which they can find fairly easily.

These are the ways in which charges of plagiarism usually begin, and they lead to what seems very much like a criminal trial before a committee that serves as judge and jury — examining evidence, hearing testimony, delivering a verdict, and (if the verdict is guilty) determining penalties. This is a dreadful ordeal, and no matter how safe and tempting the opportunity to plagiarize might appear to be, it is not worth the risk.

Unauthorized Assistance or Collaboration

Two kinds of "theft and fraud" listed in the previous section represent extreme forms of unauthorized assistance or collaboration: turning in someone else's writing as your own and using one paper to represent the individual work of more than one person.

In other forms, however, the boundaries between acceptable and unacceptable collaboration are not always so clear. Most teachers want students to discuss course material outside class, share ideas and information, and help one another grasp important concepts. Collaborative learning methods have become increasingly common in higher education, especially in the sciences. When you graduate, most of you will need to work closely with others toward common goals, including the production of reports and other documents. Most teachers show drafts of our writing to colleagues and rely on one another for substantial help before we send our work to publishers.

For these reasons, teachers often explicitly *authorize* assistance or collaboration on research projects, lab reports, and problem sets. Writing teachers frequently advise students to exchange drafts of their papers, to help one another with revision in pairs or small groups, and to visit writing centers.

But the value of cooperation sometimes conflicts with the value of individual effort. I know a science major who was formally charged with plagiarism for receiving unauthorized help from a friend on the revision of a paper for a humanities course. Collaborative writing is very common in the sciences, where students might also work together on problem sets, labs, other research projects, and reports. But individual authorship is the norm in the humanities, and teachers in fields such as English, history, and philosophy tend to assume that a paper will represent the work of a single writer.

Because collaboration is such a valuable life skill and aid to learning, I do *not* advise you categorically to avoid helping one another with assignments out of fear that you will violate rules. I encourage you instead to *make sure that you know where the boundaries between authorized and unauthorized assistance lie in every course, with awareness that these boundaries will differ.*

If a teacher, course syllabus, or assignment does not make these expectations clear, ask for clarification. **[Exercise 5]**

Lazy Citation and Paraphrase

Years ago I knew a teacher who became embattled with his small class of six students over an elaborate research paper he assigned in stages: topic selection, a note card system for recording information, outlines, first drafts, and so on. The teacher became very fussy about these procedures; his students put up resistance to his demands. At the end of the semester the students were supposed to turn in with their finished papers all of their note cards, outlines, and drafts. Then I saw the teacher heading off to the library with all of this material in a cardboard box, intending to look up every reference, to check every quotation, citation, and page number.

When he had completed this onerous task, he charged five of the six students with plagiarism. Because he presented evidence that the students had violated the campus code, his department had to pursue the charges, which were upheld in the hearing.

The most serious offense was a passage copied directly from a source without quotation marks or citation. Even in this case, however, the student claimed that he had plagiarized accidentally, by failing to use quotation marks on his note card and therefore assuming, when he wrote the paper, that the writing was his own. There were also individual sentences and phrases borrowed from sources, uncomfortably close paraphrases without acknowledgment, a quotation from one source attributed to another, and inaccurate titles or page numbers. Most of these violations were minor, and the students were sentenced only to rewrite the papers.

Because these cases resulted partly from bad relations in the class, the teacher and students were probably equally to blame for the resulting "plagiarism." In the end, however, the students had to bear the consequences of their careless documentation. If all college teachers became equally fanatical about the rules for citation and quotation, I suspect that they could find similar kinds of faulty reference in a large proportion of student research papers.

When you are writing under time constraints and find a passage in a source that says essentially what you want to say, when you find a useful quotation in your notes but didn't record the source, or when you forgot to write down the page number for a reference you need, what should you do?

- You should either quote the source directly or cite it after your own paraphrase.
- You should either find the missing reference or not use the quotation.
- You should go back to the reference and find the page number.

I know that these efforts might seem to require more time than the problems are worth and that the chances a teacher will notice a faulty reference are slim. But a larger question is involved, regardless of your attitudes toward the teacher and the task: What kind of student, scholar, and writer do you want to be?

Accurately crediting and documenting the work of others will be essential in most of the professions you pursue, and if you maintain high standards now you will learn to keep track of this information carefully in the future. Habits of carelessness and disregard, in turn, are difficult to break.

Loss of Voice

Both deliberate and accidental forms of plagiarism often result from the central challenge student writers face, especially in research papers: establishing a voice and perspective of their own. I've already explained that if you have not established your own authority over the subject and a reason for writing, it will be difficult to identify the boundaries between your ideas and language and those of other writers. What you have to say will be what others have already said. Everything you write will come directly from sources and will seem to need citation.

In their effort to avoid these strings of citations, students who are writing directly from research notes often drift into plagiarism, closely paraphrasing sources without citing them, or "borrowing" exact phrases and sentences without quotation. The following is a passage from Steven Pinker's book The Language Instinct (1995):

> But household robots are still confined to science fiction. The main lesson of thirty-five years of AI [artificial intelligence] research is that the hard problems are easy and the easy problems are hard. The mental abilities of a four-year-old that we take for granted —

recognizing a face, lifting a pencil, walking across a room, answering a
question — in fact solve some of the hardest engineering problems
ever conceived. (192–93)

And here is an uncomfortably close paraphrase that, when passed
off as the writer's own work, drifts into plagiarism:

> *The helpful household robots of science fiction have not become a*
> *reality. Over thirty-five years of research, the field of artificial intelli-*
> *gence has demonstrated that the hard problems are easy to solve and*
> *the easy problems are hard. A four-year-old can easily recognize a*
> *face, walk across a room, pick up objects, and answer simple ques-*
> *tions, but these are some of the hardest problems AI engineers have*
> *tried to solve.*

Like other experienced teachers, I can usually hear these patch-
works of voices running through individual passages and whole
papers, creating the impression that no one in particular is the
author. When I convey my suspicions, the writers usually admit that
they were writing directly from sources and had trouble avoiding
close, continual paraphrasing and quotation.

You cannot reliably avoid this patchwork plagiarism simply by
rewording a passage from sources. You can avoid it only by establishing your own voice in reference to the text you are using. Referring directly to the author and text will also remind you that you
must cite paraphrases, to tell the reader how to find this source of
information.

If you want to use paraphrase rather than quotation, therefore,
it's a good idea to read the passage until you establish your own
understanding and then put it aside. Then explain to your reader
what the author said in your own words, and if you find that you
want to use specific phrases from the source, put them in quotation
marks:

> *In* The Language Instinct, *Steven Pinker explains why robots have*
> *not become common household appliances, in spite of predictions in*
> *computer science and science fiction. These predictions failed to*
> *materialize, he says, because in the field of Artificial Intelligence, even*
> *the most basic mental and physical skills of children, such as walking,*
> *turned out to be "some of the hardest engineering problems ever*
> *conceived" (193).*

Because this paragraph begins with reference to the source, the reader knows it is a paraphrase of information in Pinker's book on page 93. Even without the quotation at the end you would need to include this page number.

Integrating References

If you were telling someone a story that involved other people and what they said, you would naturally explain to the listener who those other people were and indicate when you were quoting them. You would not let their voices become confused with yours or simply drop quotations from others into your story without reference to the speaker. The same principles apply to the "stories" you tell readers about your research and what other writers have said on the subject.

When you have established your voice as the narrator and introduced other writers in the text of your paper, you will have tremendous freedom to paraphrase and quote from these sources, without risk of plagiarism. As long as you use quotation marks around the language you have included from references, you can splice borrowed words, phrases, whole sentences, or passages into your own writing for your own purposes. Suppose, for example, that you are writing a paper on population control policies and want to refer to this passage from Joel Cohen's book *How Many People Can the Earth Support?* (1995):

> My first discovery was that I was not alone in not knowing how many people the Earth could support. Numerical estimates produced over the past century have ranged widely — so widely that they could not all be close to right — from less than 1 billion to more than 1,000 billion. More than half of the estimates fell between 4 billion and 16 billion people.
>
> I also learned that the question "How many people can the Earth support?" is not a question like "How old are you?" which has exactly one answer at any given time. The Earth's capacity to support people is determined partly by processes that the human and natural sciences have yet to understand, and partly by choices that we and our descendants have yet to make. (10–11)

You might want to include the entire passage in a block quotation, as I did here, but there are dozens of other possibilities for using portions of Cohen's writing within your own. You might begin, for example, by paraphrasing the central purpose of his book and then quote portions that underscore the main points you want to convey:

> In How Many People Can the Earth Support?, *Joel Cohen explains that all efforts to calculate sustainable population growth depend on diverse assumptions and variables that yield radically different answers to the question posed in the title of his book. As a result of these variables, Cohen notes, "Numerical estimates produced over the past century have ranged widely — so widely that they could not all be close to right — from less than 1 billion to more than 1,000 billion." Because sustainability will depend on "processes that the human and natural sciences have yet to understand" and on "choices that we and our descendants have yet to make," Cohen recognizes that this central question raises hundreds of others, some of which we cannot yet answer (10–11).*

Note that you can splice whole sentences onto your own or quote parts of sentences within yours. In the first sentence quoted here, the capital *N* and the period tell readers that the writer has quoted the whole sentence, without alteration. In the next sentence, lowercase initial letters and the absence of end punctuation indicate that the writer has quoted portions of sentences. "Tags," such as *Cohen notes* or *recognizes,* simply remind the reader of the source and sometimes express the author's viewpoint.

If necessary, you can leave out language within a quotation or add language to it, as long as you indicate to readers that you have done so. You can indicate missing language with an *ellipsis* (. . .) and added language with square brackets ([ ]). For example, if you do not want to include the words between dashes (*so widely that they could not all be close to right*), you can insert an ellipsis to let readers know you have dropped them:

> *As a result of these variables, Cohen notes, "Numerical estimates produced over the past century have ranged widely . . . from less than 1 billion to more than 1,000 billion" (10).*

If you cut off the end of a sentence in ways that make it look complete, you should let the reader know you have done so by using an ellipsis and the period at the end:

As a result of these variables, Cohen notes, "Numerical estimates produced over the past century have ranged widely . . ." (10).

Brackets allow you to supply information that clarifies a quotation or makes it fit grammatically with your sentence. When you take sentences out of a longer passage, for example, you might need to add words that clarify pronouns: *"Apparently they [Pearl and Reed] did not at first know that Verhulst had derived the same curve . . ."* (85). Or you might need to substitute words that allow the quotation to mesh with your sentence: *Cohen's "first discovery was that [he] was not alone . . ."* (10).

Only three rules limit your freedom to integrate quotations within your own sentences and passages:

1. The readers should always know whose language they are reading.
2. Sentences you assemble with quotations should read grammatically.
3. Your use of quotation (including splices, ellipses, and brackets) should not distort the original meaning of the quoted material.

These methods of integrating quotations and references will require more experimental tinkering than the practice of simply dropping quotations, as "mysterious voices," into the middle of your work, but they are necessary if you want your research papers to sound like real academic writing and if you want to avoid plagiarism. With practice, weaving references and quotations into your own writing will also become a natural way to compose. **[Exercise 6]**

Here is the beginning of a finished research paper in which the student has clearly introduced focused research questions, established her own voice, integrated quotations and references appropriately, and set a direction for further discussion. This paper on the roles of "working memory" in learning and mental disorders was written for an introductory course in cognitive science.

What limits our capacity to learn? Why don't we have unlimited access to the supposedly infinite number of memories stored in our long-term memory (LTM)? And what prevents those with serious disorders from learning and remembering normally? Part of the answers to those questions lie in working memory

(WM), a model for short-term memory first proposed in 1978 by Alan Baddeley and Graham J. Hitch. Baddeley (1986) describes working memory as a "system for the temporary holding and manipulation of information during the performance of a range of cognitive tasks such as comprehension, learning, and reasoning" (p. 39). The capacity for learning and memory depends on the amount of information one can manipulate simultaneously in WM. Working memory is used for everyday cognitive tasks and is our first approach to understanding new ideas and concepts. Our long-term memory, which derives meaning and concepts from information, comes into play based on the information currently stored in WM (Brainerd, 1983). Working memory can be seen as the "work space" for storing and processing information and has a limited capacity for the amount of information it can process.

This paper will explore the evidence for working memory and its importance in common cognitive tasks. It will also study how WM affects development of learning from childhood to maturity and its gradual deterioration in the elderly.

Conclusions

Research papers are not just collections of information you gathered from other writers. They are essays that present information and ideas to readers from a particular perspective, for a specific reason: *your perspective and your reason*. Like these reasons, the forms of a research paper will vary greatly from one field and course to another. In the sciences, business, and some social science courses they might be organized as formal reports on your investigations, with section headings, charts, and graphs. In many cases the sequence of questions that structure lab reports might be a reliable guide to organization:

- What were you investigating and why?
- How did you do this research?

- What did you find out?
- What conclusions can we draw from the study?

In other courses an equally good research paper might sound like an informative magazine article, beginning with anecdotes or leading questions that draw readers into a casual, continuous discussion of the subject.

Like other essays, however, all research papers should have a clear beginning, middle, and end. As "stories" you tell readers about your research, they should introduce the central questions or issues you intend to pursue, give readers a sense of direction, follow that direction, and arrive at a destination.

The process of completing a research paper does require some special strategies:

- Approach this task as an opportunity to explore the topic, with a sense of open curiosity. Let yourself become interested for your own reasons, with attention to the questions the topic raises.
- Begin this task early, shortly after the paper is assigned, and schedule blocks of time to work on it in the following weeks. Research papers begun shortly before the deadline are frustrating to write and usually a disappointment to everyone.
- When you have chosen a topic, immediately begin to narrow and focus research questions, and continue to do so while you are reading and composing.
- Search for materials strategically, using a few good sources to find others and asking for help when you need it.
- Read this material strategically as well, always with a purpose and with a variety of methods.
- Record bibliographical information and page numbers as you take notes, and keep notes also on your own perspective and plans for writing.
- Compose the paper in your own voice, addressed to your readers, introducing references when you choose to include the voices and viewpoints of others.
- Allow time for substantial revision, to move central ideas you have discovered to the beginning of the paper.
- Choose a consistent format for documentation.
- Proofread carefully before you turn in the paper.

If you follow this advice and enter the writing process with an inquisitive interest in the subject, a research paper can become one of the most valuable, memorable experiences you have in college.

EXERCISES

Exercise 1.   In a page or two, evaluate the accuracy of my guess about the typical procedures you have learned or developed for writing research papers (pp. 153–54). Are these the methods you learned in high school? Did you use them? If your methods differed from this sequence, explain the differences.

Exercise 2.   Here are some general, unfocused research topics from a variety of disciplines:

- Welfare reform

- The American beaver

- The Boston Tea Party

- The Cultural Revolution in China

- Human memory

- The search for extraterrestrial intelligence

Even without doing research you can probably think of questions that would narrow these topics and begin the process of focusing. Choose a general topic of this sort from one of your courses and list ten specific questions you might ask about it for the purpose of conducting research.

Exercise 3.   Try Web searches on the topics listed in Exercise 2 and on the topic you chose from one of your courses. How many references did each of these searches turn up? How many of the first twenty appear useful for writing a research paper?

Exercise 4.   The following are two passages that drop quotations. Rewrite them in ways that introduce and integrate the references, which I've provided at the end.

> *Like their colleagues in anthropology, sociologists who lived in the communities they studied had to redefine their roles as observers and their relations with the subjects of their research. "My relationship with Doc changed rapidly in this early Cornerville period. At first he was*

simply a key informant — and also my sponsor. As we spent more time together, I ceased to treat him as a passive informant. I discussed with him quite frankly what I was trying to do, what problems were puzzling me, and so on. Much of our time was spent in this discussion of ideas and observations, so that Doc became, in a very real sense, a collaborator in the research" (Whyte, 1943, p. 300). *These collaborative relations characterized research methods known as "participant observation."*

From William F. Whyte, Street Corner Society *(Chicago: University of Chicago Press, 1943).*

Black conservative leaders have urged their communities to move beyond the legacies of dependency, helplessness, and victimization. They believe the time has passed for holding white Americans and government wholly responsible for these afflictions. "We must believe that our fellow citizens are now truly ready to allow us an equal place in this society. We must believe that we have within ourselves the ability to succeed on a level playing field if we give it our all. We must be prepared to put the past to rest; to forgive if not forget; to retire the outmoded and inhibiting role of the victim" (Loury, 1995, p. 30).

From Glenn C. Loury, One by One from the Inside Out *(New York: The Free Press, 1995).*

Exercise 5. Try to describe the boundaries between authorized and unauthorized collaboration in two of the courses you are currently taking. To what extent are you allowed to get help from other students on writing assignments, problem sets, and other homework that is turned in for grades? Have the teachers made these boundaries entirely clear?

Exercise 6. For practice, write a paragraph that includes paraphrases and that splices quotations from the following passage, taken from the essay "Learning from the Beatles" in Richard Poirier's book of literary essays. *The Performing Self* (New Brunswick, N.J.: Rutgers University Press, 1992). In your quotations use at least one ellipsis.

There are few other groups in which even one or two of the members are as publicly recognizable as any one of the Beatles, and this can't be explained as a difference simply in public relations. It is precisely this unusual individuation which explains, I think, why the Beatles are so much stronger than any other group and why they don't need, like the Who, to play at animosities on stage. The pretense doesn't communicate the presence of individual Who but rather an anxiety at their not instinctively feeling like individuals when they are together.

The Beatles, on the other hand, enhance the individuality of one another by the sheer elaborateness by which they arrive at a cohesive sound and by the musical awareness of one another that isn't distinguishable from the multiple directions allowed in the attainment of harmony. Like members of a great athletic team, like such partners in dance as Nureyev and Fonteyn, or like some jazz combos, the Beatles in performance seem to draw their aspirations and their energy not from the audience but from one another. *(122–23)*

7 Rules and Errors

> The person who has acquired knowledge of a language has internalized a system of rules that relate sound and meaning in a particular way. The linguist constructing a grammar of a language is in effect proposing a hypothesis concerning this internalized system.
>
> — Noam Chomsky, *Language and Mind*

The Secret Book

If you are a typical student, you believe that there are all sorts of rules for correct writing that you should follow, rules that you vaguely remember studying in lower grades but have largely forgotten. You probably imagine that your teachers *do* know all of these rules and use this knowledge to identify errors in your writing when they evaluate your papers. Their comments and corrections tell you what these teachers think is right or wrong, and over the years you have probably used these evaluations to develop versions of the rules for writing that you believe teachers want you to follow. And as you move from one grade and course to another, you probably find that the rules sometimes change. A new teacher will mark errors that previous teachers ignored or will tell you not to do something former teachers told you to do. Types of sentence structure, punctuation, word choice, and organization that were once right now appear to be wrong. Having been taught in high school English that you should introduce your topic with a background of general discussion, you might receive a comment from a college teacher to "get straight to the point!" And what does this comment mean exactly? That you should *always* get straight to the point when you begin an essay? That you should always follow this advice for this teacher, in this course? Or does the comment apply only to this paper?

If you are a typical student, therefore, you will feel that each of your teachers has access to a Secret Book of Rules for Writing — rules that you should know and that your teachers use for determining what is right or wrong with your papers. Yet students are never allowed to see this Secret Book, and you can only guess at what it contains from the comments and corrections on your papers, through trial and error. Some of these rules seem to apply to all writing; others apply specifically to writing in this field of study, in this course, or for this teacher. But it is very difficult to distinguish the general rules from the specific ones.

College writing teachers and others who assign lots of writing will probably ask you to buy a version of this Secret Book: a college handbook of grammar and composition. This book will include the most common rules and constructions for the use of Standard Written English, along with guidelines for writing and documenting research papers and other advice for writing papers in college courses. Because college teachers commonly believe that students should have learned this material by the end of high school, they rarely teach or review the contents of these handbooks. Instead, they will tell you to consult the handbook when they notice particular types of errors or stylistic problems in your papers.

If a teacher clearly identifies the error or the section of the handbook you should consult, this reference can be very helpful. As I indicated in Chapter 6, handbooks are also essential references for citation and documentation of sources in research papers. Ideally, you will use this book on your own, for the review of rules and structures you have probably forgotten and as a reference for all of the writing assigned in your courses. This is at least what teachers hope when they tell you to buy a college handbook or assume that you already own one.

If this is the Secret Book, however, it remains largely a mystery to most students even when they own it. Even the most concise, efficient versions look like a maze of rules, guidelines, examples, and exceptions, often presented in technical terms such as *indefinite pronouns* and *predicate nominative*. If you feel that you should remember all of this information, negotiating this maze will make you feel ignorant, as though you are failing a grammar test you should have passed in the sixth grade. And a handbook will not directly explain all of the "errors" teachers point out in your papers. If a comment beside a sentence only says "ungrammatical," "awkward," or "unclear," you can't locate the problem in a handbook unless you know enough about sentence structure to identify the problem first;

and if you do know this much, you can probably solve the problem on your own. Many structural and stylistic problems that teachers mark do not have names and are not even "errors" in a technical sense. The idea that a handbook contains all of the information you need for writing effectively is false.

To this point I've emphasized the misconceptions, half-truths, and confusion that surround the subject of rules and errors in writing. In following sections I'll try to reduce this confusion.

Two Kinds of Rules and Knowledge

To write with any sense of confidence, you need to recognize that there are two kinds of knowledge about the way language works and two kinds of "rules" based on this knowledge:

1. When you are directly composing sentences, in writing or in speech, you are using what linguists call "internal rules" or "intuitive knowledge" of the way the language works.
2. When you study grammar in school or in textbooks you are acquiring "analytical" or "descriptive knowledge": the ways in which linguists have tried to analyze and describe how fluent speakers (or writers) of a language use it.

The freewriting exercise I described in Chapter 3 demonstrates that you possess the first kind of knowledge and that you can use this knowledge in writing without the second kind. If you write continuously for a few minutes without pausing to think about what you are going to say, sentences just tumble out onto the page. The writing you produce in this fashion might not be well organized and polished, but you are composing sentences, connected in passages. You insert periods at the ends of these sentences, and most of you also place commas within them when you hear pauses. I know from reading the freewriting students produce that most of these sentences and punctuation marks are correct according to the rules contained in handbooks.

How do you know how to structure and punctuate these sentences?

In freewriting, composing is just thinking on paper. You are not pausing to construct sentences deliberately before or while you write them, according to formal rules for grammar and syntax, and you are not considering the rules for punctuation to figure out where to put commas and periods. In order to construct a correct sentence you do not need to think: "I have a singular noun subject for the clause with an adjective modifier, so I should begin with the definite article *the*. Now I need a present-tense verb, and because the subject is third-person singular, I should add an *s* to the end of the verb. This transitive verb will need a direct object," and so on.

In fact, most of you could not think about writing with this second kind of knowledge even if you wanted to do so, because you have forgotten (or never learned) the linguistic terms and rules that describe the structure of written English. If you *could* think in such complex sentences about writing one, you could just write it, without going through all this deliberation. And this is what you *are* doing when you compose, with or without technical, linguistic knowledge of grammar. You just write, and sentences come out.

The reason you can do this is quite simple. Unless you learned English as a second (or third or fourth) language through formal instruction, you began to compose complex sentences in speech long before you learned to read or write, and long before you began to study grammar in primary school. You acquired this knowledge through listening and speaking, through which you also developed an ear for pauses, breaks, and other inflections. Studying grammar in school was a process of becoming consciously aware of structures you used, heard, were beginning to read, and therefore already "knew" in a different way. Even if you learned English as a second language, you did not approach fluency through formal knowledge of grammar alone. Becoming fluent means "thinking in" a language, without having to translate words or deliberately assemble sentences.

These patterns of usage are so complex that a full descriptive grammar of English requires several hundred pages of definitions, explanations, rules, exceptions, and examples. The grammatical "basics" of a language, therefore, are not at all simple, and if you can't remember the terms for types of sentences, clauses, and phrases or all of the rules for using commas in your own native language, join the crowd. If you learned English as a second language, you are more likely to know the terms for these constructions, even if you have difficulty using some of them correctly. In any case, while you are writing or speaking you do not need this technical, linguistic knowledge *because it attempts to describe what you are already doing.*

Your ability to write or speak does not depend on formal knowledge of grammar, any more than your ability to walk depends on formal knowledge of anatomy. In both cases self-conscious effort to apply knowledge of structures and their parts can disrupt the coordinated use of knowledge you already possess. Technical knowledge is most useful for solving problems and for sharpening perception. Experienced writers who thoroughly understand grammar and sentence structure shift to this second way of thinking when they hear problems in a sentence or want to improve their writing style.

This distinction applies to most kinds of activity and knowledge. You can't really learn to play tennis or drive a car by reading books about rules and techniques. In fact, you can learn to play tennis or drive a car, through practice and observation, *without* studying terms and techniques. Yet formal knowledge and instruction can help you improve your performance in these activities.

Unless you are a trained linguist, however, *your intuitive knowledge of the way English works is generally stronger and more reliable than your formal, descriptive knowledge of grammar.* For example, you can probably recognize and correct the grammatical error in the following sentence:

Can Noel, the main character in the novel, does whatever he chooses as long as he bears the consequences?

I imagine you heard that the verb *does* should be changed to *do.* But can you explain *why* you had to make that change to correct the sentence?

Probably not. A basic rule of subject-verb agreement tells us that if the subject of a verb is third-person singular and the verb is in the present tense, we should add an *s* or *es* to the verb. *Noel* is third-person singular and *does* is present tense. Therefore the construction *Noel does* should be correct, yet you know perfectly well that in this sentence it is not. You might guess that this rule doesn't apply if sentences are questions, but the next subject-verb sequences, *he chooses* and *he bears*, follow the rule.

Even if you eventually figured out that the word *Can* (called a "modal auxiliary verb") negates the standard rule for subject-verb agreement within a clause, you could hear and correct the error *before* you could explain it. You could also sense that these two kinds of knowledge are *cognitively different*: that trying to explain what you knew to be an error required a shift to a different kind of thinking. **[Exercise 1]**

Proofreading by Ear

Your ear for language is also more reliable than your eye. Or, more accurately, you will notice more when you are not only looking at written language but also *listening* to it. When writers notice error or awkwardness in a sentence, they typically say that it "sounds wrong," not that it "looks wrong," even if they weren't reading aloud. In fact, it is very difficult to proofread and revise writing effectively without listening to the sound and flow of sentences.

A very large proportion of the errors in student papers are in this sense "typos": mistakes the writers could have caught and corrected if they had read their papers aloud or at least silently vocalized and listened while they proofread. When I ask my students to read their papers aloud and listen to the sentences, they can usually catch at least half of the errors they made, and they notice other kinds of problems as well. Why didn't they notice these problems *before* they turned the papers in? Because they just "looked over" what they had written, visually scanning the pages with the false assumption that errors would stand out.

All of us make errors, typos, and awkward sentences while we are writing. One reason is that writing is usually much slower than speech, often broken by pauses that disrupt our sense for the way sentences sound. This is probably the cause of the mistake in the following sentence from a student paper, which the teacher marked as a grammatical error:

> It is for this reason that in both "The Purloined Letter" and "The Murders in the Rue Morgue," that Dupin succeeds where the Prefect and the police failed.

By the time the writer got to the last clause in the sentence, he forgot that he had used *that* in the beginning and put in another. If you read the sentence aloud, you can hear the mistake. I'm almost certain that he could have heard it as well and avoided the kinds of careless errors that substantially lowered his grade.

If this writer had been listening even more closely, he would have noticed that the beginning of the sentence — *It is for this reason that* — sounds a bit cumbersome. If he got rid of *It is,* he wouldn't need *that.* The sentence would then read:

> For this reason, in both "The Purloined Letter" and "The Murders in the Rue Morgue" Dupin succeeds where the Prefect and the police failed.

Paying even closer attention, he might hear a pattern in the way he begins sentences. Here is the first sentence from his next paragraph:

It is thinking that separates the successful from the unsuccessful.

Once again we find an *It is . . . that* construction at the beginning; while there is nothing terribly wrong with the sentence, he could recognize the option, at least, of saying more simply, *Thinking separates the successful from the unsuccessful.*

Thinking and listening also separate successful writers from unsuccessful ones. **[Exercise 2]**

False Rules

You might imagine that there are hundreds of rules you should be following because teachers do not always distinguish real errors from ambiguities, stylistic preferences, or particular instances in which a construction doesn't work. As a consequence, specific, local advice can lead writers to invent false rules that can't be generalized, even if they apply to a particular sentence, paper, or type of writing.

The comment "run-on," for example, might mean that a teacher thinks a sentence is too long and rambling, not that it is grammatically incorrect. If you try to remedy this problem by avoiding complex sentences, in fear that they might be "run-ons," that false rule (Avoid long sentences!) will lead you to break up complex statements you would have made, and your writing might begin to sound simplistic and choppy. Then another teacher might comment beside a passage, "Sentences are too short and fragmented," even though they are grammatically complete and not sentence fragments.

By this time your intuitive sense for the diverse ways in which sentences work will be dismantled by two false generalizations or "rules" for writing:

Avoid long sentences.

Avoid short sentences.

Writing sentences can then begin to feel like walking through a minefield of potential errors, described in that Secret Book of Rules that only teachers have read.

Many errors and other weaknesses in student writing result from efforts to follow these false rules derived from specific comments. These false generalizations about what writers should *always* or *never* do concern not only grammar but also organization and style. Here are some of the rules that my students have told me they learned in high school and tried to follow in college:

False Rules

- Don't use the first person (*I* or *we*).
- Don't use the second person (*you*).
- Don't use the passive voice.
- Always use the passive voice in science classes.
- Don't begin a sentence with *because, although,* or *unless.*
- Don't begin a sentence with *and* or *but.*
- Don't use more than one *and* in a sentence.
- Don't use contractions.
- Don't use the verb *is.*
- Don't change verb tenses within a paragraph.
- A sentence should contain only one idea.
- A paragraph should contain only one idea.
- Every paragraph should begin with a topic sentence.
- Every paragraph should begin with a transition sentence.
- A paragraph should contain at least two sentences (or three, or four).
- A paragraph shouldn't contain more than four sentences (or five, or six).
- A thesis statement has to come at the end of the first paragraph.
- Show, don't tell.
- Imagine that you are speaking directly to the reader.
- Don't write the way you speak. **[Exercise 3]**

I can easily find examples from respectable published writing that falsify these rules. Some of these rules falsify one another. Yet each of them might represent good advice in a particular instance. Here are some examples:

Using first person. The comment "Don't use the first person" might be valid if you have frequently used the phrase *I think* or *I* *feel* in an argument based on readings and ideas. If you have chosen to say something, obviously this is what you think, and saying that you feel one way or another won't support an argument based on reasoning. The first person is both acceptable and useful, however, when you need to describe your own experiences, actions, or intentions.

Beginning with *because, although.* Teachers sometimes tell students not to begin sentences with *because, although,* and other subordinating conjunctions when they have made sentence fragments such as *Although the author makes one good point.* Subordinating conjunctions introduce subordinate or dependent clauses and are completely acceptable if their clauses are followed (or preceded) by another, independent clause: *Although the author makes one good point, other parts of her argument are flawed.*

Beginning with *and* or *but.* *And, but, or, yet,* and some other small words are called coordinating conjunctions because they usually link, or coordinate, independent clauses, phrases, or words. Beginning a sentence with these words breaks their coordination and sometimes creates fragments, leading some teachers to prohibit this practice. But occasionally, as in the following sentence, you can begin with a coordinating conjunction if you want to emphasize the break — occasionally even with an emphatic sentence fragment: *But not always.*

Using *is.* Excessive use of *is* and other forms of the verb *to be* can deaden your writing, because verbs enliven sentences by indicating particular kinds of action, intention, and connection between subjects and objects. In description, for example, forms of the linking verb *to be* simply tell us things are there and have certain characteristics: *The room is large. There is a door in the middle of one wall. There is also a window. There are two bookshelves.*

Other verbs help to establish connections and spatial relations in longer, more fluent sentences: *The door in the middle of one wall opens into a large room, with a window flanked by bookshelves in the opposite wall.*

It is almost impossible, however, to avoid all uses of *to be,* partly because they combine with other verbs to form passives (*is told*), progressives (*are running*), and other necessary expressions.

Limiting ideas in a sentence or paragraph.   Because *ideas* and *topics* come in all sizes, it is impossible to dictate how many a sentence, paragraph, or essay should contain. A teacher might tell you for good reasons that you should divide a long paragraph with two main ideas. But even some long *sentences* relate two ideas, and a paragraph might present three or more ideas as subtopics of its central theme. You will observe that paragraphs in published work vary greatly in length, from one sentence to ten or more, depending on their functions within the work as a whole. **[Exercise 4]**

Placing the thesis statement.   As I've observed in previous chapters, the beginning of an essay should establish an understanding of what the writing is about, along with a sense of direction. In academic writing a *thesis statement*, central question, or definition of a problem usually appears early in the work — often at the end of the introductory paragraph or section. If you examine published essays or magazine articles, however, you will find that central theses or questions do not always land at the end of the first paragraph. They might appear at the very beginning, or in later paragraphs. The beginning of an essay might pose a question that is answered only at the end, with a particular argument or conclusion. **[Exercise 5]**

Showing, not telling.   *Showing* usually means illustrating, with examples and descriptions; *telling* usually means examining or discussing. Most kinds of academic writing require both, their proportions depending on the type and purpose of the writing. A case study or autobiographical essay might consist largely of narration and description. An argument about ideas might consist largely of explanation, with a few examples used for support or clarification. The introduction and discussion sections of a scientific report *tell* readers what the experiment is about and why it is important. The methods and results sections, including figures, *show* readers how the experiment was done and the results it produced. In academic writing you might need to alter the proportions of showing and telling, but you cannot avoid either of these modes of presentation altogether.

Writing versus speaking.   Writing always retains some relation to speech, and in order to write well you need to maintain a sense for the way your "writing voice" will sound to readers. Formal writing will sound like formal speech; informal writing will sound more like conversation. These writing voices will be appropriate or inappropriate for specific occasions and audiences, just as styles of speech you use with your friends will be inappropriate for an interview with an employer. When teachers tell you not to "write the way you speak," therefore, they usually mean that you have used chatty, colloquial styles unsuitable for academic writing, not that you should sever all of the essential connections between writing and speech.

Most false rules therefore result from our tendency to turn local advice into general principles — to read "in this case" to mean "always" or "never." Because both teachers and students wish that writing were less complicated than it happens to be, we look for ways to make writing simpler, more reliably successful. If your teachers notice a pattern of usage that gets you into trouble, it's hard for them to resist telling you to avoid that pattern. If teachers find a way to avoid common errors or weaknesses in your writing, they will often prescribe that method. And when you have been told that something is wrong in a particular paper, you will tend to avoid that construction in *all* of your papers, to lower the risk of criticism or poor grades. Yet each time you turn local advice into a general rule, you narrow your range of choices and undermine your intuitive sense for the subtle ways in which language works or doesn't work in particular instances.

How to Use a Handbook

If you think that a handbook of grammar and usage contains everything you should have learned and remembered back in elementary school, you will be reluctant to use one for its real purposes. You will associate the book itself with tests and errors and with the aspects of an English class that most of us disliked. When I tell my students that I'm going to talk about grammar, I can see their eyes glaze. Some of them groan.

That's unfortunate. I won't try to convince you that studying grammar can be fascinating, like solving puzzles or math problems or figuring out how any complicated structure actually works. But I will try to convince you that you should use a handbook, without hesitation, when you need the information it contains.

To disentangle this kind of book from your old associations with grammar tests and corrections, you need to realize that it is just a reference book, like a dictionary, an almanac, or a telephone directory. In other words, it doesn't tell us what we should already know and remember; it contains information we *can't* entirely remember. That's what reference books are for.

Or you can think of a handbook of English as an owner's manual. You are the real owner of the language it describes. The Owner's Manual of Written English just helps you to understand how your language is structured, how you can use it most effectively, and how to fix some kinds of problems.

Like other references, a college handbook isn't the sort of book you will want to sit down and read from cover to cover. Authors of these books try to anticipate the kinds of information college students might need, and they organize this material with index tabs and other keys that help you find relevant sections. Handbooks are designed almost entirely for "predatory reading," and before you try to use such a book you should spend a couple of minutes examining its overall structure. Some recent college handbooks begin with sections that tell you how to find information and use the book most efficiently.

If you do not own one of these reference books, I recommend that you buy one of the concise, spiral-bound varieties designed for college students and for quick reference. Two of the most popular handbooks of this type are *A Writer's Reference*, 4th ed., by Diana Hacker (Bedford/St. Martin's, 1999) and *Keys for Writers*, 2nd ed., by Ann Raimes (Houghton Mifflin, 1999).

These and other college handbooks contain three kinds of information:

- General guidance for writing essays
- Guidance for completing and documenting research papers
- Sections on the "mechanics" of grammar, sentence structure, punctuation, and style

In addition, recent handbooks usually contain sections on using Internet sources and advice for students who use English as a second language (ESL). Because linguistic terms are to some extent unavoidable in the explanation of grammar and syntax, most include glossaries of these terms, and Hacker's *A Writer's Reference* offers a concise section called "Basic Grammar," designed for writers who want a quick review of the parts of speech and the types of phrases, sentences, and clauses. This review will make it easier for you to locate and understand more detailed explanations of specific constructions.

In Chapter 6, I emphasized the convenience of using a handbook for citing and documenting sources in research papers. These references are so convenient, in fact, that unless you have memorized all the details of documentation systems (an unlikely prospect) it is silly not to use a handbook for this purpose. Formats for books, articles, and other kinds of sources are clearly sorted out with examples, so if you need to document a newspaper article or an essay in an edited collection you can easily find the correct form in the system you are using, such as APA or MLA. Other sections show you how to integrate and cite quotations in the text of your research paper and the general format for a list of references at the end.

Handbooks aren't so easy to use for solving structural problems in your papers, unless your teacher has clearly identified the problem or referred you to a specific section of the book. Beside the following description of people at a carnival, for example, a teacher might write "unparallel" or ≠:

> *Most of them were stuffing their faces with ice cream cones, popcorn, hot dogs, or smoking cigarettes.*

If you look for *parallelism* in the index to your handbook, you will find a section that describes this kind of structural and stylistic error, which creates the impression in this case that people were devouring lit cigarettes.

Beside the following sentence below, a teacher might write "comma splice" or "run-on." Or you might find that the comma is circled, perhaps with a semicolon in its place:

> *Gribner believes he is making arguments about race, however the statistics he uses as evidence represent social and economic class.*

If you look up *comma splice, run-on sentences, commas,* or *semicolons* in the index of your handbook, all of these terms will help you identify one of the most common errors in student writing: the use of a comma to splice together two independent clauses, which could stand as separate sentences. Writers frequently use commas incorrectly before words such as *however, moreover,* and *therefore* because they think these words are conjunctions, like *and* or *but.* In fact, these are conjunctive adverbs and are often used to introduce independent clauses. As a consequence, the comma creates an error — a "comma splice" — and the standard punctuation in this case is a semicolon.

The effort to solve problems in your own writing is the best way to review grammar, sentence structure, and punctuation — features of the language that are almost always related. While you try to locate the explanations for such problems, let one section lead you to others, in an exploratory fashion. In the run-on case, if you turn first to the explanation of a *comma splice*, that definition will invite you to review the types of *clauses*. In another section you will find a definition and lists of *conjunctive adverbs* used in this kind of sentence. If you wonder why a semicolon works in this sentence while a comma does not, turn to the section on *semicolons*. You can easily find all of these terms in the index or key to the contents of your handbook. One sentence can therefore direct the review of substantial areas of grammar, syntax, and punctuation.

As I previously noted, however, comments and marks on your papers will not always steer you so directly to information in a handbook, and these reference books do not explain all of the problems teachers observe in student writing. When I examine papers teachers have returned to students, I find many comments such as

awkward sentence	wordy	rambling
unclear	unnecessary	organization
vague	redundant	logic?
wrong word	syntax?	evidence?
diction	grammar	

In their haste, teachers sometimes abbreviate these words to *awk, unc, ww, gr,* or *org.* I find many question marks beside underlined sentences or phrases, along with words and phrases that are simply circled, indicating that *something* is wrong. But what, exactly? Many other comments, such as *Is this true?*, refer to particular statements the writer has made, to the way those statements are phrased, or to a contradiction between statements in different parts of the essay.

Handbooks offer very little help in identifying and solving these problems. To figure out what is wrong in these instances, you need to use your intuitive sense for language, along with your knowledge of the material you are writing about in this course, for this teacher. Question marks, circles, and underlining, like many brief comments in the margins, indicate that the teacher wants you to read over and reconsider what you said or the way you said it. Especially helpful teachers might rephrase a sentence for you, but you can often learn more from less explicit indications that there is room for improvement. For example, in the following sentence the teacher simply underlined the sentence, added the brackets, and wrote "rephrase" in the margin:

This knowledge [brings a] transformation [to the psychology of]
Douglass from a simple slave to a complex thinker.

What was this teacher noticing about the sentence? What did she want the writer to do?

If you read the sentence aloud you can probably hear that it sounds a bit awkward, or "wordy." The brackets suggest that the words within them can be eliminated. How can you change the sentence to make it sound more direct and concise?

If you can't figure out what your teacher has noticed and wants you to do, ask the teacher to explain or go to the writing center on your campus and get help from its staff. Occasionally students show me comments they can't understand because the teacher's handwriting is illegible, and in these cases you really do need to bring the problem to the teacher's attention, even if you feel uncomfortable about doing so. These teachers need to realize that the time they invest in reading and responding to student papers is wasted if the writer can't read their scribbled comments.

EXERCISES

Exercise 1. Here are some further examples that demonstrate your intuitive knowledge of grammar. Read each sentence aloud, identify the error, and correct it.

- Have Alex find out whom wants to go with us to the park.
- Tending the gardens were entirely the responsibility of women in the village.
- Every man and woman are responsible for the actions of public officials.
- If Johnson have known the consequences, would he have launched the war in Southeast Asia?
- After two hours, the dough had been risen and was ready for the pans.

Now, try to explain in grammatical terms why these are errors.

Exercise 2.   The following sentences do not violate formal rules of grammar, but if you read them aloud you can probably hear that they don't sound very clear or direct. Can you restructure them in ways that make them more clear and fluent? You might have to try two or three versions before you find one that really works.

- It is not only Garvin's central point that is flawed, but it is also the kind of evidence used to support that point that calls it into question.

- A student's poor time management can sometimes be the real cause of academic problems that are considered to result from other causes such as lack of intelligence or motivation.

- Patients of physicians in an HMO can still receive attention to their individual needs, in a system designed to control costs and regularize decisions, according to supporters of these organizations.

Exercise 3.   Did you learn any of the "false rules" before you came to college? List the ones you learned and try to use them in your writing. Then list other rules for writing that you try to use, or feel you should use, when you complete assignments.

Exercise 4.   Look closely at a passage (two or three paragraphs) from one of your textbooks or from a magazine article. How many sentences do these paragraphs contain? How many ideas? Is it possible to find the boundaries between these ideas, to count them, or to construct a "rule" that this passage follows?

Exercise 5.   Now look at the beginnings of two essays or magazine articles. Go straight to the end of the first paragraph in each. Do you find a "thesis statement"? If you do not, start reading from the beginning. How does each piece start? How and where do you figure out what the essays are about?

8 Looking Ahead

Judgment stops thought.

— S. I. Hayakawa, *Language in Thought and Action*

The Value of Uncertainty

College application forms typically ask you to describe the career goals and interests you hope to pursue in college. In response, admissions officers get hundreds of essays that begin like this: "For as long as I can remember, I have wanted to be an engineer [or doctor/lawyer/commercial artist/historian/veterinarian/psychologist/ software designer/novelist/architect]." The sentences that follow describe the formative experiences (playing with Legos, participating in school debates, drawing cartoons in class notebooks, reading *The Red Badge of Courage*, caring for a dying pet) that led to these goals.

I know that some of you can write such essays with ease and honesty, because you really do know the career you want to pursue and can trace this goal to earlier interests and experiences. Some of you will follow unswerving paths to these goals throughout your undergraduate studies and will enter professions you chose in high school or before.

When admissions officers and teachers read these essays, however, they know that the majority are at least partly fabrications, designed to convince that the applicants are highly focused students on a clear trajectory. And admissions committees shouldn't be surprised. After all, this is what questions of this sort invite you to do: to pretend that you are entirely clear and certain about your reasons for going to college. Although uncertainty is a completely acceptable response, very few applicants have the courage to say *I'm still undecided about my career goals and major. I look forward to college as a chance to explore many possibilities.*

This won't be the last time you are invited to pretend that you know exactly what you are doing and where you are going as a college student. "What's your major?" is one of the most common questions freshmen ask one another. The question itself suggests that you *should* know the answer, and while there is nothing wrong with saying, "I don't know yet," you might find yourself declaring a major just to avoid the appearance of doubt. Although colleges and universities attach great value to inquiry and exploration, you will often feel pressured to make up your mind and conceal your uncertainty.

Regardless of the ways you reply to these questions, I encourage you to keep your mind as open as possible to new perspectives and opportunities. I say this because the first year of college is an especially poor time to make up your mind about things. I believe that the greatest hazard most of you will face as college freshmen is that you might jump to hasty conclusions about your interests and abilities, about fields of study, and about your future.

Throughout this period of transition, which often extends through the sophomore year as well, tentative goals can give you a sense of direction. Your courses and teachers can give you useful information about the choices available to you and about your own strengths and weaknesses. Like an explorer in unfamiliar terrain, you can use this information to make necessary decisions about the areas you will next investigate. But tentative plans and investigative strategies differ from the kinds of judgments that close doors and narrow vision.

Every semester I talk with college freshmen who are making these judgments on the basis of scanty evidence, first impressions, or bad experiences. A poor grade in biology leads them to conclude that they aren't good at science or that they will never get into medical school. Following criticism of their papers in an English course, they decide they are bad writers and should avoid courses that assign papers. For reasons of avoidance rather than attraction, they head toward majors in the sciences or economics, "where you don't have to write." One boring professor kills their interest in the entire field of study. Occasionally they have decided to transfer to a different school or to drop out of college altogether, because their courses seem too difficult or because they haven't yet figured out how to manage their time. These hasty conclusions largely explain why attrition is highest in the freshman year of college.

These judgments are unreliable for two basic reasons:

- In this period of transition you are reorganizing your skills, interests, and strategies. Because you are certain to change a great deal over the following months, decisions that make perfect sense to you at the moment might seem completely irrational next semester or next year.

- Introductory courses do not accurately represent fields of study or related careers. The skills required to pass a freshman political science course differ from the skills most important in the professions of political science, law, and government. Your performance in Physics 100 will not reliably predict your success as a physicist. Your experience in introductory sociology will not tell you much about the challenges of a career in social work.

I can give you many examples of these "uncertainty principles" from the perspectives of college seniors, professors, and people in other professions who look back on their experiences as college freshmen with a radically different viewpoint. "In my freshman bio lab," a Ph.D. in biology once told me, "I was one of the students who just didn't get it! I could never understand the point of what we were doing." Describing another version of the "Euclidean myth" I associated with writing in Chapter 3, a chemistry professor complained that in most introductory science labs "the definition of an *experiment* is the shortest distance between a known problem and a known solution." Real scientific research is exciting (and often frustrating) because problems must be identified and solutions remain unknown. As a consequence, the process of research is creative and exploratory. As Sheila Tobias argued in her book *They're Not Dumb, They're Different*, enormous numbers of talented undergraduates prematurely abandon science careers because their freshman science courses exclude the creative, exploratory dimensions of science.

Just as many college freshmen move toward the sciences and engineering through premature judgments, to escape from writing, discussions, and other demands they associate with the humanities and social sciences. Like the ones who abandon interests in the sciences, however, these students are simply reacting to features of the freshman curriculum. Professional scientists and engineers do not spend the bulk of their time memorizing formulas, solving math problems, and following instructions in lab manuals. Writing and other communication skills are just as important in these professions as they are in English, history, law, or business. Freshmen often conclude that they dislike writing in general or that they are poor writers simply because they are writing in a particular kind of course. "I would have loved writing," an astronomer told me, "if we could have written about subjects that interested me at the time." As a college freshman he thought writing itself was the problem because his writing classes and assignments were about literature. Now, as a professional astronomer, he writes constantly, with skill and enthusiasm.

I can also testify that performance and interest in freshman courses is a weak basis for predicting the future. Now a professional writing teacher, I hated the rigid, prescriptive English composition class I was required to take as a college freshman, and I felt lucky to escape the course with a C. Although I learned in following semesters to use my ability more productively, when I was a freshman no one would have predicted that I would become a writing teacher. You might imagine that your professors all loved freshman courses in the subjects they teach, but in many cases they did not.

Genuine interest in the *subject* is usually a more reliable guide than experience in a particular course. Although he jumped to false conclusions about writing, the astronomer did follow his real interests. He could then organize his writing and speaking skills around pursuits he really cared about. Social scientists call these influences on our decisions "push and pull factors." Avoidance, fear, and rejection "push" us away from some alternatives; interest, attraction, and success "pull" us toward others. As a rule, the motives that pull you toward fields of study are more positive and reliable than motives based on avoidance or fear. Research and experience tell us that we perform best in activities we enjoy and care about.

If you feel drawn toward a field of study or career, you are therefore more likely to develop the skills you need for success in that work. I met David, who had come to the United States from China at the age of twelve, at the end of his sophomore year of college. Because his English was weak, he had performed best in math and science throughout high school, and these strengths led him to the field of engineering in college. By the end of his second year, however, he realized that because of his lack of confidence in writing and speaking he had avoided fields of study he most wanted to explore, such as philosophy, history, and religion.

The following year, therefore, David transferred from engineering to a liberal arts curriculum, where he could study the subjects he most enjoyed. Writing assignments and readings in these courses were much harder for him than the problem sets and exams in his engineering courses. With hard work and help from his teachers, however, he gradually figured out how to analyze philosophical texts and write historical arguments. "I feel that I'm using parts of my brain I didn't know were there," he told me with great excitement in his senior year, before he went on to a graduate program in religious studies. When David was a freshman, this future lay completely beyond his imagination.

Versatility

For related reasons, throughout this book I've urged you to maintain flexible approaches to writing, reading, and other dimensions of your academic work.

If you doubt the value of flexibility, think of its opposite. Just as freshness seems an obvious virtue in comparison with staleness, flexibility is preferable to stiffness or rigidity. In athletics, for example, no one would encourage you to be inflexible. Training for athletic performance should increase your range of movement, your alertness, the speed and accuracy of your responses. Stiffness also increases the likelihood of injury. This is why athletes (like dancers, actors, and musicians) "warm up" before performances. Athletes who are rigid and unresponsive never do very well, even if they have learned certain forms and techniques and worked hard to be prepared.

The same principles apply to your approaches to writing assignments, readings, examinations, and other academic challenges. Because college courses require many kinds of writing, reading, and thinking, no single, "set" way of doing things will work in all cases. As you move from one assignment to another, even in the same course, you need to be alert and responsive to the actual requirements in that instance. Whatever you did in high school, in another course, or on the previous assignment is likely to be the wrong thing to do in this case. Versatility is probably the most important quality you can develop in your first year of college.

"Rehearsal" is equally important. Like athletes who go straight onto the field when they are stiff and exhausted, students who "crank out" papers in one draft, late at night, can expect bad performances. Apart from desperation, there is no reason to believe that the first thoughts that occur to you under these conditions will be the best ones or that a single draft written under pressure will be fluent and clear. It seems obvious that you need to give yourself time to think about the task at hand, write an exploratory draft as a form of "rehearsal," think about its strengths and weaknesses, and revise it before the final performance. This flexible approach is more leisurely, but it won't necessarily take more time. We've seen that writers who are working under pressure, trying desperately to make the first draft the last, often write very slowly.

If this advice makes such perfect sense, why do freshmen so routinely ignore it? I've observed that time pressures will make linear, one-draft approaches seem more efficient at the moment, especially if you have postponed work on an assignment. But I also believe that the great variety and unpredictability of demands on your time and attention in the freshman year create a desire for a Magic Formula to replace the strategies most of you learned in high school. If the five-paragraph theme no longer works, perhaps there is another, more advanced formula for completing papers in college. Finding it would greatly reduce the time and frustration necessary to figure out how you should approach every assignment for every teacher over the next four years.

If there were such a Magic Formula I would certainly tell you about it, and other college writing teachers would have discovered it long ago. Comparable recipes for writing sometimes appear to work in high school only because they prepare you for standardized tests, used for college admissions. If the audience, assignment, and standards are uniform, the approach to writing can be uniform as well.

As I've shown, however, none of these uniformities extend beyond college admissions to the realities of academic work in college. College teachers are free to define their own expectations for their own courses and assignments, and the resulting variation extends not only across the freshman curriculum but also from freshman through senior year. Even if you could find a single, invariable strategy for writing (or for reading, or for studying) in your first year, therefore, this method isn't likely to work so well in following years, in higher-level courses.

I owe the analogy to athletics partly to Greg, a junior who thought he *had* found a Magic Formula for writing papers during his freshman year. In my advanced writing course I noticed that all of his essays had the same structure and style: very orderly and correct but rather stiff and bland. Greg explained that he had developed this approach to writing papers in his freshman writing course and he had been using it ever since, regardless of the course and assignment. In every case he introduced one central point and outlined a series of supporting points, the number varying with the length of the paper. In the conclusion he referred back to these supporting points to explain why the central argument was correct. Because the structure was so predictable, he didn't need to revise his papers, beyond minor changes within paragraphs.

The only problem, Greg explained, was that since his freshman year these papers had never received a grade higher than a B, and he hoped that I could help him improve his strategy. Yet he didn't want to experiment with completely different approaches. He just wanted to refine the one he had used so reliably.

"Try beginning with a real question you *haven't* yet answered," I suggested, "and write a draft to explore possible answers." Even when I told him he was completely free to play around with new methods or to turn in a rough, exploratory draft that I would not grade, he fell back into the same routine. "It's just the way I write," he concluded, settling for the B in my course.

During a conference toward the end of that semester, Greg mentioned that he would have more time for his studies because he had quit the tennis team. When I asked him why he had quit, Greg explained that he had reached the limit of his potential in the game and was losing matches. For years he had worked on perfecting his form and position, and because he made few errors he could beat less experienced opponents. "Now I'm running into players who can psyche me out," he said. While Greg always returned to the same position, these better players were constantly in motion, changing their strategies unpredictably. It was easy for these versatile players to figure out exactly where Greg would stand and what he was going to do.

Things Can Get Easier (Even as They Get Harder)

Greg's development was blocked, in writing and in tennis, because he couldn't let himself become uncertain. He wanted to be in a predictable position at every moment, and for this reason he became entirely predictable. At higher levels of academic work, the values of uncertainty and complexity rise. Teachers will expect you to tackle more complex problems and to raise more difficult questions that do not have obvious, simple answers. This is why Greg's papers became less impressive as he moved into higher-level courses, even though he had refined the form of his essays.

Freshmen who are struggling with their courses often become discouraged when they imagine the following semesters, where they will take courses more advanced and difficult. The volume of work probably will not increase, but readings, writing assignments, problem sets, and examinations will certainly become more challenging. If you spent days completing a research paper in Introduction to American History and got a C+, how can you survive your American Foreign Policy course next year or the History of Urbanization the year after? How could you even think of becoming a history major? Why do most juniors and seniors say that coping with their work has become *easier*?

This claim makes no sense if you presume that your knowledge, skills, and strategies will remain unchanged. From your current perspective, advanced courses *are* beyond your comprehension and abilities. In *Coming of Age in New Jersey*, an anthropological study of students at Rutgers University, Michael Moffatt quoted this junior who recalled taking an honors seminar when she was a freshman:

> *After hearing some worldly-wise sophomores express interest in surrealism (?), op art (??), and composer John Cage (???), I felt like enrolling in my local community college. My first assignment in [one course] was to read fifty pages from* The Locke Reader. *"Locke who?" My knowledge of history didn't extend past America, and I had never read anything written earlier than 1850, except Shakespeare (288).*

Describing herself as an ignorant, bewildered freshman, however, this junior had obviously become a somewhat different person, capable of handling the discussions, readings, and assignments required by more advanced courses. Juniors and seniors for whom college has become easier do not just know more. They have also developed very different strategies for reading, writing, studying, organizing their time, and thinking through assignments (288).

In some respects, greater ease and composure result from increasing familiarity with the expectations of college teachers. But this is not entirely true. If it were completely true, routine strategies like Greg's would become increasingly effective. Because expectations and standards continually change, the transition to college writing, reading, and learning is an ongoing process. The so-called sophomore slump results partly from the desire of freshmen to figure out, as quickly as possible, how to succeed in this new environment. When they have developed methods that seem to work for their freshman courses, they assume that these ways of writing, reading, and studying will continue to work in following years as well. Using the same strategies as sophomores, in a new layer of courses, they find that their grades drop.

For this reason, the juniors and seniors who say that college work has become easier have become better at *adapting* to new challenges. Like Greg's opponents, they have become increasingly flexible and versatile. Continually in motion, they can quickly alter their strategies.

This is the kind of writer and the kind of student I encourage you to become. And I say this not only in the interest of your success in college, but also in thinking of your further studies and careers beyond graduation. All of the professions you might enter value adaptive learning, creative problem solving, and lively communication skills.

Works Cited

ACS Style Guide: A Manual for Authors and Editors. 2nd ed. Edited by Janet S. Dodd. New York: Oxford University Press, 1997.

Agee, James, and Walker Evans. *Let Us Now Praise Famous Men.* Boston: Houghton Mifflin, 1988.

"Attitudes and Characteristics of Freshmen, Fall 1998." *Chronicle of Higher Education Almanac Issue* 45, no. 1 (1998): 22.

Baker, Sheridan. *The Practical Stylist.* 8th ed. New York: Longman, 1998.

Barber, Elizabeth Wayland. *Women's Work: The First 20,000 Years.* New York: W. W. Norton, 1994.

Barthes, Roland. "Writers, Intellectuals, Teachers." *Image—Music—Text.* New York: Hill and Wang, 1977.

Bartholomae, David, and Anthony Petrosky. *Ways of Reading: An Anthology for Writers.* 5th ed. Boston: Bedford/St. Martin's, 1999.

Bergson, Henri. *Creative Evolution.* New York: Henry Holt, 1911.

Bernard, Jessie. "The Good-Provider Role: Its Rise and Fall." *American Psychologist* 36, no. 1 (1981): 1–12.

Boyer, Ernest L. *College: The Undergraduate Experience in America.* New York: Harper and Row, 1988.

Chomsky, Noam. *Language and Mind.* New York: Harcourt, Brace, and World, 1968.

Cohen, Joel. *How Many People Can the Earth Support?* New York: W. W. Norton, 1995.

Dillard, Annie. *The Writing Life.* New York: Harper Perennial, 1990.

Elbow, Peter. *Writing Without Teachers.* New York: Oxford University Press, 1973.

Emig, Janet. *The Composing Process of Twelfth Graders.* Urbana: NCTE, 1971.

Fine, Marshall. "Portman Finds Time to Balance Roles." *The Ithaca Journal.* 12 November 1999, sec. B.

Flower, Linda. "Negotiating Academic Discourse." In *Reading-to-Write*, edited by Linda Flower, Victoria Stein, et al. New York: Oxford University Press, 1990.

Flower, Linda, and John Hayes. "The Dynamics of Composing: Making Plans and Juggling Constraints." In *Cognitive Processes in Writing*, edited by L. W. Gregg and E. R. Steinberg. Hillsdale, N.J.: Laurence Erlbaum, 1980.

"Freshman-to-Sophomore Persistence by Institutional Level, Control and Academic Selectivity." *Postsecondary Education Opportunity* 44 (1996): 1–9.

Geertz, Clifford. "The Social Scientist as Author." *Journal of Advanced Composition* 11, no. 2 (1991): 245–68.

Gibaldi, Joseph. *MLA Handbook for Writers of Research Papers.* 5th ed. New York: Modern Language Assocation, 1999.

Hacker, Diana. *A Writer's Reference.* 4th ed. Boston: Bedford/St. Martin's, 1999.

Hart, James Morgan. Quoted by William Lyon Phelps in *The Origins of Composition Studies in the American College, 1875–1925*, edited by John C. Brereton. Pittsburgh: Pittsburgh University Press, 1995.

Hayakawa, S. I. *Language in Thought and Action.* New York: Harcourt, Brace, Jovanovich, 1978.

Hobbes, Thomas. *Leviathan.* London: Penguin, 1987.

King, Charles. "Battling the Six Evil Geniuses of Essay Writing." *PS: Political Science and Politics* (March 1998): 59–63.

Loury, Glenn C. *One by One from the Inside Out.* New York: The Free Press, 1995.

McClelland, Kathleen, et al. "College Preparatory vs. College Reality." Unpublished report to participating schools. South Coast Writing Project and Program in Composition, University of California, Santa Barbara, 1990.

Moffatt, Michael. *Coming of Age in New Jersey: College and American Culture.* New Brunswick, N.J.: Rutgers University Press, 1989.

Myers, Greg. *Writing Biology: Texts in the Social Construction of Scientific Knowledge.* Madison: University of Wisconsin Press, 1990.

Parsons, Talcott. *The Structure of Social Action.* New York: The Free Press, 1937.

Perl, Sondra. "Understanding Composing." *College Composition and Communication* 31 (1980): 363–69.

Pinker, Steven. *The Language Instinct.* New York: Harper Perennial, 1995.

Poirer, Richard. *The Performing Self.* Newark, N.J.: Rutgers University Press, 1992.

Publication Manual of the American Psychological Association. 4th ed. Washington, DC: APA, 1994.

Raimes, Ann. *Keys for Writers.* 2nd ed. Boston: Houghton Mifflin, 1999.

Rose, Mike. *Lives on the Boundary.* New York: The Free Press, 1989.

Rothenberg, David. "How the Web Destroys the Quality of Students' Research Papers." *Chronicle of Higher Education* 43, no. 49 (1997): A44.

Sklar, Robert. *F. Scott Fitzgerald: The Last Laocoön.* New York: Oxford University Press, 1967.

Sommers, Nancy. "Revision Strategies of Student Writers and Experienced Adult Writers." *College Composition and Communication* 31 (1980): 378–88.

Steinbeck, John. Letter to Robert Wallsten, February 1962. In *Writers at Work: The Paris Review Interviews,* Fourth Series, edited by George Plimpton. New York: Viking Press, 1974.

———. *Working Days.* Edited by Robert Demott. New York: Viking Press, 1989.

Stockton, Sharon. "Students and Professionals Writing Biology: Disciplinary Work and Apprentice Storytellers." *Language and Learning Across the Disciplines* 1, no. 2 (1994): 80–104.

Tobias, Sheila. *They're Not Dumb, They're Different: Stalking the Second Tier.* Tucson, Ariz.: Research Group, 1990.

Trimble, John. *Writing with Style: Conversations on the Art of Writing.* 2nd ed. Upper Saddle River, N.J.: Prentice Hall, 2000.

Welty, Eudora. *One Writer's Beginnings.* New York: Warner Books, 1983.

Whyte, William F. *Street Corner Society.* Chicago: University of Chicago Press, 1943.

Wilson, Edward O. *The Diversity of Life.* New York: W. W. Norton, 1992.

Yezierska, Anzia. *Bread Givers.* New York: G. Braziller, 1975.

Zinsser, William. "College Pressures." *Blair & Ketchum's Country Journal* 6, no. 4 (1979): 57–61.

Index

Exercises are indexed with Ex. and a number in parentheses